SHIGERU
BAN

Matilda McQuaid

FOREWORD

Shigeru Ban—architect, inventor, experimenter, engineer—is a master builder of both the old Japanese and new International School.

Ban experiments with plywood, textiles, and paper. He seeks to develop new yet universally applicable ways of building that will open doors not only for the construction industry but also for the individual who seeks to build his own house with the help of simple yet intelligent systems. Shigeru Ban is concerned with building as a whole, and is not interested only in so-called beautiful architecture: providing assistance in coping with catastrophes is just as important to him. Moreover, Ban knows that simple solutions are often the most difficult to develop—especially when using inexpensive materials.

Although it is very easy to make paper models of houses, palaces, temples, pyramids, or towers, few materials are more difficult to actually build with than recycled paper. What opportunities one would have if one could simply enlarge the models! Unfortunately, this is impossible, yet Shigeru Ban has found very real ways of building with paper. To label Shigeru Ban as the "paper architect," however, would not do him justice: he is so much more than that. As a real building artist, he knows how to use international building sciences while remaining anchored in the Japanese tradition.

Those who have rested on tatami mats and seen Japanese temples and villas with their sliding walls will never forget this architecture, set in green mini-paradises, ever lightened and refined over its two-thousand-year evolution. Today, it is largely replaced by a soulless and foreign architecture of concrete, steel, and glass, conceived by architects lacking all sensual consciousness of the places in which they build. Shigeru Ban upholds the Japanese tradition, not simply by imitating the old but rather by daring to travel new paths, seeking aesthetic perfection with the knowledge that the new cannot be perfect.

I had the honor to help him plan the Uno Chiyo Memorial Museum in Iwakuni and the Japan Pavilion at the 2000 World Expo in Hannover.

The paper experiment in Hannover was not easy in its realization, and the German officials were not as cooperative as we had hoped. Nevertheless, we came through and learned a great deal in the process. Among other things, we realized that building with paper must be entirely relearned: there is simply no highly developed technology at one's disposal, as is the case when building with wood, steel, or concrete. Building with paper can only be compared, if at all, to building with textiles.

Shigeru Ban is a friend with whom I share similar ideas and goals. He is critical and very demanding of himself and, with no superstar ambitions, goes about his work with humor and cheerfulness. He will surely play an important role in the years to come. The architecture world is waiting in anticipation of his future activity, as are the inhabitants of his future creations, his artistic sculptures, which serve simultaneously as truly liveable houses. Working with him was a unique experience: he always remains open to new ideas without ever losing sight of his goals.

Since the 1920s there has been a close relationship between Japanese and German architecture—for example, between German classic Modernism and traditional Japanese timber architecture. Max Taut was the first person to engage this relationship systematically, in a wide-ranging approach; Mies van der Rohe and many others followed. I too was able to take advantage of this bond: I had wonderful experiences working with Kenzo Tange in Arabia and the Arctic and enjoyed a good relationship with Kiyonori Kikutake. The intensive discussion on the topic of "natural construction" has also created friendships between architects, artists, and engineers from both countries. I am very pleased to be able to continue this relationship between Japan and Germany together with Shigeru Ban.

Today's architecture is at a turning point. The big trends of the last decade are outlived, and only a few buildings in the world manifest architectural perfection while paving new ways into the future. Yet it is precisely the future that holds the greatest opportunity for all those who help people settle on this planet and find a beautiful home. Shigeru Ban is the future.

INTRODUCTION

Shigeru Ban is a global architect. He thinks, travels, and works without boundaries. His work has profound relevance because of its ability to draw together both world events and personal beliefs. He is an active participant in humanitarian and ecological causes, yet he easily traverses the boundaries that often separate these from the material world. In 1995, when he started the Voluntary Architects' Network (VAN), Ban's primary concern was to establish a network of architects and other individuals who shared his awareness of housing shortages and deplorable living conditions in various parts of the world. As an architect, he acknowledges a responsibility to the built environment, understanding both the physical and emotional reconstructive potential of architecture. He has pursued these issues through both research and the construction of buildings, and the result is architecture with extraordinary variety, invention, and execution.

Ban's work reflects the influences of both American architectural training and the traditions of his native Japan. He initially studied at the Southern California Institute of Architecture (SCI-Arc), and later at Cooper Union's School of Architecture under John Hejduk. His education with Hejduk introduced him not only to the fundamental elements of architecture—grid, frame, post, beam, and so forth—but also to Hejduk's interest in "architectonic poetics," the creation of three-dimensional poetry. The work that Ban built soon after he began his own practice in 1985 reflects Hejduk's influence in its use of the basic compositional and geometric elements, specifically wall and core. Through his continuing explorations Ban began to depart from these earlier formal experiments to develop his own structural solutions.

Ban is also a Japanese architect, and his work, not surprisingly, reflects an interest in certain themes that pervade traditional Japanese architecture. For example, his transformation of interior spaces by opening or closing a sliding panel and creating a completely open floor, or in Ban's words, a "universal floor" that allows fluid continuity between inside and outside, has roots in Japanese architecture. His interest in regional crafts and techniques has inspired him to experiment with a variety of architectural interpretations and ultimately build with ordinary materials in extraordinary ways. As he has no doubt learned from centuries of Japanese architecture, structural necessities can be transformed into sculptural forms, so that the material itself is the sole adornment.

This idea relates directly to one of the most important underlying themes in Ban's work—invisible structure. He avoids overt expressions of structure, or "structure-for-structure's sake," and instead adheres to a construction method in which structure is integrated into the overall design. It is not an application of the newest materials but a system in which the expression of a concept is the most vital. The materials are always preexisting, but the concepts are as varied and individual as each specific project. The need to find the least expensive but most expedient and durable form of temporary shelter, for example, was the impetus for designing his Paper Log houses. Ban's observation about the strength and durability of furniture led him to build his Furniture House series, which uses prefabricated bookshelves and storage units as structural components—an example of mass customization that helps reduce construction costs. Even a panoramic view of the Pacific Ocean can inspire new structural solutions, which occurs in Ban's Picture Window House. He liberates the ground floor to become a viewing apparatus for the immediate and distant landscape. The circumstances may have site-specific implications, but the overall concepts have far-reaching applications that can vary with context and program.

When Ban and I were considering how to structure this book, there was an initial appeal on my part to organize it by material. The materials—paper, wood, and bamboo—lent a certain elegant simplicity to presenting his work, but in the end these are only a partial explanation of his building intentions and thinking process. In fact, throughout several long interviews, when Ban reviewed dozens of projects with me, he rarely focused on the material or even the quality of space. Rather, he explained each project in terms of its structural implications—why he chose a particular system in order to achieve a specific result. He outlined all of the advantages so that in the end it seemed impossible to consider any alternative solutions. Every one of his projects is evaluated according to a building system that is embedded in the design and at the same time has been transformed into the unexpected. Paper tubes can support a roof just as bookshelves or precast concrete piles can be primary structural components, and Styrofoam packing can work effectively as insulation material just as stacking shutters can be used as a building skin. Ultimately, what links Ban's work is the crystal-clear approach to each project and the spatial invention that he ultimately achieves. If there is a surprise factor in Ban's architecture, it is what he will do next.

ENGINEERING AND ARCHITECTURE: BUILDING THE JAPAN PAVILION

When most people think of Frei Otto, they think of a structural engineer; but in fact, he is an architect. My first meeting with Otto occurred three years ago, on July 1, 1997, when I visited him at his atelier in the town of Warmbronn. I have had great respect for Otto ever since my first years in college: I will never forget the excitement I felt on my first encounter with his Munich Olympic Stadium and his multipurpose hall in Mannheim, Germany.

So when I needed a German collaborator for the Japan Pavilion at Expo 2000 in Hannover, the first name that occurred to me was Otto, even though I had not seen his work since the 1980s and I did not know if he was still practicing, much less whether he would cooperate on the project. Nevertheless, I sent him a letter with copies of my work and subsequently paid him a visit. Up until the moment we met I was still wondering what sort of cooperation I should ask him for; but he had already arranged to have paper tubes sent to his atelier, and when I arrived he was ready to start work immediately.

The main theme of the Hannover Expo 2000 concerned the environment, following the concept of sustainable development proposed at the 1992 U.N. Conference on Environment and Development in Rio de Janeiro. The Japan External Trade Organization (JETRO), the client and general producer for the Japan Pavilion at the Expo, had approached me with the idea of building the pavilion using paper architecture. The basic concept for the Japan Pavilion was a structure that would produce as little industrial waste as possible when dismantled. As design criteria for the materials and structure, Otto and I decided that it should be possible to recycle or reuse nearly all of the materials.

Otto agreed to cooperate as a consultant in the design of the Japan Pavilion, but we also needed the services of engineering consultants. Otto specified Buro Happold, the English firm founded by Ted Happold, former leader of the special structures group at Ove Arup, which handled the design of the grid shell structure at Otto's multipurpose hall in Mannheim. Although he is not well known in Japan, Happold is the person who brought Richard Rogers together with the young Renzo Piano for the Centre Georges Pompidou. The basic structural element, paper tubes, was developed under the leadership of Wim van de Camp, technical director at Sonoco Europa, who cooperated with me on the development of emergency refugee paper shelters in Africa. The paper tubes developed in Germany were to be more waterproof than those in Africa, and were to be recyclable.

FINDING STRUCTURE AND FORM

The first structural idea was a tunnel arch of paper tubes, similar to my Paper Dome in Gifu, Japan (1997–98). However, when I designed the Paper Dome, I was bothered by the high cost of the wood joints compared to inexpensive paper tubes. With this in mind, I had an idea to take advantage of one of the characteristics of paper tubes—they can be made to any length. I proposed a grid shell without joints to Otto. The tunnel arch would be about 74 meters long, 25 meters wide, and 16 meters high. The most critical factor was lateral strain along the length of the building. To address this factor, I chose a grid shell of three-dimensional curves instead of a simple arch. The curved shape, formed by indentations along the length and width of the structure, was stronger with respect to lateral strain.

Beginning in August 1997, staff from Buro Happold participated in our monthly meetings and a large model was constructed for every meeting to illustrate the topics discussed at the previous one. Otto's daughter, an assistant at his atelier, was always present at our meetings. As the main exhibition hall began to take shape, she created models and began formal studies.

To determine the form, we adopted a building method in which straight paper tubes one meter in length would be connected in a grid by rotating joints. The grid would then be elevated, or pushed up, from below to form the grid shell. Since the final formal decision depended on the construction method, it took a long to time to program software to output the shape. In the meantime, we used custom-ordered narrow tubes to create a 1:15 scale model of the push-up construction method, to measure the intersections of the paper tubes and create elevations and cross sections.

The site was a block divided into a grid, facing a main street on the short side and an intersecting street on the long side. If the main hall had been placed there, it would not have fit into the urban block. In terms of circulation, the structure required a space leading into the main hall. We decided to surround the main hall on three sides with large stairs and three-meter-high stages, using footing boards on the scaffolding of the structure. Corridors would be formed on the stages by columns of cantilevering 5-meter-long paper tubes, with their foundations weighted down by sandbags. These corridors would serve as waiting areas for visitors about to enter the pavilion, allowing them to experience the variations of light and shadow in the paper-tube columns.

Otto and I had serious disagreements with Buro Happold about the joints between the paper tubes and about how to secure internal and external strength. We wanted to finish the entire structure using methods that were as low-tech as possible, so we argued for simple joints of fabric or metal tape. As the intersection between two paper tubes was pushed up to form the three-dimensional grid, an angle would open and a suitable amount of tension would be applied. Furthermore, since the paper tubes themselves would rotate to form a gentle S-curve, the joint needed to allow for three-dimensional movement. Tape was the appropriate solution.

Otto proposed a fixed timber frame of ladder arches and intersecting rafters that would lend strength to the paper-tube grid shell, allow the roof membrane to be attached, and be used during construction and maintenance. Buro Happold proposed metal joints into which bracing cables would be inserted at diagonal angles to tension the paper-tube grid while allowing the paper tubes to move in three dimensions.

As we developed the paper membrane and honeycomb structure, we also worked on developing the membrane material for the roof. The PVC used in conventional membranes cannot be recycled and gives off dioxins when burned. Therefore, we had to develop a membrane material that could be recycled along with the paper tubes when the pavilion was dismantled. We consulted the research and development departments at several large paper manufacturers, but were told that it was impossible to develop a paper membrane with the necessary waterproof and fireproof properties. By chance, however, we discovered a waterproof bag used by a courier service. The R&D department at the bag's manufacturer, Oji Seitai Co., told us that such a membrane might be possible. It was the first positive response we had received thus far. We asked Oji to prepare samples and had them tested for strength and usability.

The main hall of the Japan Pavilion was a single-story structure, so the paper tubes and membrane were required to meet Germany's B2-grade fireproof requirements. The paper tubes used in this project cleared the B2 requirements in a single try, without any fire-resistant coating. However, it was not easy to achieve the proper balance between strength, waterproofing, and fireproofing in the paper membranes. After preparing samples and repeating the tests ten times, we finally succeeded in achieving the required strength and performance by using fireproof paper with glass-fiber reinforcement and a laminated fireproof film of polyethylene. For strength, we used a ladder and rafter timber frame with three-meter intervals, to which battens were stapled and the paper membrane affixed with waterproofing tape.

For the two nearly semicircular end walls we used timber arches that clamped to the ends of the paper-tube grid shell, achieving the required planar strength by pulling cables at a 60-degree angle from the foundation, as in a tennis racquet. The foundation did not rely on concrete. Instead, it consisted of boxes made of steel framework and footing boards filled with sand for easy use after dismantling.

STRUCTURAL AND CONSTRUCTION PROBLEMS

Preliminary strength tests of the paper tubes were carried out by Buro Happold at Bath University, with official tests for strength, water resistance, and durability carried out later at Dortmund University in Germany. At our meeting in January 1999, when the tests were proceeding, the basic structural design firmed up, and calculations underway, Buro Happold suddenly pointed out a major structural defect. There was an unexpectedly large amount of creep in the paper tubes, which made it impossible to guarantee an adequate safety ratio for the grid shell. Buro Happold proposed several ideas as countermeasures, but at this point it was impossible to make any major changes to the form or function of the pavilion or any changes that would significantly increase costs. The paper tubes were being tested, so their size could not be changed. Although it detracted from the purity of the paper tube architecture, we decided to combine the grid shell with timber arches. This was achieved by eliminating all of the joints and bracing cables in Buro Happold's original proposal for the grid shell and enlarging the sections of the timber rafters, originally designed as a frame for the membrane and scaffolding for construction work. Structural purity is important, but we were developing a new type of structure using new methods and new materials in a limited time-frame.

CONFRONTATION WITH HANNOVER CITY AUTHORITY

Problems arose one after the other. Over the course of the year, we had consulted repeatedly with our proof engineer in Cologne, Stefan Polonyi, to verify the structural concepts as we proceeded with the design work. In August, however, the Hannover city authority suddenly ordered us to dismiss Polonyi and replace him with a local engineer. As their reason for doing so, the city cited a letter that our local architect had submitted as part of our paperwork, stating that we had obtained Professor Polonyi's "involvement" in the design work. The city objected to the word "involvement," arguing that the proof engineer should be a neutral third party. We proposed a compromise under which Polonyi would work together with the engineer nominated by the city, but this was summarily rejected.

There were essential differences between our original design concept and the concept that emerged under the new engineer. First, since the Japan Pavilion was a temporary structure, we assumed that conditions such as wind load and ground friction coefficients could be alleviated. Now we were obliged to meet the same conditions as those applied to permanent buildings. The paper-tube grid shell, ladders, and rafters were originally designed to be loosely connected and mobile. Now the entire structure was to be rigid. Although we submitted additional test results and calculations, these did not resolve the basic issue. Second, in order to create a structure that was primarily dependent on conventional materials such as wood and steel, we were obliged to enlarge the section of the rafters and add unnecessary steel reinforcement. Although it delayed the construction permit by four months, we submitted the required additional tests and calculations, hoping to avoid additional reinforcement as much as possible. Finally, an incredible restriction was placed on the push-up construction method, limiting it to two centimeters per day instead of the planned twenty centimeters. This made it impossible to meet the May opening schedule. Faced with this final, impossible demand, we made the heartbreaking decision to accept all of the city's requirements.

This was not the end of the story, however. Although the roof and paper membranes had already cleared the fire standard tests, it was widely reported that the Japan Pavilion would be made out of paper. On the pretext that the pavilion might become a target for terrorists, we were required to replace the roof and paper membranes with conventional PVC membranes rated at B1, one grade higher on the fireproof scale. We could not accept abandoning the paper membrane developed especially for this project, so we placed a transparent PVC membrane above the paper membrane. Though we now had a double membrane, the PVC membrane was at least transparent, allowing natural light to filter through the paper.

After all of these compromises, the pavilion began to go up at the end of January. In view of the construction delays and the additional structural reinforcements, the contractor and client decided to abandon the paper-tube corridors around the main hall. Ironically, the city and Expo authorities reacted to this by trying to convince the client that the corridors were important elements of the structure and should be reinstated. They even offered to issue an immediate construction permit for the paper-tube corridors, which were still untouched at that point. In the end, the corridors could not be revived.

AFTERWORD

Although the completed main hall was marked by many compromises from the viewpoint of structural purity, we were proud that it was spatially satisfactory. I was surprised by the city's reluctance to recognize new structures and new materials, and above all by its unwillingness to listen to an authority of Otto's stature and achievements. Nevertheless, I learned a great deal through our collaboration. Without Otto's cooperation, a structural advance such as paper architecture would have been impossible. Otto and I agreed that this project was only the first step in a continuing collaboration, and that we ought to work together in the future. And in fact, we did: our subsequent cooperation was on the design of the Uno Chiyo Memorial Museum projected for the city of Iwakuni, Japan.

PAPER

PAPER

Shigeru Ban has used paper, an inherently weak material, in the form of tubes, honeycomb panels, and membranes to construct dozens of structures over the past two decades, from exhibition installations and temporary shelters to monumental pavilions.

Ban challenges the assumed relationship between the strength and sustainability of a material and the corresponding strength and sustainability of a structure. For him, these factors depend on the building technique and on how much one knows about the inherent qualities of the chosen materials.

Ban refers to paper as "evolved wood," implying that wood and paper share certain similarities—the most obvious being that one is the source for the other. Paper's multistep manufacturing process begins with wood pulp saturated in water. Paper tubes, the form of paper most associated with Ban, actually begin with rolls of recycled paper. These are cut into strips, saturated with glue, and wound spirally around a short metal rod that creates the hollow core of the tube. The tube can be made in any diameter, thickness, and length, depending on its use. And used tubes can be recycled, creating an endless reincarnation cycle.

Ban was attracted to paper tubes because they are inexpensive, easily replaceable, low-tech, retain their natural color, and produce virtually no waste. He began using them as a structural material on a modest scale in 1986 for an exhibition on the furniture and glass of Alvar Aalto. Three years later, he used paper tubes again, as display panels and space dividers for an exhibition on the work of architect and designer Emilio Ambasz. The tubes could be disassembled for travel and reduced material waste.

In 1989 Ban also built his first paper-tube structure, Paper Arbor, an outdoor pavilion at the World Design Expo in Nagoya, Japan. At the close of the six-month Expo, the pavilion was dismantled and the strength of the paper tubes tested. Despite harsh weather conditions, the tubes' compressive strength had actually increased as a result of the hardening of the glue and moderate exposure to ultraviolet rays. Paper Arbor was followed in 1990 by two additional temporary structures, the Odawara Pavilion and East Gate. Ban used steel columns to support the roof of the Pavilion, with paper tubes included on the exterior and interior to withstand wind loads.

Ban constructed his first permanent paper-tube structure, Library of a Poet, in 1991; two years later the use of paper tubes was authorized in Japan under the Building Standard law. Over the next few years, no situation proved to be as challenging or appropriate for paper tubes as the temporary houses that Ban built for victims of earthquakes in Japan, Turkey, and India, and the paper shelters built for Rwandan refugees. As Ban explained, "Anyone who participates in the construction of a paper log house in that situation could not find himself spiritually untouched. Moreover, it is different to construct temporary housing with one's own labor as opposed to simply purchasing ready-made accommodations. Even if the paper log houses themselves were pulled down after several years, they will remain in the minds of the people who built and lived in them."

These projects involved close collaboration with structural engineer Gengo Matsui, who influenced Ban's thoughts about tectonics and structure and taught him how materials react under different conditions and tests—for tension, compression, bending, and condensation, among other stresses. Despite years of testing, different combinations of materials often require reevaluation. For example, Ban tested the wood joints that connected the paper tubes when he built his Paper Dome, and they were acceptable. Yet several years later, when designing the Boathouse at the Centre d'Interpretation du Canal de Bourgogne, Ban was able to eliminate the wood joint by a using die-cast aluminum joint.

Ban's largest paper tube structure to date, the Japan Pavilion at Expo 2000 in Hannover, Germany, required similar testing. However, late in the design process the Pavilion team was forced to make changes that resulted in a hybrid structure of wood arches and paper tubes. Although this detracted from the purity of the paper-tube architecture, the work of Ban and his team was extremely groundbreaking. Ban's experience in Hannover inspired him to construct a pure paper-tube structure for a temporary outdoor installation at The Museum of Modern Art in New York. Whereas in Hannover wooden arches were incorporated to withstand deformation of the cardboard-tube grid shell, Ban substituted cardboard trusses at MoMA. Finally, in the Nemunoki Children's Art Museum, which utilizes paper honeycomb panels for a lattice roof, Ban made a relatively weak material stronger by interlocking two facing honeycomb panels to form a grid core.

It is the very simplicity and banality of paper that Ban cites in describing the material's power and beauty. Ban retains the paper tube's humble character, enhancing its underlying qualities to create a solid structural material. Whether he is transforming tubes into monumental columns or majestic roof structures, he has forever changed our notion of the weakness, durability, and ephemeral nature of paper.

LEFT: Alvar Aalto exhibition, Axis Gallery, Tokyo, Japan, 1986
RIGHT: Paper Arbor, PTS-01, World Design Expo, Nagoya, Aichi, Japan, 1989

LIBRARY OF A POET

COMPLETION DATE: February 1991
LOCATION: Zushi, Kanagawa, Japan
STRUCTURAL ENGINEERS:
Gengo Matsui, Minoru Tezuka,
Kazuo Ito

OPPOSITE: Library with loft in center

The Library of a Poet was Ban's first permanent building made of paper tubes. The library is annexed to the client's house, which had been enlarged and renovated by the architect some two years earlier. The client had seen two temporary structures—a gateway and a pavilion for a festival—completed by the architect the previous year in Odawara. Ban's use of paper as a structural material related to the client's own work as a poet and his passion for collecting books.

The paper tubes, which are confined to the interior in order to maintain their texture and color, measure 10 cm in diameter and are 12.5 mm thick. A post-tensioned steel rod is used to connect the wood joints. While the temporary pavilion in Odawara had been a hybrid structure that used both paper tubes and steel, in the library the paper tubes are the exclusive structural material. In keeping with a relatively small palette of materials, Ban uses 10-cm-square pieces of timber rather than the usual steel angles to form joints.

Integral to the design are four full-height, prefabricated bookshelves arranged along two sides of the library. These perform several important functions besides holding books. Each unit has a special exterior finish to satisfy its role as an exterior wall. Each also contains insulation material, which was added during fabrication at the factory. In addition, the shelving units absorb lateral wind load independent of the paper tubes. This use of furniture as a structural component laid the framework for Ban's Furniture House system.

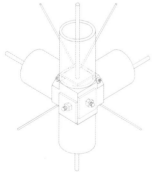

Library of a Poet,
Zushi, Kanagawa, Japan, 1991
OPPOSITE LEFT: Detail of wood joint
LEFT: View from upper loft
BELOW: Section and plan, 1:100

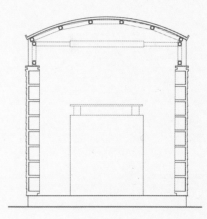

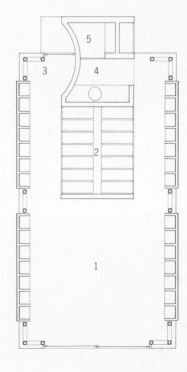

1 Library
2 Movable bookshelves
3 Entrance
4 Kitchen
5 Storage

Library of a Poet,
Zushi, Kanagawa, Japan, 1991
BELOW: Axonometric view of structure
OPPOSITE: South facade

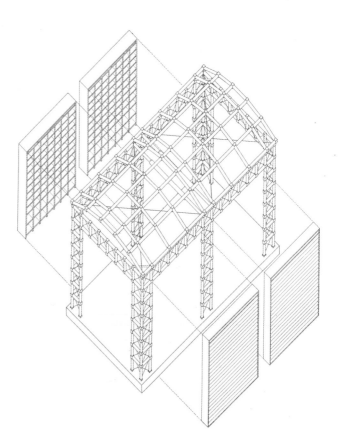

PAPER HOUSE

COMPLETION DATE: July 1995
LOCATION: Lake Yamanaka,
Yamanashi, Japan
STRUCTURAL ENGINEERS:
Gengo Matsui, Minoru Tezuka,
Kazuo Ito, Nobunori Yamada

RIGHT: North facade

This weekend house, overlooking a large lake with Mt. Fuji towering in the distance, represents the first authorized use of paper tubes as a structural material in a permanent building. Designed with the explicit purpose of introducing tubes into Japanese building regulations, Ban created a dramatic showcase for this new structural material.

An S-shaped arrangement of 108 tubes, of which nine provide vertical structural support (the remaining support lateral forces), is imposed on a 10 m x 10 m floor plan, creating a series of multifunctional interior and exterior spaces. Each tube is screwed to cruciform wooden joints in the column bases, which are then anchored to the foundation. Part of the S-curve is a circular

Paper House, Lake Yamanaka,
Yamanashi, Japan, 1995
LEFT: Interior with kitchen area at left
BELOW: Plan and section, 1:150

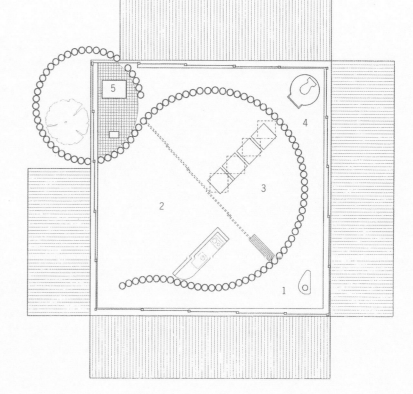

1 Entrance
2 Living/dining/kitchen
3 Bed corner
4 Corridor
5 Bath

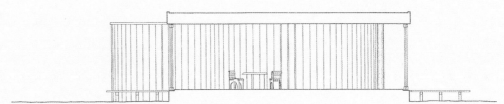

Paper House, Lake Yamanaka, Yamanashi,
Japan, 1995
BELOW: Axonometric view of structure
CENTER: Entrance area
OPPOSITE: Living/dining/kitchen

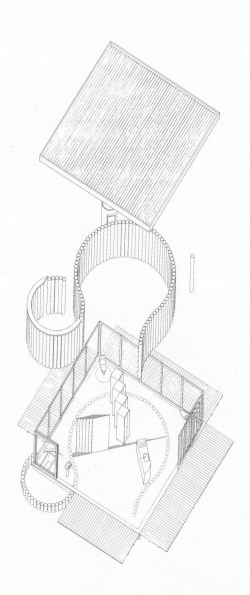

form of thirty-four paper tubes, including twenty-nine on the exterior that are non-structural. These help to enclose a small garden and interior bathing area. Seventy-four paper tubes form the larger circle that creates an internal living area and an external circulation space. Narrow slots between the tubes allow light to enter this space and allow for a partial view inside or outside. Standing independently in the circulation space are two additional tubes: The smaller one marks the entrance while the other functions as a "container" for the toilet.

The house's large universal space can be transformed into smaller units, a characteristic of many traditional Japanese houses. Separate sleeping and kitchen/dining/living areas are formed when sliding solid panels, a type of *fusuma*, bisect this central space. The sleeping area can be further subdivided with an arrangement of movable closets.

In warm weather, the large living area can be expanded by opening the sliding glass doors on its perimeter, creating a free flow of space between the circulation corridor and outdoor terraces. The completely open space has a Miesan visual emphasis, with the horizontal roofline and vertical columns underscoring the house's structural purity.

PAPER EMERGENCY SHELTERS FOR UNHCR

DESIGN AND PROTOTYPE CONSTRUCTION:
Spring 1995 – July 1996
CONSTRUCTION AND MONITORING:
February – September 1999
LOCATION: Byumba Refugee Camp,
Rwanda

BELOW: View of a typical refugee camp
RIGHT: View of camp with completed shelters

In spring 1995, Shigeru Ban became involved in the efforts of the Office of the United Nations High Commissioner for Refugees (UNHCR) to provide temporary housing for the more than two million Rwandans escaping the ongoing genocide in Tanzania and Zaire (now the Democratic Republic of the Congo). To meet these dire housing needs, Ban proposed a paper-tube shelter that would utilize the standard 4 x 6-meter plastic sheet issued to all refugees.

Ban's design came after several months of evaluating several potential materials for the shelters' frames, including bamboo, aluminum, plastic, and paper tubes. A number of factors led to the final choice of paper tubes. First, they addressed the serious problem of local deforestation which resulted when refugees cut down trees to build shelter frames. Second, they were inexpensive and carried little risk of being sold off. Finally, it was possible to produce the tubes on site, reducing transportation time, expense, and potential waste.

The first phase of the project, the construction of three prototype shelters, occurred in spring 1995. These shelters, each incorporating the 4 x 6-meter plastic sheet and encompassing a floor area of 16 square meters, were built at Vitra, the Swiss furniture manufacturer, and tested for durability, cost, and termite-resistance. One type was a standard, triangular-shaped tent with one paper tube post at each gable end and ropes and stakes providing the proper tension. Another type was an asymmetrical shelter that created more usable interior space than the first type. Paper tubes formed a V-shape at each gable end and required rope and stakes to provide tension. The final prototype, which was larger and utilized three plastic sheets (one large and two small), could be connected to other shelters of the same type at their gable ends. Its paper-tube framework allowed for the most usable floor area, making it suitable for field hospitals and other facilities. This was the prototype ultimately used. After their brief assembly time at Vitra, the shelters were transferred in July 1996 to the garden of the United Nations headquarters in Geneva for final presentation to UNHCR (Ban's work in Rwanda was also sponsored by Medecins sans Frontières/Doctors Without Borders).

Paper Emergency Shelters, Byumba Refugee
Camp, Rwanda, 1995–1999
OPPOSITE: Three prototype shelters
RIGHT: Constructing the paper tube frame
BELOW: Pages from "Annex D: Assembling
Procedure Instruction Note" of *The Monitoring
of Paper Tube Shelter at a Refugee Camp,*
a manual produced by Shigeru Ban Architects

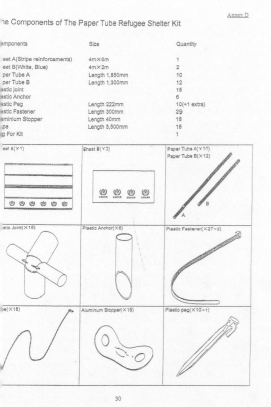

The Components of The Paper Tube Refugee Shelter Kit

Components	Size	Quantity
Sheet A(Stripe reinforcements)	4m×6m	1
Sheet B(White, Blue)	4m×2m	2
Paper Tube A	Length 1,850mm	10
Paper Tube B	Length 1,300mm	12
Plastic joint		15
Plastic Anchor		6
Plastic Peg	Length 222mm	10(+1 extra)
Plastic Fastener	Length 300mm	29
Aluminium Stopper	Length 40mm	18
Rope	Length 3,500mm	18
Bag For Kit		1

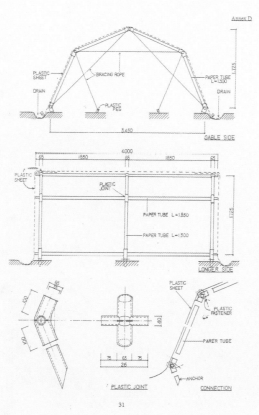

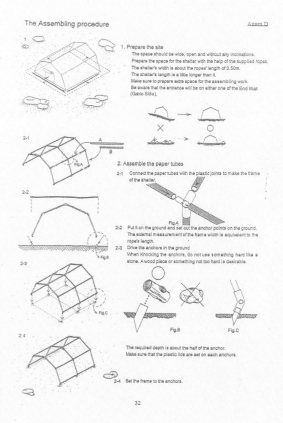

The Assembling procedure

1. Prepare the site
   The space should be wide, open and without any inclinations.
   Prepare the space for the shelter with the help of the supplied ropes.
   The shelter's width is about the ropes' length of 3.50m.
   The shelter's length is a little longer than it.
   Make sure to prepare extra space for the assembling work.
   Be aware that the entrance will be on either one of the End Wall
   (Gable Side).

2. Assemble the paper tubes

   2-1 Connect the paper tubes with the plastic joints to make the frame
        of the shelter.

   2-2 Put it on the ground and set out the anchor points on the ground.
        The external measurement of the frame width is equivalent to the
        rope's length.

   2-3 Drive the anchors in the ground
        When Knocking the anchors, do not use something hard like a
        stone. A wood piece or something not too hard is desirable.

   The required depth is about the half of the anchor.
   Make sure that the plastic lids are set on each anchors.

   2-4 Set the frame to the anchors.

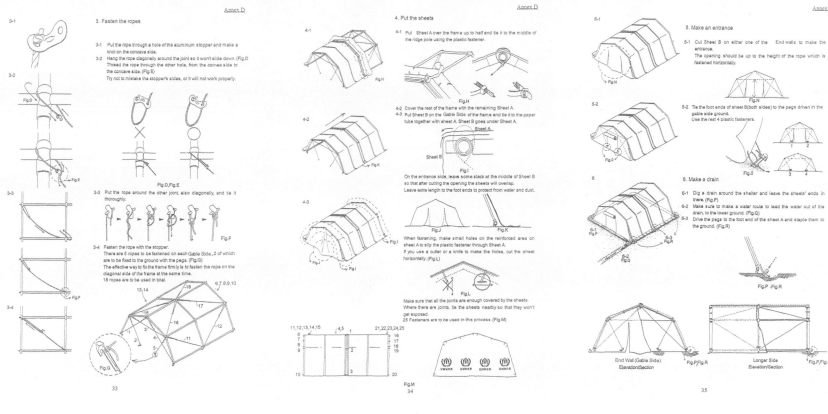

3. Fasten the ropes

3-1 Put the rope through a hole of the aluminum stopper and make a knot on the concave side.
3-2 Hang the rope diagonally around the joint so it won't slide down. (Fig.D) Thread the rope through the other hole, from the convex side to the concave side. (Fig.E)
Try not to mistake the stopper's sides, or it will not work properly.

Fig.D,Fig.E

3-3 Put the rope around the other joint, also diagonally, and tie it thoroughly.

Fig.F

3-4 Fasten the rope with the stopper.
There are 5 ropes to be fastened on each Gable Side , 2 of which are to be fixed to the ground with the pegs. (Fig.G)
The effective way to fix the frame firmly is to fasten the rope on the diagonal side of the frame at the same time.
18 ropes are to be used in total.

Fig.G

4. Put the sheets

4-1 Put Sheet A over the frame up to half and tie it to the middle of the ridge pole using the plastic fastener.

Fig.H

4-2 Cover the rest of the frame with the remaining Sheet A.
4-3 Put Sheet B on the Gable Side of the frame and tie it to the paper tube together with sheet A. Sheet B goes under Sheet A.

Fig.K

Fig.I

On the entrance side, leave some slack at the middle of Sheet B so that after cutting the opening the sheets will overlap.
Leave extra length to the foot ends to protect from water and dust.

Fig.J   Fig.K

When fastening, make small holes on the reinforced area on sheet A to slip the plastic fastener through Sheet A.
If you use a cutter or a knife to make the holes, cut the sheet horizontally. (Fig.L)

Fig.L

Make sure that all the joints are enough covered by the sheets.
Where there are joints, tie the sheets nearby so that they won't get exposed.
25 Fasteners are to be used in this process. (Fig.M)

Fig.M

5. Make an entrance

5-1 Cut Sheet B on either one of the   End walls to make the entrance.
The opening should be up to the height of the rope which is fastened horizontally.

Fig.N

5-2 Tie the foot ends of sheet B(both sides) to the pegs driven in the gable side ground.
Use the rest 4 plastic fasteners.

Fig.O

6. Make a drain

6-1 Dig a drain around the shelter and leave the sheets' ends in there. (Fig.P)
6-2 Make sure to make a water route to lead the water out of the drain, to the lower ground. (Fig.Q)
6-3 Drive the pegs to the foot end of the sheet A and staple them to the ground. (Fig.R)

Fig.P .Fig.R

End Wall (Gable Side) Elevation/Section   Fig.P,Fig.R

Longer Side Elevation/Section   Fig.P,Fig.R

Paper Emergency Shelters, Byumba Refugee
Camp, Rwanda, 1995–1999
OPPOSITE: Pages from assembly manual by
Shigeru Ban Architects
OPPOSITE AND BELOW: Completed paper tube
frame, positioning the plastic sheet over paper
tube frame, and completed shelter

In the second phase, on-site production was explored. In February 1997, specialists from Sonoco, a paper-tube manufacturer, were sent with tube-making machinery and raw materials to Medecins sans Frontières' (MSF) logistics center in Bordeaux, France. The Sonoco representatives trained MSF staff to operate the machinery, demonstrating the feasibility of producing large quantities of tubes on-site in an emergency situation. For Ban, the final phase of the project took place in 1999 and consisted of monitoring the construction of fifty shelters.

At the same time Ban was working on the temporary shelters for Rwandan refugees in Tanzania and Zaire, he also worked with the volunteer organization he established—Voluntary Architects' Network (VAN)—as a design advisor to provide more permanent housing for refugees returning to Rwanda. The Rwandan government established the architectural program: a 42-square-meter space with sun-dried bricks for walls, a wooden framework, and corrugated-steel sheets for the roof. Ban changed the plan to a more elongated rectangle, thereby decreasing the amount of bricks used for the walls and minimizing excavations into the region's hillsides. He also recommended bamboo for the roofing as it was easily available, ecological, and less expensive.

PAPER LOG HOUSES

JAPAN
COMPLETION DATE: September 1995
LOCATION: Nagata, Kobe, Japan
STRUCTURAL ENGINEERS:
Minoru Tezuka,
TSP Taiyo — Eiichiro Kaneko

TURKEY
COMPLETION DATE: January 2000
LOCATION: Kaynasli, Turkey
ASSOCIATE ARCHITECTS:
Mine Hashas, Hayim Beraha,
Okan Bayikk

INDIA
COMPLETION DATE: September 2001
LOCATION: Bhuj, India
ASSOCIATE ARCHITECTS:
Kartikeya Shodhan Associates—
Kartikeya Shodhan

RIGHT: Log Houses at Minamikomae Park,
Nagata, Kobe

Natural disasters have provided the context for some of Ban's most publicized and challenging projects, particularly three great earthquakes that struck Kobe, Japan (1995), Kaynasli, Turkey (1999), and Bhuj, India (2001). After each of these tragedies, his Paper Log House answered the dire housing needs of dozens of families left homeless. In Kobe, the shelters were primarily built for Vietnamese refugees who remained in the vicinity because of jobs, schools, and a supportive community. In Turkey and India, earthquake victims also wished to remain near their destroyed homes for the sake of their community and to begin the process of rebuilding. In all these instances, Ban responded immediately and creatively, ultimately providing temporary relief for dozens of families.

On January 17, 1995, a strong earthquake tore through Kobe, leaving more than 5,000 people dead and many others without safe shelter. Ban's first temporary paper-tube housing was designed to meet the city's needs. Soon after the quake, he established criteria for temporary housing: inexpensive materials, simple construction methods, satisfactory insulation, and an end result that was aesthetically pleasing. By July 1995 the first of approximately twenty-seven paper log houses were completed in Minamikomae Park (other houses were located in Shin Minatogawa Park). It was built by a team of volunteers who had come to help with the construction of Ban's Paper Church, sited a few hundred feet away.

The 4-square-meter log house was of ridge-beam construction, with walls made out of paper tubes 108 mm in diameter and 4 mm thick. Self-adhesive, waterproof sponge tape between the paper tubes insured a watertight fit. The plinth was constructed of borrowed beer crates filled with sandbags. The ceiling and roof, each made out of a PVC tent membrane, were separated so that air could circulate between them—cooling the interior in the summer, when the gable ends of the roof were open, and retaining warm air in winter when the ends were closed. In some cases, when a large family required two linked units, a 2-meter space between the two units formed a common area when the roofs were joined.

A team of ten volunteers, including one construction leader, was chosen for each house. Prefabricated elements were prepared inside the partially constructed Paper Church, then were trucked to the site on the morning of assembly. The first six houses were completed after only eight hours and approximately twenty-one were built within the month. At a cost of ¥250,000 each, Ban's Paper Log houses met the financial constraints and physical needs of a very critical situation. They were cheaper and more easily assembled than other temporary, prefabricated housing, and the fact that they were also recyclable contributed to the project's success.

Paper Log House, Nagata, Kobe, Japan, 1995
OPPOSITE (left to right): View of temporary
shelters erected before paper log houses;
a volunteer constructing roof of paper log house;
volunteers installing walls of paper log house
ABOVE LEFT: Living space in a completed log house
ABOVE RIGHT: Paper log houses adapted to
residents' daily use
LEFT: Plan and sections, 1:100
BELOW: Exploded axonometric view

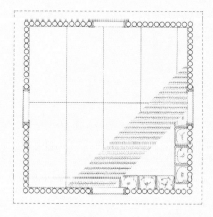

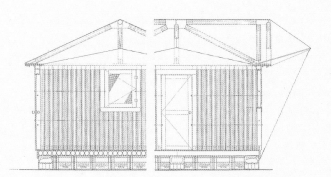

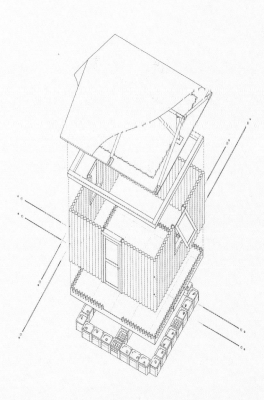

Four years later, Ban participated in relief efforts in western Turkey, where a catastrophic earthquake and its aftershocks left more than 20,000 people dead and some 200,000 homeless. When the first earthquake occurred in August 1999, Ban and other members of the Voluntary Architects' Network (VAN), which Ban had founded in 1995, immediately gathered supplies for emergency shelters. He appealed to leaders in the building industry for contributions and donations, specifically seeking the kind of plastic sheets and tarpaulins used in construction. The 643 sheets he received were shipped to Turkey in September, where they were distributed to villages around the earthquake's center. At that time many of the victims were living in old military cotton tents; the plastic sheets helped to waterproof them.

The most serious of the aftershocks struck the northwestern part of Turkey on November 12, leaving 80,000 additional people homeless. One of Ban's log houses was constructed in coordination with a local volunteer organization, and with the financial support of private individuals such as the owners of the contemporary furniture company Mozaik. Although it was based on the shelter in Kobe, certain improvements were made for Turkey's weather and lifestyle. The floor area, for example, measured 3 x 6 meters, a different and slightly larger configuration. This change was due primarily to the standard size of plywood in Turkey, as well as to the country's larger average family size. There was also more insulation than at Kobe—wastepaper was inserted inside the tubes along the walls and fiberglass in the ceiling. In addition to window frame sealant inserted between the tubes, cardboard and plastic sheets were used to add insulation according to the residents' needs. By December, seventeen of these houses had been built, with the help of donated materials from Turkey and Japan and the labor of architecture students and residents.

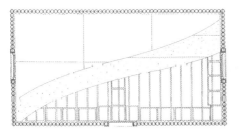

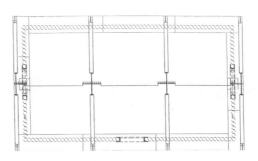

Paper Log House, Kaynasli, Turkey, 1999
OPPOSITE AND ABOVE: Volunteers
constructing roof of paper log house;
volunteers constructing foundation of paper
log house; interior view of typical house;
exterior view
LEFT (clockwise from top left): Floor plan,
roof framing plan, longitudinal section,
cross section, 1:100

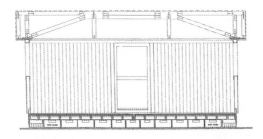

THICK PLASTIC
(TARPAULINE)

CANE MATTING
(CHATAI)

PLYWOOD TOP
CONNECTOR

SPLIT BAMBOO
PURLINS

PLASTER OF
PARIS POURED IN
CORNER TUBES

6mm DIA.
STEEL RODS

WHOLE BAMBOO
MAIN MEMBERS

PAPER TUBE
WALL

G.I.CHANNEL

VERTICAL STEEL
ROD 10mm DIA.

PRE-CAST CONC.
FOUNDATION BASE

VERTICAL BAMBOO
SUPPORT

MAIN BAMBOO MEMBERS

SPLIT BAMBOO FOR
VAULTED ROOF

PLYWOOD
FRAME FOR
WINDOW
W

CORNER PLYWOOD
BRACING

6mm DIA. M.S.
RODS PASSING
THROUGH EACH
PAPER TUBE

CONCRETE
PEDESTAL

GROUND
LEVEL

RUBBLE FILLING

3.27m
3.16m

PLYWOOD FRAME
FOR WINDOW

PLYWOOD
TRIANGLE
AS CORNER
STIFFENER

MUD +
COWDUNG
FLOOR

5.01m
4.90m

INDOOR
SPACE
3.05m X 4.80m

G.I.CHANNEL
AT BASE

PLYWOOD
FRAME FOR DOOR

CONCRETE
PEDESTAL AT
CORNERS

1.80m

SEMI-OPEN SPACE
(VERANDAH)
3.27m X 1.80m
10'-9" X 6'-0"

SECONDARY
ROOF
MEMBERS OF
SPLIT BAMBOO

PLINTH
PLATFORM
MADE OF
RUBBLE

MAIN ROOF MEMBERS
OF WHOLE BAMBOO

Paper Log House, Bhuj, India, 2001
ABOVE LEFT: Axonometric view
LEFT: Section and plan, 1:80
BELOW: Section detail, 1:30

ABOVE: Interior view of log house used as
a classroom; living and sleeping area
OPPOSITE: Paper log houses adapted to
traditional Indian customs

SPLIT BAMBOO MEMBER

MAIN BAMBOO MEMBERS

CORNER PLYWOOD

10mm DIA. M.S. ROD PIERCED
THROUGH BAMBOO
INTERSECTION & BENT OVER
AT 90 DEGREES

DETAIL AT A

PAINTED WITH RED OXIDE
ANTI-CORROSIVE PAINT

MUD + COWDUNG FLOOR

DETAIL AT B

RUBBLE FILLING

CONCRETE
PEDESTAL

GROUND LEVEL

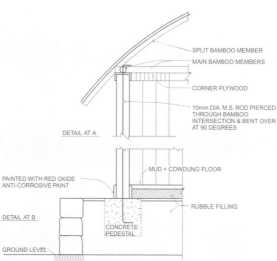

On January 26, 2001, India experienced the worst earthquake in its history. Over 20,000 people died and more than 600,000 were left homeless by the 7.9 quake, with its epicenter near Bhuj, Gujarat, in western India.

Ban was soon contacted by a Mrs. Neeta Premchand, a businesswoman who asked him to work with a local architect, Kartikeya Shodhan Associates, to construct twenty temporary housing units for some of the victims. She also sponsored the project, and although she had not known of Ban's previous work with emergency shelters, she had seen his Japan Pavilion in Hannover and thought his work appropriate for the situation. Here, Ban used paper tubes for the walls of a 3.2 x 4.9-meter structure, but he had a difficult time finding appropriate materials for the foundation and roof. Beer crates had been used successfully in Kobe and Turkey, but it was impossible to find them in Bhuj. Ultimately he chose to use rubble from destroyed buildings for the foundation, with a traditional mud floor on top. For the roof, Ban used split bamboo for the rib vaults and whole bamboo for the ridge beams. A locally woven cane mat was placed over the bamboo ribs, followed by a clear plastic tarpaulin to protect against rain, then another cane mat. Ventilation was provided through the gables, where small holes in the mats allowed air to circulate. This ventilation also allowed cooking to be done inside, with the added benefit of repelling mosquitoes.

PAPER CHURCH

COMPLETION DATE: September 1995
LOCATION: Nagata, Kobe, Japan
STRUCTURAL ENGINEERS:
Gengo Matsui, Shuichi Hoshino,
TSP Taiyo — Mihoko Uchida

BELOW: Night view to the north
RIGHT: Interior hall, with
elliptical space formed by paper
tubes and membrane ceiling

This community center and house of worship was built on the site of Takatori Church, which had been destroyed by fire after the great earthquake in Kobe in January 1995. The congregation consisted primarily of Vietnamese refugees, whose nearby homes had also been destroyed. Ban and some 160 volunteers worked to rebuild this small community, building thirty paper-log houses as temporary housing and the Paper Church as a temporary center to fulfill spiritual and communal needs.

Because the design and construction of the church had to occur within a very short time frame, Ban adopted the paper-tube structural techniques he had developed in previous projects. Like the Paper Log houses, the cost had to be kept low and assembly had to be easy enough for volunteers to complete without using heavy machinery. Ban also thought that the church could be easily disassembled and transported to another disaster area after it had fulfilled its use in Kobe.

The rectangular 10 x 15-meter building has a skin of translucent polycarbonate panels. The entire front and half of each side of the church can be completely opened, providing cross ventilation as well as additional space for crowded events. The interior space, a dynamic oval in the spirit of seventeenth-century Baroque architect Giovanni Lorenzo Bernini, counteracts the orthogonal exterior. The oval, made of fifty-eight paper tubes each 5 meters high, 33 cm in diameter and 15 mm thick, accommodates eighty people. Opposite the tubes, a corridor runs around the perimeter of the building. Half of the tubes along the oval's longer axis are closely spaced to form a backdrop for the altar; they also create storage behind the altar. The remaining tubes are spaced widely; when the doors are opened along the front and side facades, they allow for an integration of interior and exterior. The oval creates a compressed entrance sequence that helps to draw one's eyes up toward the ceiling, which is made of a tent material that allows daylight inside and emits a golden glow at night.

The needs of the church and its congregation now include many different kinds of community services. There have been ongoing discussions about preserving the existing church and celebrating its tenth anniversary in 2005, when Ban and church officials will unveil a proposal for another structure that will accommodate the church's larger role.

Paper Church, Nagata, Kobe, Japan, 1995
OPPOSITE (left to right):
Volunteers assembling paper tube structure;
installing the roof membrane
BELOW (clockwise from top left): Axonometric
view; plan, 1:150; section, 1:150;
paper-tube-to-roof detail, 1:20

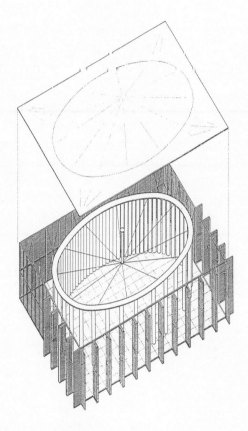

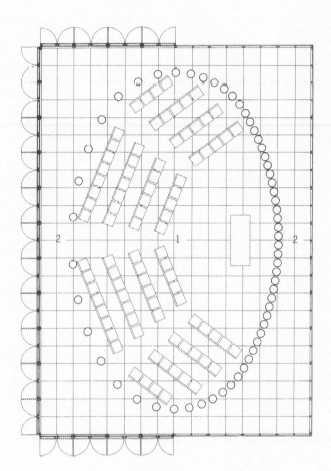

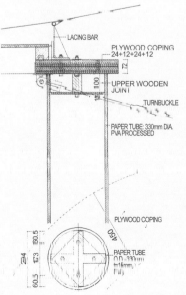

LACING BAR
PLYWOOD COPING
24+12+24+12

UPPER WOODEN
JOINT

TURNBUCKLE

PAPER TUBE: 330mm DIA.
PVA PROCESSED

PLYWOOD COPING

PAPER TUBE
O.D. 330mm

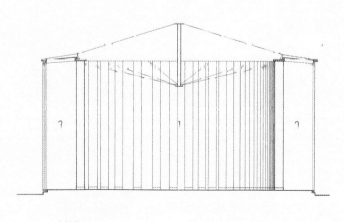

2 Corridor

Paper Church, Nagata, Kobe, Japan, 1995
OPPOSITE: Exterior enclosure of
corrugated polycarbonate sheeting
BELOW: Interior ellipse formed by
58 paper tubes

PAPER DOME

COMPLETION DATE: January 1998
LOCATION: Masuda, Gifu, Japan
STRUCTURAL ENGINEERS:
Minoru Tezuka,
VAN Structural Design —
Shigeru Ban, Satoshi Higuchi

RIGHT: Completed dome, view from east

Paper Dome, Masuda, Gifu, Japan, 1998
BELOW: Wood joint; connecting
the split joint at the vertex of the arch
OPPOSITE: Detail of paper tubes connected
by wood joints; detail diagram of assembly
at wooden joint

This permanent paper shelter was designed for a contractor of wooden houses who had met Ban
in 1995. As a trained architect, the client appreciated Ban's interest in new building materials that
were both ecologically sound and had some relationship to his own material of choice, wood.

The requirements for the building were straightforward. The 28 x 25-meter shelter was intended for
outdoor work, particularly in snowy weather, and its structural system had to be simple enough
to be assembled by the client's crew of carpenters. Ban's design was a three-layered arched roof spaning
27.2 meters, with a peak height of 8 meters at the center. Since paper tubes cannot be produced as
curved elements without loss of structural integrity, each row of the arch is formed by eighteen straight
paper tubes, each 1.8 meters long with an external diameter of 29 cm, connected by laminated
wood joints. The twenty-eight rows that make up the arch are in turn connected by a series of tubes
0.9 meters long and 14 cm in diameter. Waterproofing the paper tubes with clear polyurethane
before construction minimized their expansion and contraction due to humidity and extreme changes
in temperature.

Lateral stiffness was achieved with a layer of structural plywood over the paper-tube frame. Each
panel of plywood contains a hole 50 cm in diameter to allow natural light inside. The plywood was
covered by sheets of corrugated polycarbonate. Additional steel tension cables and braces were
used as a precaution against sudden changes of load that occur, for example, when accumulated snow
breaks loose and drops suddenly from the roof.

Although Ban had already obtained official approval to use paper tubes as a structural material several
years earlier for the Paper House project, he was still required by the authorities to provide testing
data for the joint connecting the paper and the laminated wood joint. This was primarily a shearing
test to assure that the wood and paper were compatible at the connection point.

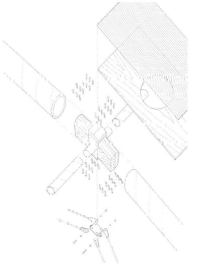

Paper Dome, Masuda, Gifu, Japan, 1998
OPPOSITE: Sheltered lumber
supplies under arch
LEFT: Diagram of roof composition
BELOW: Section, 1:300
BOTTOM: View of exterior with
corrugated polycarbonate roof panels

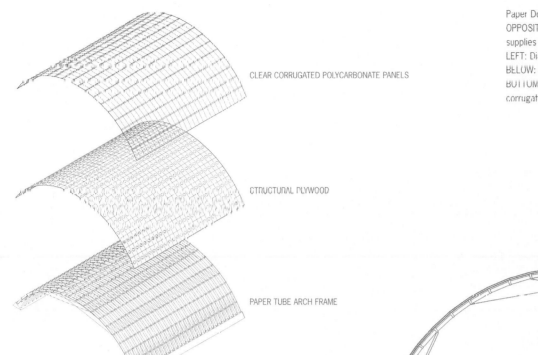

CLEAR CORRUGATED POLYCARBONATE PANELS

STRUCTURAL PLYWOOD

PAPER TUBE ARCH FRAME

NEMUNOKI CHILDREN'S ART MUSEUM

COMPLETION DATE: May 1999
LOCATION: Kakegawa, Shizuoka, Japan
STRUCTURAL ENGINEERS:
Minoru Tezuka,
VAN Structural Design —
Shigeru Ban, Naoyuki Sasaki

RIGHT: Northwest façade viewed from road
BELOW: Site plan, 1:1000

Nemunoki Children's Art Museum, Kakegawa,
Shizuoka, Japan, 1999
BELOW (counterclockwise from top):
Axonometric view of structure;
plan 1:400; section 1:400; detail of
connection at aluminum joint

RIGHT AND OPPOSITE: Assembling
the paper honeycomb roof; view of
ceiling; gallery interior showing paper
honeycomb roof

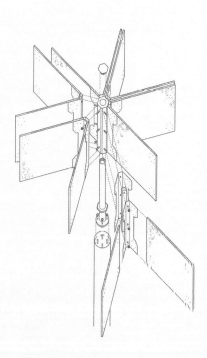

1 Gallery
2 Reception
3 Entrance
4 Washroom
5 Mechanical

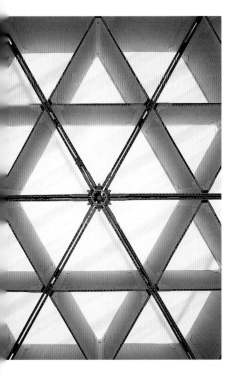

The Nemunoki Children's Art Museum, located in a beautiful forested valley a few hours southwest of Tokyo, is associated with a school and home for mentally and physically challenged children. Studio art is an extremely effective form of therapy for many of the children and the school has gained a national reputation in the field of art education. The client and founder of the school, Mariko Miyagi, wanted a facility where the children could exhibit their art, primarily works on paper.

The approach to the museum is along a narrow road that winds through a network of bamboo forests, green tea fields, and flower gardens. Where the road reaches a cul-de-sac, the single-story triangular building is nestled on a similarly shaped site. The entrance, at the north corner, leads into a 300-square-meter gallery space, glazed on all three sides, and completely open except for a small storage room next to the entrance and a red cylinder containing the restroom at the southwest corner. Art is displayed on freestanding paper honeycomb walls in the central part of the gallery.

The most striking element of the building is its beautiful lattice roof, made of a triangular grid of paper honeycomb panels and supported by fifteen steel columns. Conventional honeycomb board is produced by gluing paper on both sides of the honeycomb material; but in Grid Core, the product used in this structure, the honeycomb and paper are molded together as one unit. Two of these panels are glued together so the honeycomb faces are interlocked, which creates a much stronger material.

The roof's basic unit is made by inserting a 60 cm x 15 cm x 15 mm piece of plywood between the two reinforced honeycomb boards, which measure either 60 cm x 1 m or 60 cm x 3 m. The plywood and panels are then sandwiched together by aluminum plates to form a 60-degree triangle open on one side. This unit is attached to others like it to form the roof. The roof units work together so effectively because the three types of joints were designed specifically for this project. The first joint connects the basic unit of two panels together; the second attaches three of these units to a triangular aluminum die-cast pipe; and the third connects six of these larger units to a hexagonal aluminum die-cast pipe.

On top of the grid core is a translucent PVC membrane and transparent, corrugated fiber-reinforced plastic (FRP) decking to diffuse the natural light, the only source of illumination for the gallery. The overriding impression of the roof is that of a giant honeycomb—the material is used as inspiration for the entire structure.

Nemunoki Children's Art Museum, Kakegawa,
Shizuoka, Japan, 1999
OPPOSITE: Entrance on north facade
BELOW LEFT: Museum interior
BELOW (top to bottom): Detail plan
of paper honeycomb roof, showing joints,
1:50; various joint types J1, J2, J3

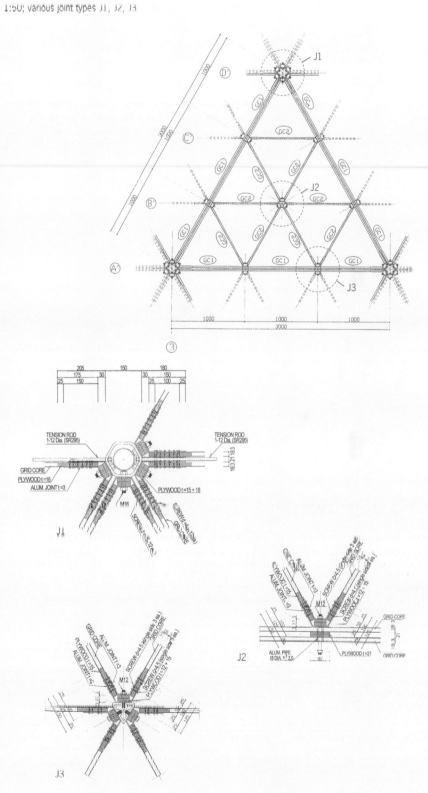

JAPAN PAVILION, EXPO 2000

COMPLETION DATE: May 2000
LOCATION: Hannover, Germany
CONSULTANT: Frei Otto
STRUCTURAL ENGINEERS:
Buro Happold — Michael Dickson,
Paul Westbury, Paul Rogers,
Greg Hardie, Klaus Leiblein

BELOW: South facade,
with paper membrane and PVC
membrane on exterior

The theme for Expo 2000, a world's fair held in Hannover, Germany, was "Humankind-Nature-Technology: A New World Arising." The fair focused on the idea of sustainable development, a theme that originated with the U.N. Earth Summit held in Rio de Janeiro in 1992. Japan's contribution to the Expo was this 3,100-square-meter paper-tube pavilion, designed by Ban. The temporary pavilion used recycled paper tubes as its primary structural material; at the end of the Expo it could be completely recycled.

Early in the design process Ban consulted with the renowned architect and structural engineer Frei Otto, who has a studio outside of Stuttgart. Ban proposed to Otto a tunnel arch that measured 74 x 25 x 16 meters. Since paper tubes can be fabricated to any length, Ban also thought they should employ a three-dimensional grid shell using long paper tubes without joints. This would avoid the cost of fabricating expensive wood joints, a necessity in his recently completed Paper Dome, and it would also reduce the lateral force along the Pavilion's long (south and north) sides. A grid shell of three-dimensional curved lines with indentations in the height and width provided stronger support against lateral forces. Ultimately the tubes were fabricated in 20-meter lengths for transport and then connected using a wooden splice rather than a joint.

The pavilion's construction method was integral to its form. Ban, Otto, and the structural engineers, Buro Happold, decided that by using a flexible joint system, the grid could be lifted up from below to form the grid shell. Ban and Otto also wanted the joints to be made out of low-tech material—fabric or metal tape—in keeping with the Expo's theme. The tape would allow the angle between the tubes to open up in order to create a three-dimensional curve. Otto also proposed a fixed timber frame of ladder arches and intersecting rafters, which would give further stiffness to the grid shell and allow the roof membrane to be attached. These ladders could also be used during construction and for maintenance.

Japan Pavilion, Expo 2000, Hannover,
Germany, 2000
OPPOSITE AND BELOW: Constructing the
paper tube roof, sequential views
ABOVE (left to right): Using GPS equipment
to accurately form grid shell;
detail of paper tube grid shell with fabric tape
connections; scaffolding system supporting
paper tube grid shell
BELOW: Axonometric view of
structural composition

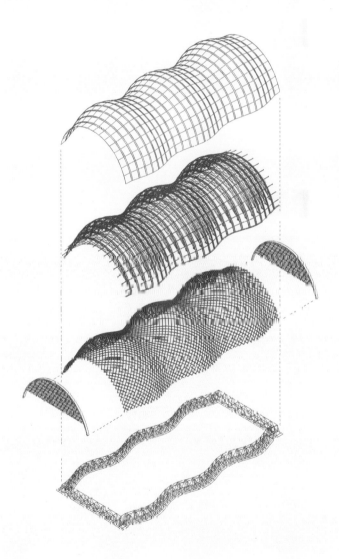

Japan Pavilion, Expo 2000, Hannover,
Germany, 2000
BELOW: Longitudinal section, cross
section, plan, 1:800
RIGHT: Interior detail, paper tube grid shell
and timber ladder arches
OPPOSITE: Main exhibit space, upper level

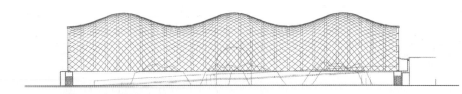

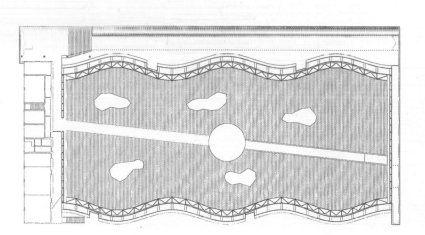

Ban intended the roof membrane to be paper, similar to the type used in waterproof envelopes. After much experimentation and testing, he and his team succeeded in achieving the necessary strength using a fireproof paper with glass fiber reinforcement and a laminated fireproof film of polyethylene.

In the end, all of the new materials and techniques passed the requirements of the German authorities. Although Ban had to make numerous compromises to accommodate these requirements and other security concerns, the pavilion was an enormous building achievement. Not least, it fulfilled its environmental obligations as a completely recyclable structure.

PAPER ARCH, THE MUSEUM OF MODERN ART

COMPLETION DATE: April 2000
LOCATION: The Museum of Modern
Art, New York, United States
ASSOCIATE ARCHITECTS:
Dean Maltz, Architect — Dean Maltz,
Kamonsin Chathurattaphol
STRUCTURAL DESIGN:
Preliminarily Design: Takenaka
Corporation — Yoshio Tanno,
Keiichi Hasegawa
CONSTRUCTION DESIGN:
Buro Happold Consulting Engineers
PC, New York — Craig Schwitter,
Cristobal Correa, Laura Fuentes

BELOW: Detail of two paper tube trusses
OPPOSITE: Completed arch in the Abby
Aldrich Rockefeller Sculpture Garden, view
to the north

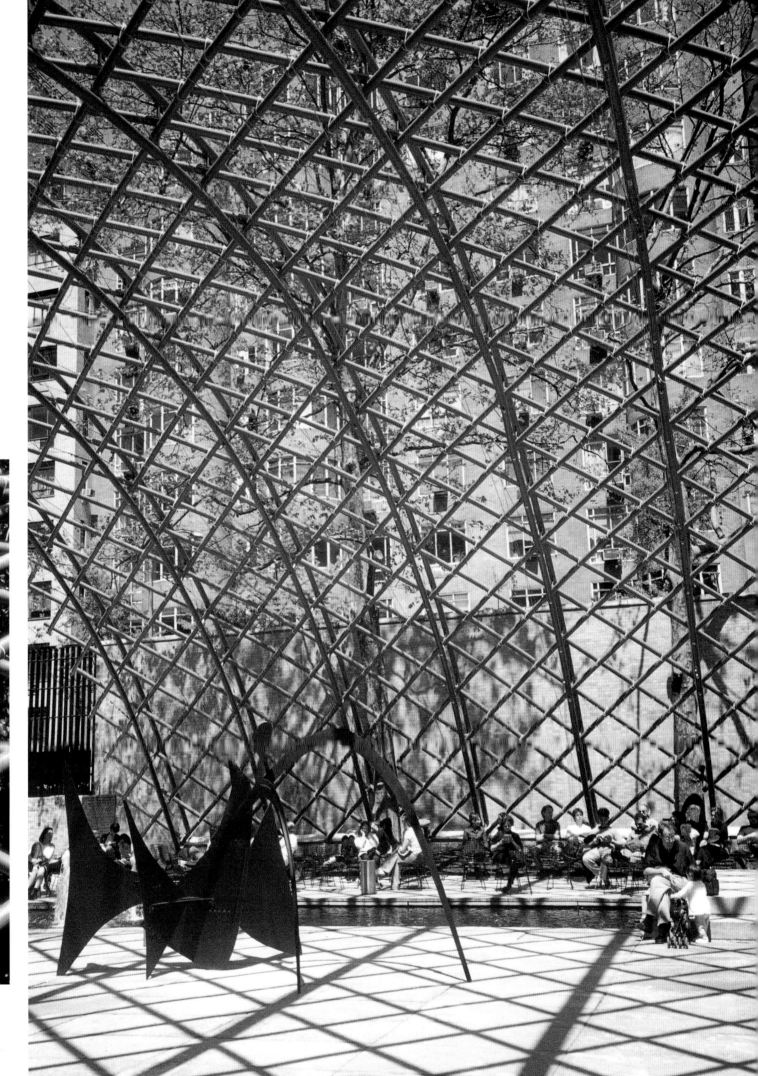

Paper Arch, The Museum of Modern Art,
New York, 2000
BELOW LEFT: Lifting a truss over the
garden wall on 54th Street for installation
BELOW RIGHT: Detail of a paper tube truss

OPPOSITE LEFT: Detail of paper tube
truss connection, 1:20
OPPOSITE RIGHT: Isometric view of
paper tube structure
OPPOSITE BOTTOM: Completed arch,
aerial view toward 54th Street

The Paper Arch was a 9.1-meter-high (30 feet) structure made entirely out of paper tubes and
commissioned by the Museum of Modern Art in New York as part of its celebration of the
new millennium. Spanning 26.5 meters (87 feet) over the central part of the Abby Aldrich Rockefeller
Sculpture Garden, the arch transformed the space into a monumental outdoor room.

When the museum asked Ban to design the project, its intention was for Ban to build upon its
exhibition history of contructing temporary houses and other structures in the garden. Beginning with
the first House in the Garden in 1949 by Marcel Breuer and ending ten years later with Three
Structures by Buckminster Fuller, the museum had commissioned works pertaining directly to current
building practices and advances. In Ban's original proposal, he used the entire garden as his floor plate,
designing a large paper-tube roof to cover it. Financial constraints reduced the size of his proposal
to one-third of the garden, but the effect of a grand enclosure was not diminished.

Fabrication of the structure took place offsite in Maspeth, New York, where a scaffolding company
assembled the Paper Arch and then cut it into eight segments. These segments were transported
to the museum, lifted into place by crane, then spliced together. The eight trusses braced by grid shell
tubes created a segment of an elliptical curve with an 18-meter radius (59 feet). The natural bend of the
tubes was a result of the weight of the tubes and the structure's geometry.

As in some of the architect's other projects, such as the Daycare Center in Odate and the Japan
Pavilion in Hannover, the Paper Arch featured the roof as its most expressive architectural element.
Its purpose was not only to cover but also to create a new context, complete with animated surfaces,
for the sculpture underneath.

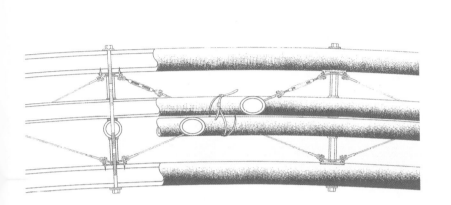

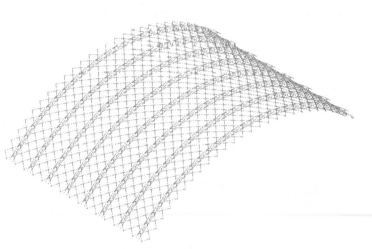

BOATHOUSE, CENTRE D'INTERPRETATION DU CANAL DE BOURGOGNE

DESIGN DATES:
September 1998 – August 2002
PROJECTED COMPLETION: 2004
LOCATION: Pouilly-en-Auxois, France
ASSOCIATE ARCHITECT:
Jean de Gastines Architecte DPLG —
Jean de Gastines, Damien Gaudin
STRUCTURAL ENGINEERS:
Buro Happold — Paul Westbury,
Geoffrey Werran;
Terrell Rooke and Associates —
Eric Dixon

BELOW: Studies of various aluminum joints
OPPOSITE TOP: Model
OPPOSITE BOTTOM: Plan and section, 1:600

Ban was commissioned to build a boathouse (phase 1) and an institute (phase 2) dedicated to the history of the Canal de Bourgogne in a community of small villages in Burgundy. The canal dates to the seventeenth century, but it was not completed until more than two centuries later, in 1832, when for the first time the north and south of France and the Seine and the Rhône were connected.

Ban's two buildings are sited at the summit of the canal, near its famous 3.2-kilometer tunnel. The boathouse is a paper-tube structure that will shelter a historically significant canal boat. The 20-meter-long tunnel arch is comprised of a grid shell that uses a triangular lattice of paper tubes. The outer diameter of the arch, 11 meters, is about the same as the tunnels that are found along the canal. For the first time Ban used a die-cast aluminum joint in order to utilize the same size paper tubes as at the Japan Pavilion and the same testing data for approval in France. This framework is covered by corrugated polycarbonate panels, but otherwise the structure is completely open.

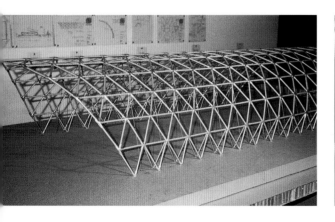
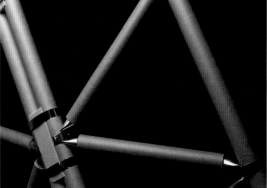
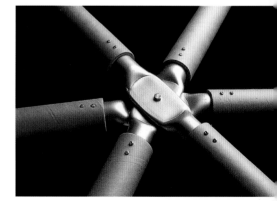

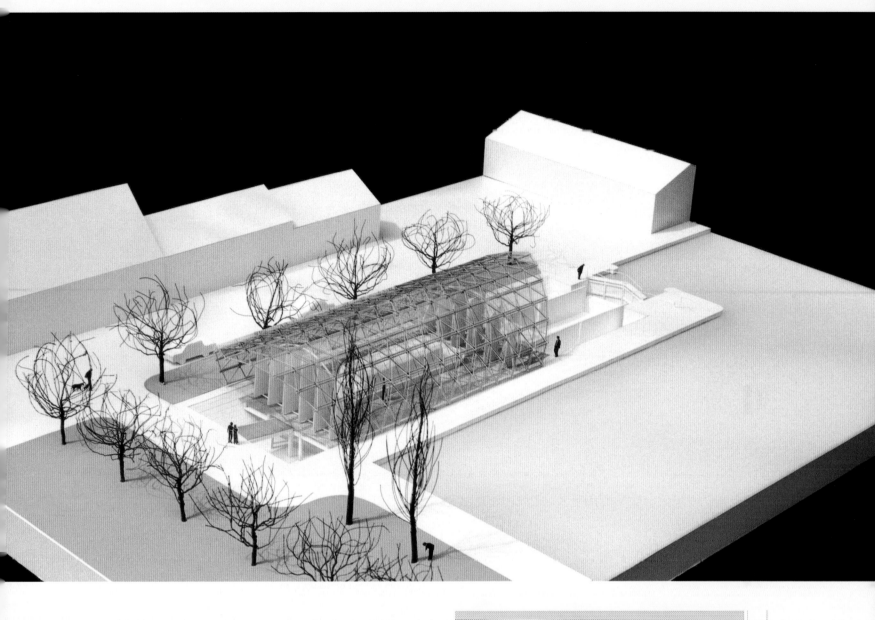

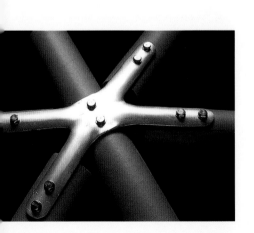

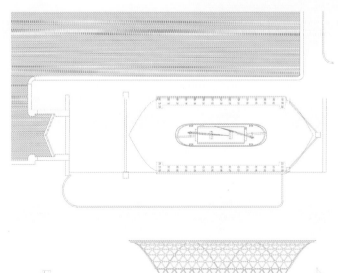

■ LIBRARY OF A POET

Experiment date	August 1990 – August 1991
Location	Waseda University Department of Architecture School of Science and Engineering Tokyo, Japan
Performed by	Dr. Minoru Tezuka Mr. Kazuo Ito

Test Report Profile

The purpose of this experiment was to determine the long-term effect of creep of the paper tubes under a constant axial load. The paper tubes under constant load were left in a room, and their dimensional changes in length were measured regularly over a period of one year.

Dimensional changes in length were measured regularly over a period of one year.

The Long-term Behavior of Paper Tubes under Constant Axial Load

1-1 _____ Test Specimens

Five paper tubes with a diameter of 100 mm, a wall thickness of 12.5 mm, and a length of 400 mm were used.

Axial force (=1000 kgf) was determined on the condition that it was less than a third of the compressive strength of the paper tube, as shown in Table 1.

Compressive strength of the paper tube was 103.2kgf/cm².

TABLE 1 Compression test results with Poisson's ratio and Young's modulus measured at Pmax/3.

Specimen	A (cm²)	P (kgf)	δ max (kg/cm²)	E (x10⁴kg/cm²)	
a-1	33.26	3335	100.3	1.86	0.192
a-2	33.5	3640	108.7		
a-3	33.5	3405	101.7	1.88	0.18
a-4	33.2	3452.5	104	1.89	0.197
a-5	33.65	3405	101.2	1.82	0.187
Averages			103.2	1.86	0.189

Area of a paper tube (A) $A = \dfrac{\pi}{4} \times (10^2 - 7.5^2) = 34.3\,cm^2$

Axial force (N) $N = \dfrac{34.3cm^2 \times 103.2kgf/cm^2}{3} = 1180\,kgf \longrightarrow \mathbf{1000\,kgf}$

Elastic deformation (ΔE) $\Delta E = \dfrac{1000kgf \times 40cm}{34.3cm^2 \times 1.86 \times 10^4 kgf/cm^2} = 0.0627\,cm \longrightarrow \mathbf{0.627\,mm}$

Operation of axial force-applied torque wrench. Its measured value equivalent to 1000 kgf was 310 kgfcm.

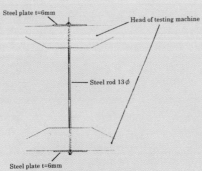

FIGURE 1 Measurement of tensile force in steel rod by testing machine,

The Long-term Behavior of Paper Tubes under Constant Axial Load

1-2 _____ Test Procedures

The specimen (paper tube) was inserted between two plates, and a steel rod was passed through the plates (Fig.2). This rod was fastened at 310kgfcm by a torque wrench, then a rectangular timber member with a dial gauge was inserted between the plates to measure the dimensional changes in length (Fig.3). To record the value of the gauge, the steel rod was refastened to 310kgfcm, then recorded. The temperature and relative humidity were also measured each time. Measurements were taken at intervals of about one week for the period of one year.

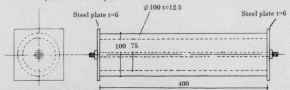

FIGURE 2 Specimen set (mm).

The rod was fastened at 1000kgf (29.2kgf/cm²) by a torque wrench.

FIGURE 3 Operation of axial force by torque wrench.

The Long-term Behavior of Paper Tubes under Constant Axial Load

1-3 _____ Test Results

Figures 4 shows the changes in temperature and relative humidity. Figure 5 shows the dimensional changes of the specimens. From Figure 5, it was determined that a large percentage of dimensional change in length is caused by relative humidity, and that dimensional changes due to creep are minimal.

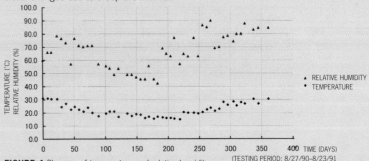

FIGURE 4 Changes of temperature and relative humidity.

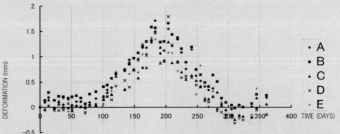

FIGURE 5 Dimensional changes in length of paper tube under long-term axial load.

A large percentage of dimensional change is caused by relative humidity.

■ PAPER HOUSE

Time of Experiment _____	October 14 – November 20, 1991
Location _____	Waseda University, Department of Architecture School of Science and Engineering Tokyo, Japan
Performed by _____	Chiba Polytechnic College Housing Environment Department Lectureship Dr. Minoru Tezuka Lectureship Nobumichi Yamada Mr. Kazuo Ito

Test Report Profile

The paper tubes are used as columns in Paper House. The purpose of this experiment was to investigate the short-term strength of the paper tube through a bending test, compression test, and a single shear strength test (on the lag-screws of the single shear wood-to-paper connections). Since moisture content has a great influence on paper strength, the moisture content of each specimen was measured.

1 _____	Paper Tube Compression Test
2 _____	Paper Tube Bending Test
3 _____	Single Shear Strength Test

All paper tubes' outer/inner diameter: ## 280mm/250mm

Paper Tube Compression Test
1-1 _____ Test Specimens

Five paper tubes were provided as specimens for this experiment. All specimens were accurately measured to obtain their inner diameter, outer diameter, and length. All paper tubes were 600mm in length and the cross-sectional area of each specimen was 126.0cm². The specific gravity of the paper tubes ranged from 0.81 to 0.82.

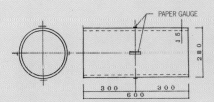

Four paper gauges (length=60mm) were bonded to the surface of each tube, as shown in Figure 1, in order to measure Young's Modulus and Poisson's Ratio.

FIGURE 1 Compression test specimen (mm).

Paper Tube Compression Test
1-2 _____ Test Procedures

The specimen was mounted between a base and a pressure plate on the testing bed. The tests were made by operating a compressor (REH-200) at loading speed 5–7kg/cm²/min at compressive stress.

Machine-rolled paper is wound up on a steel core with a space in between.

FIGURE 2 Compression test overview.

Paper Tube Compressive Test
1-3 _____ Test Results

Failure conditions: Assuming that σmax. is the compressive strength, the specimen showed visible wrinkles at 0.88σmax.

In particular, the specimen's ends were markedly warped, as though twisted. Wrinkles were also apparent along the spiral winding edges of the machine-rolled paper. The cause of this phenomenon is linked to the manufacturing process when machine-rolled paper is wound up on a steel core. In this process a space is left between the layers in order to maintain the prescribed paper tube thickness.

 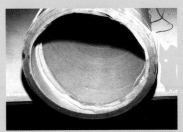

Specimen showed visible wrinkles at 0.88 times the compressive strength

FIGURE 3 Compression test results: (left) Failure condition, external view. (right) Internal view.

Figure 4 shows load-strain relations. The ● marked curve represents longitudinal strain (negative value), and the ▲ marked curve represents lateral strain (positive value). The load-strain relations of the paper tube resemble those of concrete.

The data summary of the test results is shown in Table 1, with Young's modulus and Poisson's ratio based on longitudinal and lateral strains measured at 1/3 compressive strength. The moisture content on average was 8.8%.

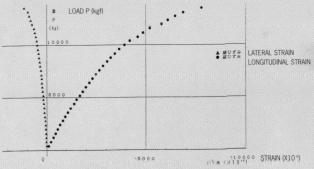

FIGURE 4 Compression test results: Relationship between load and strain.

TABLE 1 Compression test results.

SPECIMEN NO.	C - 1	C - 2	C - 3	C - 4	C - 5
COMPRESSIVE STRENGTH σC (kgf/cm²)	108.1	115.4	116.3	114.9	114.9
	AVERAGE=113.9				
YOUNG'S MODULUS .1 (X10⁴kgf/cm²)	2.55	2.40	2.34	2.45	2.33
	AVERAGE=2.41				
POISSON'S RATIO .1	0.113	0.155	0.150	0.135	–
	AVERAGE=0.138				
MOISTURE CONTENT (%)	8.3	8.8	8.9	9.2	8.8
	AVERAGE=8.8				

The average compressive strength of the paper tube was 113.9kgf/cm².

Since moisture content has a great influence on the specimen's strength, a small chip from the center of each specimen was cut and weighed after the test. The chips were later dried in a thermostatic chamber at 105 degrees Celsius for 7 days and were weighed again. To measure the moisture content the following formula was used:

$$\text{Moisture Content (\%)} = \frac{W1 - W2}{W2} \times 100$$

W1: Weight of the chip after compressive test
W2: Weight of the chip after drying at 105℃ for 7 days

Paper Tube Bending Test
2-1 _____ Test Specimens

Five paper tubes 4 meters in length were used, each having identical diameters, as mentioned previously. The span in the bending test was lengthened in order to minimize the partial deformation of the paper tube at supporting points and loading point.

Paper Tube Bending Test
2-2 _____ Test Procedures

A wooden block was put on either side of the tube, 1860mm from the center of the loading point. The specimen was stressed by a vertical force (P) at the midpoint of its length. Figure 5 shows the detail of the bending test. The loading speed was set out at 3–7kgf/cm²/min at extreme fiber stress. REH-200t was the test machine.

A small chip was cut out to record the moisture content of each specimen in the same way as the specimens for the compression test.

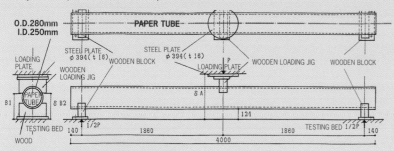

FIGURE 5 Bending test procedure (mm).

FIGURE 6 Bending test overview.

Paper Tube Bending Test
2-3 _____ Test Results

Failure conditions: Figure 8 shows the paper tube at maximum stress just touching the testing bed at the span center. The vertical force (P) on the specimen was increased until it unloaded at this point of maximum stress. In review of the test results however, the maximum strength under load is at the vertical displacement of 124mm from span center.

Results showed that wrinkles run along the spiral winding edge of the machine-rolled layers of paper. Further, the wrinkles are limited to the upper part of the span center.

Wrinkles are limited to the upper part of the span center.

FIGURE 7 (left) Loading point at center of span.
FIGURE 8 (right) Bending test results: Paper tube just touching testing bed at span center.

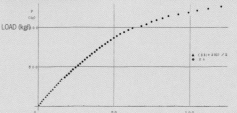

FIGURE 9 Bending test results: Relationship between load and displacement.

Bending strength, Young's modulus: The central displacement relation was obtained from the average of δB1 and δB2 (between the wooden loading jig and testing bed) and δA (between the loading plate and testing bed) as shown in Figure 5. The difference between δA and δB is negligible. The value of δB is more accurate. The range of measurement of δB is below the maximum 20mm displacement, therefore the value of δA was subsequently used.

fb > 1.42 × fc

TABLE 2 Results of bending tests.

SPECIMEN NO.	B – 1	B – 2	B – 3	B – 4	B – 5
BENDING STRENGTH	172.4	151.3	158.4	158.8	165.7
σb (Kg/cm²)	AVERAGE=161.3				
YOUNG'S MODULUS *1	2.18	2.15	2.26	2.20	2.29
(× 10⁴Kg/cm²)	AVERAGE=2.22				
MOISTURE CONTENT (%)	9.3	9.3	8.6	8.7	8.5
	AVERAGE=8.9				

Due to partial deformation, Young's modulus was equivalent to 92% of the result obtained in the compression test.

The bending strength is more than 1.42 times the compressive strength.

Single Shear Strength Test
3 _____ Test Report

In the design of Paper House, the paper tubes act as cantilevered columns in case of earthquakes or strong winds. When this occurs, the connection to the floor at the base of the column is subjected to bending moment. The aim of this experiment was to obtain the effect of the single shear wood-to-paper connections on the strength of the lag screws.

3-1 _____ Test Specimens

Paper tubes cut into 600mm lengths were used as specimens. Wooden joints of western hemlock were connected to the paper tubes by lag screws. Eight 12mm lag screws (D=12mm) were used in each specimen. The space between lag screws and from the edge of the paper tube was 7D. Wax was applied to the points of contact between the paper tube and the wooden joint.

Lag screws were used in the single shear wood-to-paper connection.

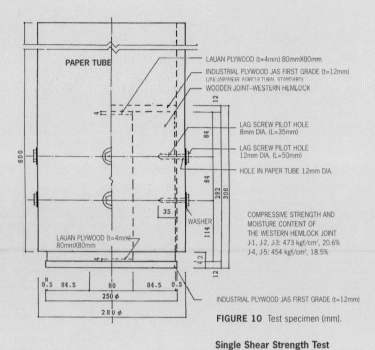

FIGURE 10 Test specimen (mm).

PAPER TUBE

LAUAN PLYWOOD (t=4mm) 80mmX80mm

INDUSTRIAL PLYWOOD JAS FIRST GRADE (t=12mm)
(JAS:JAPANESE AGRICULTURAL STANDARD)

WOODEN JOINT—WESTERN HEMLOCK

LAG SCREW PILOT HOLE
8mm DIA. (L=35mm)

LAG SCREW PILOT HOLE
12mm DIA. (L=50mm)

HOLE IN PAPER TUBE 12mm DIA.

COMPRESSIVE STRENGTH AND
MOISTURE CONTENT OF
THE WESTERN HEMLOCK JOINT
J-1, J-2, J-3: 473 kgf/cm², 20.6%
J-4, J-5: 454 kgf/cm², 18.5%

WASHER

LAUAN PLYWOOD (t=4mm)
80mmX80mm

INDUSTRIAL PLYWOOD JAS FIRST GRADE (t=12mm)

Single Shear Strength Test

3-2 _____ Test Procedures

The method followed that of the compressive test. Relative displacement between paper tube and wooden joint was assumed to be the same as the displacement between the testing bed and loading plate. The loading speed was 1.5–2.5 kg/cm²/min.

Single Shear Strength Test

3-3 _____ Test Results

Failure conditions: Figure 11 shows the deformation of the tube under low pressure. Figure 12 shows the failed condition of the specimen. The tube was greatly deformed at the head of the lag screw, as it was no longer perpendicular to the paper tube with increasing load.

FIGURE 11 (left) Condition of specimen at the start of the experiment.
FIGURE 12 (middle) Condition of specimen after the experiment.
FIGURE 13 (right) Failed condition of the wooden joint after the experiment.

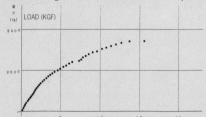

FIGURE 14 Load-displacement relationship.

LOAD (KGF)

DISPLACEMENT (mm)

TABLE 3 Results of single shear strength test.

SPECIMEN NO.	J－1	J－2	J－3	J－4	J－5
MAXIMUM LOAD	4625	4395	4500	4865	4865
	AVERAGE=4650				
LOAD AT 2mm OF DISPLACEMENT	1611	1424	1561	1483	1786
	AVERAGE=1573				
MOISTURE CONTENT OF PAPER TUBE	9.5	9.4	9.1	8.8	9.3
	AVERAGE=9.2				

The single shear strength was 581kgf per lag screw.

■ PAPER DOME

Experiment date _____ July 1997

Location _____ Chiba Polytechnic College
Housing Environment Department

Performed by _____ Assistant Prof. Dr. Minoru Tezuka

Test Report Profile

The paper tubes are used as arch members in the Paper Dome. The purpose of this experiment was to investigate the short-term strength of the paper tube through a compression test, bending test, and compression tests at different moisture contents, and to determine the connection strength through a shear test and bending test.

The paper tubes are manufactured under a constant production process in order to achieve high strength. Each paper tube is made from recycled paper, rolled at 74.5 degrees in 2mm intervals using a polyvinyl compounded bond. The bond accounts for 7–10% of the total tube weight. The data in Table 1 is provided by the paper tube manufacturing company.

TABLE 1 Mechanical properties of original paper.

Items		Results	Testing methods
Basis weight (g/m²)		521	JIS P 8124-1976
Thickness (mm)		0.728	IIS P 8118-1976
Bulk density (g/cm³)		0.72	
Moisture (%)		6.6	IIS P 8127-1979
Tensile strength (kgf/cm²)	MD*	890	JIS P 8113-1976
	CD**	253	
Compressive strength (kgf/cm²)	MD*	232	JIS P 8126-1987
	CD**	142	
Stöckigt sizing degree (sec.)		4545	JIS P 8122-1976
Young's modulus (×10³ kgf/cm²)	MD*	70–80	JIS P 8113-1998
	CD**	20–25	

Note: MD*: Machine direction. CD**: Cross direction. Related articles: Method of sampling paper for testing (JIS P 8110-1965). Conditioning of paper and paperboard for test (JIS P 8111-1976). JIS: Japanese Industrial Standard.

1 _____ Paper Tube Compression Test
2 _____ Paper Tube Bending Test
Compression Test of Paper Tubes at
3 _____ Different Moisture Contents
4 _____ Connection Shear Strength Test
5 _____ Connection Bending Strength Test

The outer/inner diameter of all paper tubes:
280mm/250mm

Paper Tube Compressive Test

1-1 _____ Test Specimens

Five specimens 600mm in length were provided. A strain gauge was used to read Young's modulus and Poisson's ratio, as in the Paper House experiments. Due to the large diameter of the specimens and their relative thickness, the edges could not be cut smoothly. Therefore, both ends of each tube were capped by applying epoxy adhesive on each cut surface and pressing a steel plate to each end.

FIGURE 1 (left) Application of epoxy adhesive to cut surface of paper tube.
FIGURE 2 (right) Capping the paper tube by pressing steel plate to adhesive.

Epoxy adhesive was used in capping the cut surfaces of the paper tubes.

Paper Tube Compression Test

1-2 _____ Test Procedures

The same procedures were followed as in the Paper House experiments, with the exception of the loading speed, which was 5–7kg/cm^2/min.

Paper Tube Compression Test

1-3 _____ Test Results

Aspects of failure are similar to the results of the compression test for Paper House. The local damage at both ends of the tube was reduced by the epoxy adhesive capping. Young's modulus and Poisson's ratio were calculated from the load-strain relationship by the same means as in the compression test for the Paper House. The results are shown in Table 2.

TABLE 2 Compression tests results.

	$D=291$		$d=250$		
Specimens	$(\sigma_c)_{max}$	E	ν	W	ρ
C-1	97.9	21.8	0.134	10.2	0.816
C-2	101.6	20.9	0.138	9.9	0.821
C-3	101.4	21.4	0.140	9.9	0.819
C-4	97.7	19.8	0.142	9.8	0.811
C-5	97.7	21.6	0.151	10.2	0.817
Means	99.3	21.1	0.141	10.0	0.817

D: Outer diameter (mm).
d: Inner diameter (mm).
$(\sigma_c)_{max}$:Compressive strength (kgf/cm^2).
E: Young's modulus ($\times 10^3$ kgf/cm^2).
ν: Poisson's ratio.
W: Water content in percentage of total weight(%)
ρ: Density (g/cm^3).

Compressive strength was 99.3kgf/cm².

Paper Tube Bending Test

2-1 _____ Test Specimens

Five paper tubes, 1758mm each, were used as specimens. Stiffeners were inserted at the loading and bearing points of every specimen to prevent local deformation.

Stiffeners were inserted to prevent local deformation.

Paper Tube Bending Test

2-2 _____ Test Procedures

Vertical displacements were measured at the two loading points and at the center of the span, which was nearly the same condition as loading on three equidistant points, confining the specimen's span to 1708mm.

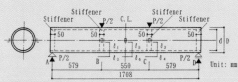

FIGURE 3 Bending test procedure.

Paper Tube Bending Test

2-3 _____ Test Results

The center of the specimen touched the test bed and wrinkles formed at the upper part of the specimen near the center of the span before failure occurred, just as in the results of the Paper House test. Values for Young's modulus obtained from the bending displacement were similar to the results from the compression test.

TABLE 3 Results of bending test.

	$D=291$	$d=250$	
Specimens	$\sigma_b{}^{**}$	E	W
B-1	149.2	22.9	10.5
B-2	150.7	21.9	10.4
B-3	157.5	20.1	10.0
B-4	155.5	19.7	10.1
B-5	147.0	22.7	10.1
Means	152.0	21.5	10.2

Young's modulus in the bending test was equal to that in the compression test.

D: Outer diameter (mm).
d: Inner diameter (mm).
$\sigma_b{}^*$: Bending stress at $\delta=124$ mm (kgf/cm^2).
$\sigma_b{}^{**}$: Bending stress at $\delta=36$ mm (kgf/cm^2).
E: Young's modulus ($\times 10^3$ kgf/cm^2).
W: Water content in percentage of total weight(%).

Bending strength was more than 1.53 times greater than the compressive strength.

Compression Test of Paper Tubes at Different Moisture Contents

3-1 _____ Test Specimens

Forty-five smaller paper tubes with an outer/inner diameter of 95mm/85mm and a length of 259mm were provided for this test. These tubes were made from the same original paper used to produce the specimens for the previous tests, but were produced by a different paper rolling machine with a different rolling angle.

The specimens were divided into nine groups according to their weight at absolute dry condition. Two groups of the nine were coated with a waterproofing agent, urethane-resin. The resin was diluted with thinner, which corresponded to 40% of the total weight of the diluted agent. Each cut surface was dipped in the diluted agent at a depth of 15mm from the edge for five minutes. Furthermore, external and internal walls of the tube were coated with the same agent. A second coat, this time with a 10% diluted agent, was applied using the same method, after the first coat had dried. These two groups of coated paper tubes varied in their moisture contents between 0.2% and 19.2% after the coating process.

Compression Test of Paper Tubes at Different Moisture Contents

3-2 _____ Test procedure

Compression tests were performed with the loading speed set to 7–8kgf/cm^2/min. The displacement between the paper tubes and the test bed was recorded. Moisture contents for the specimens coated by the waterproof agent were calculated by the following formula:

$$\text{Moisture Content (\%)} = \frac{W1-W2'}{W2} \times 100$$

W1: WEIGHT OF WATERPROOF AGENT COATED SPECIMEN, AT THE TIME OF TEST
W2': WEIGHT OF WATERPROOF AGENT COATED SPECIMEN, AT ABSOLUTE DRY CONDITION
W2: WEIGHT OF SPECIMENS AT ABSOLUTE DRY CONDITION, BEFORE BEING COATED WITH WATERPROOF AGENT

Compression Test of Paper Tubes at Different Moisture Contents

3-3 _____ Test Results

Figures 4 and 5 show the test results. It is important to note that the resulting Young's modulus figures are apparent values, because it was computed by applying Hooke's law to the displacement between the specimen and the test bed. The displacement had some frictional influence on the cut surfaces of the specimens. Under such circumstances, compressive strength and Young's modulus decreased in an inverse ratio to the rise in moisture content. Decreasing ratios of compressive strength and modulus gradually increased until the 7% moisture content level, but then increased acutely between 7% and 13%. The values then decreased gradually above the 13% moisture content level. The compressive strength and Young's modulus of the paper tubes at varying water contents can be estimated by the use of the aforementioned ratios.

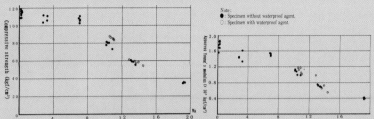

FIGURE 4 (left) Relationship between compressive strength and water content.
FIGURE 5 (right) Relationship between apparent Young's modulus and water content.

Compressive strength and Young's modulus decreased in an inverse ratio to the rise in moisture content.

Connection Shear Strength Test
4 _____ Test Profile

In the design of the Paper Dome, the compressive forces in the structure are resisted by the epoxy adhesive applied at the wooden joints, and by the compressive strength of the paper tube. The tensile strengths of the lag screws in the wood-paper connections resisted the tensile forces of the structure, thus it was necessary to perform tests for the strength of the wood to paper connection by lag screws.

4-1 _____ Test Specimens

Round joints made of laminated wood were inserted into one end of a paper tube and fixed using lag screws. Five specimens were made of Type-J2 using eight lag screws (M12, L=75mm), and five specimens were made of Type-J3 using twelve lag screws (M12, L=75mm), as shown below in Figure 6. The top cross-sectional surface (the compressive plane) of each tube was dipped in epoxy-resin adhesive for capping. The round laminated joint was inserted into the paper tube with 30mm of the joint remaining outside. The surface of the exposed portion of the joint became the compressive plane at the bottom.

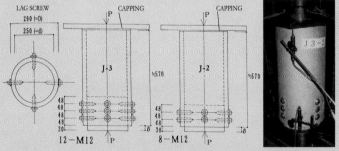

FIGURE 6 Shear test of lag screws (single shear wood-to-paper connection).

Connection Shear Strength Test
4-2 _____ Test Procedure

The shear test was carried out by applying pressure to the specimen's capping plane and the wooden base plane. Compressive load acting on the capping plane is transferred to the round wooden joints through the lag screws subjected to the shear force. The displacement between the paper tube's lower edge and the lower test bed was measured in order to obtain the relative displacement (δ) of the lag screws caused by shear. The loading speed was 200–300kgf/min. for Type-J2 specimens and 300–450kgf/min. for Type-J3 specimens.

Connection Shear Strength Test
4-3 _____ Test Results

Table 4 shows the test results. The relative displacements (δ) of Type-J2 specimens at P=1530kgf, 6120kgf, and 8568kgf are shown. Results show that the relative displacement of Type-J3 specimens at 1.5 times the loads applied to Type-J2 are similar. The relative displacements of Type-J2 at P=6120kgf and those of Type-J3 at P=9180kgf are similar. Among all the specimens, J2-3, J2-4 and J3-2 have comparatively large relative displacements. This dispersion of the data was possibly caused by different fastening forces of the lag screws, which consequently generated varying frictional forces between the round wooden joint and the paper tube.

TABLE 4 : Results of connection shear strength test.

Test Specimen	Outer Diameter	Inner Diameter	Pmax/nkgf /screw (n=8)	Moisture Content (%)	Relative Displacement (mm)		
					at P=1530kgf	at P=6120kgf	at P=8568kgf
J2-1	289.95	249.85	1396	10.40	0.195	2.115	4.2275
J2-2	289.75	249.80	1327	10.18	0.1975	2.4475	4.8725
J2-3	289.85	250.10	1344	10.31	0.4175	3.235	6.6825
J2-4	290.03	249.93	1321	10.51	0.4038	2.985	5.7175
J2-5	289.88	250.03	1556	10.55	0.16	1.83	3.985
Average			1389	10.39	0.2748	2.5225	5.097

Test Specimen	Outer Diameter	Inner Diameter	Pmax/nkgf /screw (n=12)	Moisture Content (%)	Relative Displacement (mm)		
					at P=2244kgf	at P=9180kgf	at P=12852kgf
J3-1	290.23	250.13	1267	10.23	0.2713	2.7613	7.0925
J3-2	289.83	249.88	1210	10.21	0.3288	3.41	7.315
J3-3	289.85	250.00	1247	10.07	0.2438	2.6038*	5.935**
J3-4	290.08	250.03	1261	10.47	0.265	2.405	4.8788
J3-5	289.98	250.20	1231	10.40	0.2638	2.18	4.7825
Average			1243	10.28	0.2745	2.672	6.0008

* : RELATIVE DISPLACEMENT AT P=9177kgf
** : RELATIVE DISPLACEMENT AT P=12845kgf

The connection strength was 1240kgf per lag screw.

Connection Bending Strength Test
5-1 _____ Test Specimens

A wood joint made from a laminated wooden block with dimensions 290mm (W) X 290mm (D) X 180mm (H), was fabricated to the shape of a cylinder (249ØX150mm) at both sides. Paper tubes (outer/inner diameters 290/250mm), with epoxy compound adhesive were inserted into the cylinders and fixed by twenty lag screws (M12, l=5mm). Four specimens were provided for this test, two BJ4 type specimens, with the screws fixed at the location of maximum bending stress, and two BJ5 type specimens, with the screws fixed at the neutral axis location of the paper tubes.

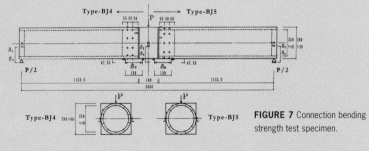

FIGURE 7 Connection bending strength test specimen.

Connection Bending Strength Test
5-2 _____ Test Procedure

The bending test was conducted by applying a centrally concentrated load on a span of 2450mm. Vertical displacements at the loading point (δ5, δ6) and at the bearing points (δ1, δ2, δ3, δ4), and the relative displacement (δ7, δ8) between the tensile side of the paper tube and the wooden block were measured. The loading speed was maintained at less than 64kgf/min.

5-3 _____ Test Results

Table 5 shows the bending strength of the specimens and Figures 9 and 10 show the Load-displacement relationships. Central displacement, excluding the amount of partial deformation at the points of support, is displayed in the bold plot in Figures 9 and 10, whereas the small plot displays the change in the amount of relative displacement ($\delta_7 + \delta_8$) caused by the shear force of the lag screw on the tension side of the specimen.

FIGURE 8 Failure condition of a specimen.

TABLE 5 Results of connection bending test.

Test Specimen	Outer Diameter	Inner Diameter	Pmax (kgf)	Moisture Content (%)
BJ4–1	289.78	249.66	2873	10.47
BJ4–2	290.13	249.79	2776	10.50
BJ5–1	289.99	249.96	2868	10.45
BJ5–2	290.20	249.91	2841	10.31
Average	——	——	2840	10.43

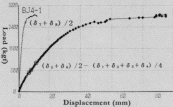
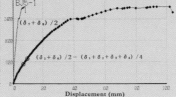

FIGURE 9 Load-displacement relationship for Type-BJ4 and Type-BJ5.

The bending strength of the connections Type-BJ-4 and Type-BJ5 was 1610kgfm.

■ NEMUNOKI CHILDREN'S ART MUSEUM

Experiment date _____ October 1998

Location _____ Chiba Polytechnic College
Housing Environment Department
Chiba, Japan

Performed by _____ Assistant Prof. Dr. Minoru Tezuka

Test Report Profile

In the Nemunoki Art Museum, the roof beams were constructed from Grid Core Panels, which are produced by gluing together two form-compressed "sub-panels" made from recycled resources such as paper and cardboard. For these tests, Grade-A Grid Core Panels, which are mainly composed of cardboard, were used to carry out a tension test, compression test, bending test, shear test, and skin-to-plywood adhesion test. Furthermore, the connection between the adhesive skin-to-plywood connection and aluminum joints was also tested.

On the premise that the museum would be climate-controlled at 20℃ and 60% relative humidity, the tests were carried out on specimens that were controlled at those conditions.

In this experiment, the water content rate of the panel at 20℃, 60% RH was 9.26%.

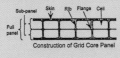

Standard Dimension
Nominal Dimension: 4×10 feet×3/4 inch (1,219×3,048×18.3mm)
A, B: Considered directions in picking the specimens

FIGURE 1 Grid Core Panel.

The rib portion of a sub-panel was carved off to leave just the skin. This skin, considered to be a thin board, had a thickness ranging from 0.8–1.4mm, with a tensile strength of 121kgf/cm², and Young's modulus of 40.1x10³kgf/cm², at 20℃ and 60% relative humidity. The specific gravity was 1.00g/cm³, and the estimated weight of the adhesive was supposed at 0.0044g/cm³.

TABLE 1 Basic performance of Grid Core Panel.

Test Item		Unit	Test Result			Remarks
			Standard state 20℃, 60%RH	State of Moisture absorption 20℃, 90%RH	Damp condition 1hr. water steep	
Apparent density		-	0.241			
Water content		%	9.5	15.8		JIS A 5905,5.5
Coefficient of moisture absorption		%	5.7			Standard→Moisture absorbing state
Coefficient of water absorption		%	85.2			JIS A 5905,5.9
Coefficient of water absorptive expansion		%	12.2			JIS A 5905,5.10
Compressive strength		kgf/m²	3.1	1.9	0.53	JIS A 6931,7.4
Bending strength	Length direction	kgf/m²	83.5	48.3		JIS A 5905,5.7
	Width direction	kgf/m²	81.6	48.5		JIS A 5905,5.18
Impact resistance	Dent diameter	mm	15.1	16.7	18.1	JIS A 1421,3.1
	Surface defect	-	None	None	None	
Heat conductivity		kcal/mh°C	0.0783			JIS A 1412,5.3
Moisture permeability		g/m²hmmHg	0.038			
Peel strength		kgf/m²	1.97	1.32		JIS A 5905,5.12
Wood screw retaining strength	At rib	Kgf	25.3	21.4		JIS A 5905,5.13
	Cell center	Kgf	15.0	14.4		

Test Item		Unit	Standard →Moisture absorbent	Moisture absorption →Dry	Standard →Damp	Remarks
Dimension change rate	Length	%	0.080	-0.73	0.43	
	Width	%	0.082	-0.74	0.41	
	Thickness	%	0.019	-3.82	12.0	

1 _____ Full-Panel Tension Test
2 _____ Full-Panel Compression Test
3 _____ Full-Panel Bending Test
Tension Test on Skin and Plywood
4 _____ Connection

Full-Panel Tension Test
1-1 _____ Test Specimens

Three specimens (Type-A) in the A-direction of width 36mm and length 440mm, and three specimens (Type-B) in the B-direction of width 32mm and length 400mm were cut from a full-panel of Grid Core Panel. Furthermore, epoxy was filled on both ends of the long direction of the full panel in order to prevent breakage in the connection between the full panel and the testing apparatus.

Full-Panel Tension Test
1-2 _____ Test Procedures

The ends of the full panel were pinched by chucks of the testing apparatus and pulled apart at a constant rate of 6.0kgf/min. Young's modulus was determined from readings measured by strain gauges attached to the full panel.

FIGURE 2 Test procedure: Specimen pinched on both ends by testing apparatus.

Full-Panel Tension Test
1-3 _____ Test Results

The results of the tensile strength and Young's modulus of the A-direction specimens were greater than the results for the B-direction specimens. There was a large difference in those specimens.

FIGURE 3 Failure conditions of Type-A specimen (A-direction) and Type-B specimen (B-direction).

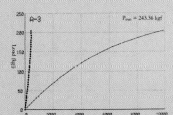
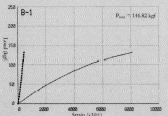

FIGURE 4 Load-strain relationship Type-A specimen (A-direction) and Type-B specimen (B-direction).

TABLE 2 Results of full-panel tension test.

Specimen No.	Thickness (cm)	Width (cm)	Weight* (g/cm²)	Area** (cm²)	Tensile Strength f t (kgf/cm²)	Young's Modulus E (x10⁵kgf/cm²)
A-1	1.91	3.60	0.5422	1.952	158.0	28.5
A-3	1.88	3.525	0.4962	1.749	139.1	29.1
A-4	1.8775	3.610	0.4929	1.779	102.7	25.2
Avg.	—	—	—	—	133.3	27.6
B-1	1.845	3.10	0.4340	1.345	109.2	26.3
B-2	1.855	3.135	0.3865	1.212	106.5	20.8
B-3	1.84	3.215	0.3657	1.176	99.4	26.7
Avg.	—	—	—	—	105.0	24.6

* Value of assumed wieght of adhesive 0.0044g/cm² subtracted from full-panel's weight of unit area (g/cm²)
** Assumed cross-sectional area = Weight x Width
Young's modulus(E) was secant modulus of elasticity at 1/3 P$_{max}$.

Average tensile strength was 105kgf/cm².

Full-Panel Compression Test

2-1_____Test Specimens

Three specimens (Type-C) in the A-direction with a width of 36.4mm and length of 126mm, three specimens (Type-D) in the B-direction with a width of 31.5mm and length of 127.3mm, three specimens (Type-I) in the A-direction with a width of 87mm and length of 179mm, and three specimens (Type-J) in the B-direction with a width of 86mm and length of 184mm were cut from a full panel of Grid Core Panel. For all specimens, capping was done by filling the cavities with epoxy at both ends of the long direction of the full panel in order to prevent local damage to the areas where loads are applied. For Type-I and Type-J specimens, in order to obtain accurate readings of the elastic constant, 60mm-long strain gauges were attached to the surface of the full panel (Figure 5), vertically and horizontally, at different locations of the rib arrangements.

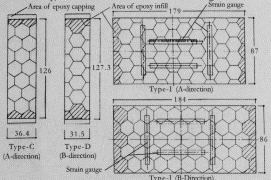

FIGURE 5 Test specimens: Type-C and Type-D, Type-I, and Type-J.

Full-Panel Compression Test

2-2_____Test Procedure

Figure 6 shows the specimens undergoing the test. Load was applied at a constant rate of 6.0kgf/min. for Type-C and Type-D specimens, and 15.0kgf/min. for Type-I and Type-J specimens.

FIGURE 6 Compression test procedure for Type-C, Type-D, Type-I, and Type-J specimens.

Full-Panel Compression Test

2-3_____Test Results

The compressive strength of the B-direction was greater than that of the A-direction in the test results for Type-C and Type-D specimens, contrary to that of the tension test. There is little difference in the values for Young's modulus between the A-direction and B-direction specimens. Also, there is little difference in the values of Young's modulus from the full-panel tension test.

There is little difference in Young's modulus between the A-direction and B-direction specimens, as well as in the full-panel tension test. 24.6–28.8 x 10³kgf/cm².

FIGURE 7 Failure condition of Type-C and Type-D specimens.

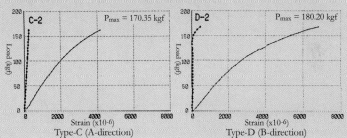

FIGURE 8 Load-Strain Relationship of Type-C and Type-D specimens.

Average compressive strength was 94.5kgf/cm².

TABLE 3 Full-panel compression test results for Type-C and Type-D.

Test specimen No.	Thickness (cm)	Width (cm)	Weight* g/cm²	Area** cm²	Tensile strength ft (kgf/cm²)	Young's Modulus E (×10³ kgf/cm²)
C-2	1.915	3.62	0.5172	1.872	91.0	28.0
C-3	1.9225	3.76	0.5387	2.026	93.7	27.6
C-4	1.9025	3.6975	0.5321	1.967	98.7	30.9
Average					94.5	28.8
D-1	1.80	3.0575	0.5101	1.500	104.0	(26.5)***
D-2	1.9125	3.1225	0.5210	1.627	110.8	25.1
D-4	1.8925	3.10	0.5517	1.710	110.0	29.4
Average					108.5	27.3****

* Value after estimated weight of adhesive 0.0044g/cm², is subtracted from full panel weight(g/cm²)
** Estimated section area = Weight* × Width   Same as Table 2.
*** Value according to the strain on one side.
**** Average value of D-2 and D-4
The Young's Modulus was secant modulus of elasticity at 1/3 P$_{max}$.

From the test results of Type-I (A-direction) and Type-J (B-direction), the values for Young's modulus and Poisson's ratio were respectively similar. Therefore, the shear modulus was calculated based on the assumption that the full panel was isotropic.

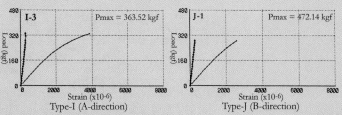

FIGURE 9 Load-strain relationship of Type-I and Type-J specimens.

TABLE 4 Elastic constants of full panels for Type-I and Type-J.

Specimen No.	Thickness (cm)	Width (cm)	Weight* (g/cm²)	Area (cm²)	Young's modulus $E(\times10^3 kg/cm^2)$	Poisson's Ratio ν	Shearing modulus $G(\times10^3 kgf/cm^2)$
I-1	1.825	8.535	0.4208	3.592	25.0	0.111	11.3
I-2	1.843	8.5875	0.5098	4.378	32.6	0.103	14.8
I-3	1.870	8.6775	0.5389	4.676	26.9	0.135	11.9
Average	–	–	–	–	28.2	0.116	12.7
J-1	1.877	8.555	0.4895	4.188	30.3	0.125	13.5
J-2	1.886	8.5825	0.4841	4.155	32.5	0.127	14.4
J-3	1.849	8.660	0.4452	3.855	23.0	0.095	10.5
Average	–	–	–	–	28.6	0.116	12.8

*Value after estimated weight of adhesive 0.0044g/cm², is subtracted from full panel weight(g/cm²)
Same as Table 2.
Young's Modulus (E) was the secant modulus of elasticity and Poisson's ratio (ν) was the horizontal strain/vertical strain at 1/3 P_{max}.
Shear Modulus(G) = E / 2(1+ ν)

TABLE 5 Full-panel bending test results for Type-E and Type-F.

Spec-imen No.	Thick-ness (cm)	Width (cm)	Weight* (g/cm²)	Area (cm²)	τ_{max} (kgf/cm²)	Z (cm³)	f_b (kgf/cm²)	I (cm⁴)	E ($\times10^3$kgf/cm²)
E-1	1.835	8.926	0.4275	3.816	17.0	5.677	152.7	25.34	32.9
E-3	1.840	8.980	0.4131	3.710	21.2	5.552	189.2	24.93	33.9
E-5	1.830	8.921	0.4592	4.097	24.3	6.091	217.7	27.17	41.7
Avg.					20.8	—	186.5		36.2
F-1	1.9125	9.455	0.4816	4.554	25.9	7.176	218.9	33.92	30.5
F-2	1.850	9.5275	0.4419	4.210	21.6	6.685	181.6	31.85	25.9
F-3	1.865	9.470	0.4454	4.218	22.7	6.657	191.5	31.52	26.9
Avg.					23.4		197.3		27.8

*Value after estimated weight of adhesive 0.0044g/cm², is subtracted from full-panel weight (g/cm²)
Area = Weight* x Depth τ_{max} =(Q_{max}/Area) x 1.5   Z=Weight* x (Depth)2/6.0   same as Table 2
fb = P_{max} / 2 x 20cm / Z   I = Weight* x (Depth)3 / 12.0
E: was determined by the constant increment of θ between 1/3P_{max} and 1/2P_{max}.
E = ΔP x 10cm x 20cm / I x θ

Full-Panel Bending Test
3-1 _____ Test Specimens

Three specimens (Type-E) in the A-direction with a width of 91mm and length of 1100mm, and three specimens (Type-F) in the B-direction with a width of 95mm and length of 1100mm were cut from a full panel of Grid Core Panel. For all specimens, the cavities of the full panel where loads were applied were filled with epoxy to prevent local damage.

Full-Panel Bending Test
3-2 _____ Test Procedure

As shown in Figure 10, the bending test was performed with the span set to 900mm. The loading speed was 2.0kgf/min. and Young's modulus was obtained by measuring the rotational angle of the zone subjected to constant bending moment.

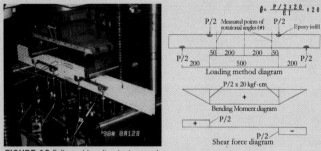

FIGURE 10 Full-panel bending test procedures.

Full-Panel Bending Test
3-3 _____ Test Results

There was a large difference in the resulting bending strengths, with the lowest strength being specimen E-1 (A-direction). Those of the other five specimens, independent of the direction of the ribs, were almost equal. There was also a large difference in Young's modulus. The Type-E (A-direction) specimens generally had a greater value than Type-F (B-direction) specimens. But, the Young's modulus of Type-F (B-direction) was similar to the resultant Young's modulus of the full-panel tension tests and full-panel compression tests.

Type-E (A-direction)   Type-F (B-direction)

FIGURE 11 Failure condition of Type-E and Type-F specimens.

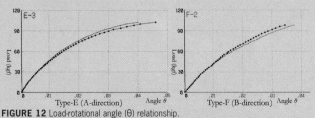

Type-E (A-direction)   Type-F (B-direction)

FIGURE 12 Load-rotational angle (θ) relationship.

Tension Test on the Skin and Plywood Connection
4-1 _____ Test Specimens

Five specimens (Type-K) were prepared as shown in Figure 13, where the rib portion was scraped out 45mm from both ends of the full panel, and plywood was inserted into that cavity and glued to the remaining skin using Resorcinol adhesive. The gluing process for the two skins and the plywood was accompanied by continuous pressure of 10kgf/cm² applied for twenty hours.

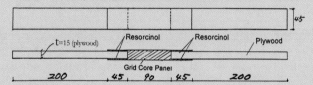

FIGURE 13 Tension test specimen Type-K.

Tension Test on the Skin and Plywood Connection
4-2 _____ Test Procedure

This tension test was performed by clamping the two open ends of the plywood using the chucks of the testing apparatus, and pulling them apart at a loading speed of 4.0kgf/min. (Figure 14). The specimen was clamped approximately 70mm from the end of the plywood on both ends. The distance between the two clamped ends (440mm) was set as the span.

FIGURE 14 Tension test specimen undergoing the test.

Tension Test on the Skin and Plywood Connection
4-3 _____ Test Results

All specimens had breakage occurring in the full panel (Figure 15). The adhesion strength between veneer plywood and skins was found to be greater than 7.32kgf/cm². The relationship of the load-displacement between the two clamped ends is shown in Figure 16, and the test results are shown in Table 6.

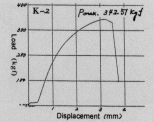

FIGURE 15 Failure condition.
FIGURE 16 Relationship of the load-displacement between the two clamped ends.

Specimen	Full panel					Adhered face
	Thickness (cm)	Width (cm)	Weight (g/cm²)	Area (cm²)	Tensile strength ft(kgf/cm²)	Shearing stress intensity (kgf/cm²)
K 1	1.82	4.4825	0.5133	2.135	121.3	7.32
K-2	1.8375	4.505	0.5237	2.359	145.2	8.46
K-3	1.8175	4.5025	0.5389	2.426	146.7	8.79
K-4	1.8375	4.50	0.5399	2.430	142.4	8.55
K-5	1.8275	4.4975	0.4916	2.211	134.3	7.33
Average	–	–	–	–	138.0	8.09

TABLE 6 Tension test results of the skin and plywood connection.

The adhesion strength between plywood and skins was greater than 7.32kgf/cm².

Experiment date _____ September 1998

Location_____ Kokan Keisoku K.K.
Instrumentation Department
Kawasaki, Kanagawa, Japan

Performed by_____ Mr. Kazuya Hashimoto
Instrumentation Engineer
Kokan Keisoku

Test Report Profile

The connection between the adhesive skin-to-plywood connection and aluminum joints was tested.

Connection Test

5-1_____Test Specimens

The purpose of this test was to verify the bearing force of wood screws. Two independent series of specimens were investigated, A-series and B-series. The A-series specimens were used to study the bearing force of one screw. The B series specimens were fabricated in particular detail with the prospect of being introduced to real structures. These were used to investigate the bearing force of a group of wood screws.

Five specimens of each of the two series were produced, and one end of each specimen was designated as the test end. The other end was connected with more than double the number of screws with the aim that it would have no effect on the test. Figure 17 shows the A-series and B-series specimens.

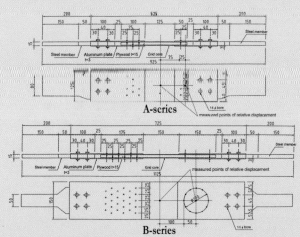

FIGURE 17 A-series and B-series test specimen.

Connection Test

5-2_____Test Procedure

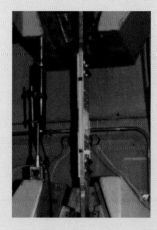

A constantly increasing loading test was conducted by clamping steel plate ends of the specimen with the chucks of the testing apparatus. The displacement between the grid core and the aluminum plate was read by PI displacement meters. Figure 17 shows the measured points of relative displacement.

FIGURE 18 Connection test procedure.

Connection Test

5-3_____Test Results

Inclined and pulled-out screws were found on all of the specimens after the tests; however, there were no accompanying fractures on the screw heads or other serious phenomena. As expected, fairly constant test results were obtained, without a large differential of ultimate loads and its load-displacement relationship.

The average strength per screw for A-series specimens was 290.7kgf, and for B-series specimens 259.0kgf. Therefore, the average strength of a B-series screw is close to 10% less than that of an A-series screw.

FIGURE 19 Failure condition of specimen.

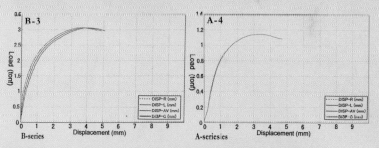

FIGURE 20 Load-relative displacement relationship of A-series and B-series specimens.

TABLE 7 Connection test results.

Test piece	Max. load (tonf)	Load per screw (kgf)	Breaking area/state
A-1	1.217	304.25	Slope/drawing of screw
A-2	1.134	283.50	Slope/drawing of screw
A-3	1.118	279.50	Slope/drawing of screw
A-4	1.144	286.00	Slope/drawing of screw
A-5	1.200	300.00	Slope/drawing of screw
Average	1.162	290.70	
B-1	3.091	257.58	Slope/drawing of screw
B-2	2.964	247.00	Slope/drawing of screw
B-3	3.064	255.33	Slope/drawing of screw
B-4	3.359	279.92	Slope/drawing of screw
B-5	3.062	255.17	Slope/draw of screw
Average	3.108	259.00	

■ JAPAN PAVILION

Experiment date _____ November 10, 1991

Location _____ University of Dortmund
Faculty of Building
Dortmund, Germany

Performed by _____ Dr. Ing. Klaus Block

Test Report Profile

The pavilion is an arc structure spanning approximately 35m with a maximum height of approximately 15m. A corridor is adjacent to the main structure on three sides. Its columns are about 8m high. For this arc structure, paper tubes with a diameter of 120mm and a wall-thickness of 22mm are applied.

The main load of the arc structure is its own dead load. This loading as well as snow load lead to predominantly compressive stresses. The horizontally acting wind load causes single-sided tensile stresses.

The purpose of these experiments was to test the structural behavior of the load-bearing paper made for the Japan Pavilion at Expo 2000, in Hannover.

Durolene paper in combination with glue PVA (resistance-class D2 of the German Industrial Standard DIN EN 204), with outer/inner diameters of 120/76mm, was selected as the building material.

In the experiment, unlike in the Paper House, Paper Dome, and Nemunoki Children's Art Museum tests, the following equation was used to calculate Moisture Content*:

$$\text{Moisture Content (\%)}^* = \frac{W1 - W2}{W2} \times 100$$

W1: Weight after testing
W2: Weight after drying

1 _____ Short-Term Axial Compression Test
2 _____ Long-Term Axial Compression Test
3 _____ Short-Term Bending Test
4 _____ Long-Term Bending Test
                           Axial Compression Test after Assembly
5 _____ Simulation
6 _____ Torsion Test
                           Applicability Test of the Damp Proof
7 _____ Membrane

Short-Term Axial Compression Test

1-1 _____ Test Specimens

Paper tube diameter/thickness: 120mm/22mm
Paper tube length: 240mm
Paper tube quantity: 5

Short-Term Axial Compression Test

1-2 _____ Test Procedures

The load was applied at a speed of 0.05 N/mm²/s. To determine the modulus of elasticity, special strain gauges (DDI) were utilized. They measure the changes in distance between two reading points at an initial distance of 100mm.

Short-Term Axial Compression Test

1-3 _____ Test Results

Failure of samples with diameters of 120mm is characterized by warping of the material (Figure 1).

TABLE 1 Results of the short-term axial compression test (Moisture content*: 8.7%)

test	strain [‰]	stress [N/mm²]	E-modulus [N/mm²]	evaluation of E-Modulus [N/mm²]		max. stress [N/mm²]	evaluation stress [N/mm²]	
							mean value	9.53
00	2.40	4.03	1550	mean value	1570	9.46	standard deviation	0.15
01	2.37	4.00	1560	standard deviation	21	9.60		
02	2.30	3.99	1610			9.76	5%-fractile	9.01
03	2.35	3.98	1570	minimum	1550	9.41	minimum	9.40
04	2.34	3.99	1580	maximum	1610	9.40	maximum	9.76

Compressive strength and Young's modulus were 9.53N/mm² (97.2kgf/cm²) and 1.57x10³N/mm² (16.0kgf/cm²) respectively.

FIGURE 1 Warping of the material due to axial compression, diameter/thickness 120/22mm.

Long-Term Axial Compression Test

2-1 _____ Test Specimens

Paper tube diameter/thickness: 120mm/22mm
Paper tube length: 240mm
Paper tube quantity: 8

Long-Term Axial Compression Test

2-2 _____ Test Procedures

To determine the influence of creep, the samples were loaded with a constant force. Its magnitude was chosen according to preceding studies of the strength as well as a decrease of the load in 5% increments. The starting magnitude was the strength determined in short-term tests. This load was lowered to a level where no failure occurred.

The load was applied at a speed of 0.05 N/mm²/s until the load level was reached. It was then kept constant. The time until failure occurred was recorded.

Long-Term Axial Compression Test

2-3 _____ Test Results

Failure was revealed by a rise in the deformation speed.

TABLE 2 Results of long-term axial compression test.

load [kN]	[%]	time [s]	moisture content* %
64.34	100	0	
61.13	95	4	7.8
57.91	90	9	7.6
54.69	85	110	7.9
51.47	80	200	7.8
48.26	75	510	7.4
45.04	70	5000	8.2
41.82	65	5600	7.3
38.61	60	36000	6.8

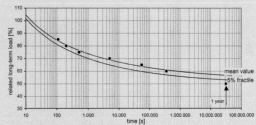

FIGURE 2 Results of the long-term axial compression tests.

Short-Term Bending Test

3-1_____Test Specimens

Paper tube diameter/thickness:	120mm/22mm
Paper tube length:	1000mm
Paper tube quantity:	5

Short-Term Bending Test

3-2_____Test Procedure

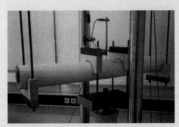

The span was 1m. The supports and the load implementation point were manufactured from wood in a so-called "saddle-shape." This minimizes local deformations on the sample. The load application and the constraining of the sample were obtained by a section, which was loaded with the maximum moment, but no shear force (Fig.3).

FIGURE 3 Bending test on tubes with diameter/thickness 120/22mm.

Short-Term Bending Test

3-3_____Test Results

Failure was preceded by a local failure of the compression zone (Fig.4) that led to a sudden failure of the tension zone. The load and the deflection of the testing machine were recorded as well as the deflection in the middle of the cross-section. In this case the deflection of the testing machine was similar to the deflection due to the applied load. The results of these tests are presented in Table 3

FIGURE 4 Bending test; local failure of the compression zone.

TABLE 3 Results of bending strength tests under short term load (Moisture content*: 10.1%).

test	Deflection [mm]	force [kN]	E-modulus [N/mm²]	evaluation of E-Modulus [N/mm²]		max. Stress [N/mm²]	evaluation of Stress [N/mm²]	
00	12.69	6.51	1430	mean value	1460	14.35	mean value	14.52
01	12.23	6.51	1480	standard deviation	29	14.34	standard deviation	0.2
02	12.27	6.53	1480			14.70	5%-fractile	13.84
03	12.59	6.51	1440	minimum	1430	14.45	minimum	14.34
04	12.14	6.50	1490	maximum	1490	14.76	maximum	14.76

Bending strength was 1.52 times greater than compressive strength.

Long-Term Bending Test

4-1_____Test Specimens

Paper tube diameter/thickness:	120mm/22mm
Paper tube length:	1250mm
Paper tube quantity:	9

Long-Term Bending Test

4-2_____Test Procedures

To determine the creep strength the same testing arrangement was used as in the bending tests. Similar to the creep tests, the load was stepped in 5% intervals using the short-term strength as base value.

Long-Term Bending Test

4-3_____Test Results

Failure starts with a yielding of the compression zone, which then leads to a breaking of the tension zone. The magnitude of the load level and the measured time until failure are shown in Table 4.

TABLE 4 Results of the bending strength tests under long-term load.

load [kN]	[%]	time [s]	moisture* content %
10.90	100	272	
10.36	95	310	9.3
9.81	90	449	10.0
9.27	85	727	10.0
8.72	80	2461	10.0
8.18	75	9137	9.6
7.63	70	47018	9.6
7.09	65	87790	9.6
6.87	63	1500000	8.3
6.54	60	10000000	9.2

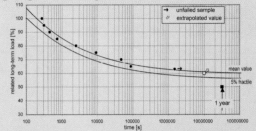

FIGURE 5 Results of the bending strength tests under long-term load.

Axial Compression Test after Assembly Simulation

5_____

Test Report Profile

During the assembly process bending stresses occur. The aim was to identify any damages that might have occurred during the assembly process.

Axial Compression Test after Assembly Simulation

5-1_____Test Specimens

Paper tube diameter/thickness:	120mm/22mm
Paper tube length:	1000mm
Paper tube quantity:	4

Axial Compression Test after Assembly Simulation

5-2_____Test Procedures

These tests were similar to those investigating the creep response with tubes of diameter/thickness 120/22 mm. However, instead of applying a force, deformation was applied to the specimen. The magnitude of the deformation was determined based upon the maximum radius of curvature (10m), which is reached on completion of the structure as well as in intermediate steps. The span was 1m.

In an elastic state the relation between curvature and deflection can be formulated as:

$$S'' = K = \frac{1}{r} = \frac{8}{l^2} S_{max} \longrightarrow S_{max} = \frac{l^2}{8r}$$

S_{max} = deflection at mid-span
r = radius of the structure
l = span

In the first step a radius of 30m was used; after 48 hours it was bent further to a radius of 8m. Based on this experience, a second test was carried out. There, the curvature was directly adjusted to 8m. It was then released to a radius of 10m. The time span between bending and releasing was shortened to 24 hours in a fourth test.

02 -bending to a radius of 30m (48 h), afterward bending to 8m (moisture content* 9.5%)
03 -bending to a radius of 8m (48 h), afterward bending to 10m (moisture content* 8.9%)
04 -bending to a radius of 8m (48 h), afterward bending to 10m (moisture content* 8.9%)
05 -bending to a radius of 8m (24 h), afterward bending to 10m (moisture content* 8.9%)

Following the assembly simulation tests the samples were cut and tested for their respective compression strength. The tests were performed similar to the short-term axial compression tests.

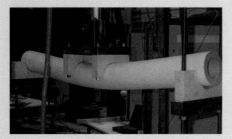

FIGURE 6 Simulation of the assembly process: relaxation.

Axial Compression Test after Assembly Simulation
5-3 _____ Test Results

No irreversible loss in material strength could be detected. The body stress due to the curvature has a magnitude of max. 2.25 N/mm², which was preceded by noticeable creep.

TABLE 5 Results of axial compression tests after assembly simulation.

test	strain [‰]	stress [N/mm²]	E-modulus [N/mm²]	evaluation of E-modulus [N/mm²]		max. stress [N/mm²]	evaluation of stress [N/mm²]	
031	2,38	3,47	1.460	mean value	1.470	9,23	mean value	9,56
032	2,32	2,47	1.500	standard deviation	37	9,32	standard deviation	0,28
033	2,33	3,46	1.490			9,46		
041	2,33	3,47	1.490			10,18	5%-fractile	8,61
042	2,47	3,47	1.410	minimum	1.340	9,39	minimum	9,23
043	2,28	3,49	1.530	maximum	1.530	9,57	maximum	10,18
051	2,29	3,49	1.520			9,91		
052	2,60	3,47	1.340			9,57		
053	2,38	3,46	1.460			9,45		

No irreversible loss in material strength could be detected.

Torsion test
6-1 _____ Test Specimens

Paper tube diameter/thickness: 120mm/22mm
Paper tube length: 1500mm
Paper tube quantity: 6

Torsion Test
6-2 _____ Test Procedure

The tests were carried out in the coiling direction as well as in the opposite direction. Tubes with diameter/thickness 120/22mm were utilized. For the tests the samples were fitted into wooden cylinders and mounted in a lathe. The load was applied via a lever 1m in length. The distance between the fixed support and the load application location measured 1.35m. Deformation was recorded at a distance of 1.20m. The distortion due to shear was recorded by monitoring the deformation at the outer circumference. Compared to monitoring the shear deformation due to shear force, this method allows for a simpler approach to obtaining the modulus of shear. The modulus of shear was computed using the following equations:

$$\tau = G\gamma = \frac{M_T}{W_T}$$
$$\Rightarrow G = \frac{M_T}{W_T\gamma} \quad \text{mit} \quad W_T = \pi r_m{}^2 (D-d)$$

G   modulus of shear
γ   shear distorsion
M_T torsional moment $M_T = P*l$
W_T torsional resistance moment
r_m radius of the middle surface
D   outside diameter
d   inside diameter

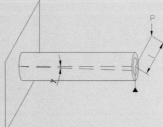

FIGURE 7 Torsion test.

Torsion Test
6-3 _____ Test Results

TABLE 6 Results of the torsion test.

a) in coiling direction

test	shear modulus [N/mm²]	mean value	140
		standard deviation	12,47
00	156		
01	131	minimum	131
02	141	maximum	156

b) opposite coiling direction

test	shear modulus [N/mm²]	mean value	180
		standard deviation	9,33
00	169		
01	188	minimum	169
02	177	maximum	188

Shear modulus in the coiling direction was 140N/mm² (1.43x10³kgf/cm²); in the opposite coiling direction it was 180N/mm² (1.84x10³kgf/cm²).

Applicability Test of the Damp Proof Membrane
7-1 _____ Test Specimens

Paper tube diameter/thickness: 120mm/22mm
Paper tube length: 2400mm
Paper tube quantity: 5

To test the resistance of the moisture protection the samples were coated with two layers of acrylic paint. The cut surfaces were covered with Perspex and silicone. Subsequently, the samples were exposed to a weathering cycle according to EOTA[1]. However the testing time was reduced from 28 to 7 days because of the limited length of the useful life of the structure. The testing cycle is typically used to investigate facade elements with a life cycle of 50 years. The mean rainfall per year (645l/m²) was applied within one week.

Note 1: ETAG Draft Nr. 14, February 1999, guideline for European Technical Approval for External Thermal Insulation Composite Systems with Render.

The weathering was performed in the following steps:

Day 1–5:   3 hours at 70°C and 15% humidity
             1 hour rainfall
Day 6–7:   2 hours at 15°C and 15% humidity
             Frost-defrost cycle without rainfall at +50°C and –20°C

Applicability Test of the Damp Proof Membrane
7-2 _____ Test Procedures

(a) The compression strength after weathering (length: 240 mm, quantity: 20).
The tests were similar to those measuring the deformation of the strength under axial compression.

(b) The bending strength after weathering (length: 1000mm, quantity: 5).
The tests were similar to those measuring the deformation of the strength in bending.

Applicability Test of the Damp Proof Membrane
7-3 _____ Test Results

TABLE 7 Results of short-term tests after weather conditions.

a) Axial compression tests (Moisture content*: 9.6%)

test	strain [‰]	stress [N/mm²]	E-modulus [N/mm²]	test	strain [‰]	stress [N/mm²]	E-modulus [N/mm²]	evaluation of E-modulus [N/mm²]		max. stress [N/mm²]	max. stress [N/mm²]	evaluation of stress [N/mm²]	
11	2,55	3,70	1452	33	2,46	3,70	1504	mean value	1440	8,93	9,06	mean value	8,70
12	2,60	3,73	1435	34	2,66	3,73	1406	standard deviation	55	8,75	8,63	standard deviation	0,19
13	2,60	3,72	1435	41	2,52	3,70	1471			8,67	8,98		
14	2,68	3,72	1389	42	2,68	3,71	1386	minimum	1359	8,67	8,65	5%-fractile	8,30
21	2,38	3,71	1561	43	2,53	3,75	1486	maximum	1561	8,76	8,95	minimum	8,39
22	2,74	3,72	1359	44	2,63	3,72	1416			8,55	8,67	maximum	9,06
23	2,62	3,73	1427	51	2,65	3,74	1411			8,59	8,70		
24	2,71	3,70	1366	52	2,67	3,70	1387			8,39	8,42		
31	2,43	3,73	1540	53	2,52	3,71	1474			8,89	9,01		
32	2,51	3,70	1476	54	2,55	3,69	1450			8,64	8,55		

b) Bending tests (Moisture content*: 9.2%).

test	Deflection [mm]	stress [N/mm²]	E-Modulus [N/mm²]	evaluation of E-Modulus [N/mm²]		max. stress [N/mm²]	evaluation stress [N/mm²]	
01	5,02	4,34	1.800	mean value	1.780	15,64	mean value	15,67
02	5,16	4,45	1.800	standard deviation	25	15,79	standard deviation	0,2
03	5,14	4,34	1.760			15,57	5%-fractile	15,01
04	5,10	4,27	1.740	minimum	1.740	15,98	minimum	15,47
05	5,18	4,45	1.790	maximum	1.800	15,47	maximum	15,98

Experiment date _____ July 15, 1999

Location _____ Institut für Baustoffe, Massivbau und Brandschutz (iBMB)
(Institute for Building Materials, Concrete Structures and Fire Protection)
Braunschweig Civil Engineering Materials Testing Institute,
Technical University Braunschweig, Germany

Performed by _____ RD. Dr.–Ing. Wesche

Officers in charge _____ DR.–Ing. Dobbemack
Techn. Ang. K. Feustel-Prause

Test Report Profile

In the Japan Pavilion at Expo 2000, in Hannover, Germany, a custom-made paper membrane was used as the main exterior envelope covering the primarily paper-tube arc structure. The purpose of this experiment was to determine the structural behavior of the load-bearing paper membrane and to obtain the Inflammable Standard B2 approval as set in DIN 4102 Part 1 – 6.2 (May 1998) for the "Paper Membrane Type C."

Fire Protection Performance of Paper Membrane

8-1 _____ Test Specimens

Description: "Paper Membrane Type C" is composed of the following superimposed layers:
–Foil 'Polylon incombustible film' from Sekisui Film Co. Ltd., Japan approx. weight: 48 g/m²

–Paper layer 'OK Cosmo' from Oji Paper Co. Ltd., Japan approx. weight: 150 g/m²

–Interior Fiberglas fabric, WLA90C103 from Nitto Boseki Co. Ltd., Japan approx. weight 86 g/m²

–Paper layer 'OK Cosmo' from Oji Paper Co. Ltd., Japan approx. weight: 150 g/m²

–Foil 'Polylon incombustible film' from Sekisui Film Co. Ltd., Japan approx. weight: 48 g/m²

Cumulative thickness: approx. 0.56 mm

Total weight: approx. 0.04 kg/m²

Five specimens 90mm wide x 190mm tall were required for the edge ignitibility test.

These specimens were conditioned according to DIN 50014-23/50-2 standard atmosphere for at least two weeks prior to testing. A gauge mark was drawn across the entire width on each specimen, 150mm above the bottom edge.

Fire Protection Performance of Paper Membrane

8-2 _____ Test Procedures

The test was carried out according to DIN 4102 Part 1 –6.2.5. The ambient temperature of the test room is to be about 20°C. Each specimen was placed in the testing apparatus as shown in Figure 8. The test consisted of 5 trials of applying the flame to the bottom edge of the specimen at the center of its width and thickness. The flame was applied for 15 seconds and then the burner pulled back, making sure not to create a draft. As soon as the specimen was exposed to the flame, time was measured to determine how long it took for the flame tip to reach the gauge mark (unless the flame extinguished beforehand).

This test was deemed passed if, for any of the five specimens tested, flaming did not reach the gauge mark within 20 seconds after flame application.

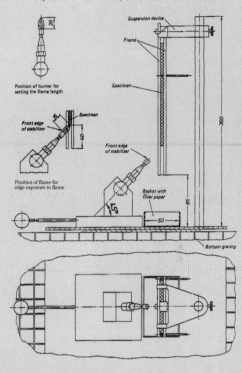

FIGURE 8 Arrangement of ignitibility test for building materials of Class B2.

While performing the edge ignition test, Class B2 materials are also to be tested for molten dripping. If within 20 seconds after exposure to the flame, the filter paper ignites, or if drops of the specimen that have fallen onto the filter paper burn for more than two seconds, then molten dripping has occurred.

Fire Protection Performance of Paper Membrane

8-3 _____ Test Results

In all tests, the requirements as set in DIN 4102 Part 1 –6.2 (May 1998) were fulfilled. In all of the tests, the flame did not reach the gauge mark. In all tests, there was no indication of molten dripping, as there was no ignition of the filter paper nor was there any burning drip-off of more than two seconds. Hence, the examined material was designated as standard inflammable Class B2. The material was indicated with the following qualification: DIN 4102 - B2.

TABLE 8 Test results for edge ignition test.

Specimen No.		1	2	3	4	5
Time taken to ignite specimen	[s]	1	1	1	1	1
Time taken to reach gauge mark	[s]	–	–	–	–	–
Time taken for flame to self-extinguish	[s]	–	–	–	–	–
Maximum flame height	[cm]	11	12	12	12	11
Time until end of smoldering	[s]	–	–	–	–	–
Time taken for flame to extinguish	[s]	30	30	25	25	30
Smoke development		with all tests moderate				
Occurance of molten dripping		–	–	–	–	–

WOOD

WOOD

In the past two decades, new high-performance wood construction materials have replaced many traditional building products. In the building industry these advanced materials are referred to as engineered wood products (EWP). They are variations on plywood—a material first made in ancient Egypt and China, though modern versions first appeared in the nineteenth century. Among these new products are laminated veneer lumber (LVL), laminated strand lumber (LSL), and oriented strand board (OSB).

LVL, first developed for airplane propellers and other aircraft parts during World War II, became widely used in the building industry during the 1970s. Today it is used as a high-strength component for all types of construction applications. LVL is made of parallel laminations of veneer glued together and processed to form a material that has a thickness similar to sawn timber. The difference between LVL and plywood is the orientation of the veneer layers: The direction of the plies in LVL is the same while in plywood it alternates.

LSL, developed within the last twenty years, is made of low-grade logs not normally used for conventional wood products. Debarked logs provide the material for flaked strands, up to 300 mm long, which are dried, coated with resin, and pressed into large billets by a process that includes steam injection.

In the manufacture of OSB, wood strands about 75 mm long are bonded with adhesives to form a mat. As with plywood, the mats are layered and oriented for maximum strength and stiffness. Recent innovations in the manufacture of OSB provide for a higher degree of water resistance and larger panel sizes.

Each of these products is manufactured from small lumber, making use of faster-growing trees and undesirable timber. Ban has used several varieties of engineered wood over the last twelve years, beginning with his first case study house, I House, in 1991. There Ban used structural plywood as both an interior finishing material and bracing. For Tazawako Station, Ban decided to use laminated timber as a structural support, but due to strict regulations, the client prohibited the use of structural timber. Skirting this restriction, Ban created a composite beam system employing steel plates sandwiched between laminated timber; the timber provided stiffness and insulated the steel plates. Ban employed wood for the first time as a fireproofing material in the GC Osaka Building after a change in building law allowed him to clad the steel frame of the building in particleboard with a plywood finish.

The Uno Chiyo Memorial Museum, a collaboration between Ban and Frei Otto, is designed for a site in Iwakuni, a scenic area near Hiroshima. The region's buildings are known for their distinctive *kawara*, or roof tiles, which define the curved shape of a traditional Japanese roof. This curved line usually consists of timber columns, beams, and rafters, so every structural member is working in compression. Ban and Otto, however, thought this form resembled the curve of a tension structure, so they created one from timber. As Ban explained, "In this way, form and structure became rational." Ban and Otto based their building technique on *ajiro*, a traditional Japanese wickerwork used to make ceilings and small crafts for the home. By weaving thin sheets of LVL and supporting the roof at the ridge (the uppermost point) and at the eaves (the lowest point), a large curve was formed. As a result, the roof was thinner and lighter and used less timber than a conventional one. Kawara roof tiles were laid on top so the structure harmonized with its surroundings.

Ban's Imai Hospital Daycare Center employed a different bentwood technique, *magewappa*, ordinarily used for small objects. Bentwood is used on the interior roof, while translucent polycarbonate panels form the exterior. On the interior, sheets of LVL form a light-filled tunnel and the scent of wood creates intimacy and warmth. Much larger than the daycare center, Ban's Atsushi Imai Memorial Gymnasium combines LSL with a truss-and-arch structural system to create a modest dome. He again applied translucent polycarbonate panels on the exterior and wood on the interior to admit natural light.

For the Wickerwork House, Ban employed a structural technique similar to the one used at the Forest Park Pavilion, substituting laminated wood for bamboo. Using Uno Chiyo as the main reference point, he refined the technique and construction. As with the daycare center and gymnasium, Ban translated two of the most outstanding and significant architectural elements of the traditional wooden Japanese house—the roof and ceiling—into a new, contemporary vocabulary.

Ban's design solutions are innovative without being high-tech, incorporating preexisting materials that he often refines to suit particular purposes. His ability to combine materials and techniques to make strong, innovative architectural creations is reminiscent of Aesop's fable of the father and his sons. In the tale, a father tries to heal the disputes of his quarreling sons by showing them the strength of a bundle of sticks and the weakness of a single one. Ban's work demonstrates the versatility and power of wood both as an individual material—itself a composition of multiple layers and fibers—and an integral component of the larger whole.

LEFT: Detail of laminated strand lumber (LSL)
RIGHT: Uno Chiyo Memorial Museum, Iwakuni, Yamaguchi, Japan, 1999–2000 (design)

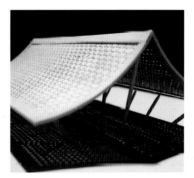

GC OSAKA BUILDING

DESIGN DATES: June 2000
LOCATION: Chuo, Osaka, Japan
ASSOCIATE ARCHITECTS:
Marunouchi Architects and Engineers —
Mitsuaki Matsuo
STRUCTURAL ENGINEERS:
VAN Structural Design Studio —
Shigeru Ban
FIRE ENGINEERS: Kajima Corporation —
Tomio Oouchi

OPPOSITE: Entrance facade,
view from street

The GC Corporation, an eighty-year-old company engaged in the research and development of dental products and equipment, commissioned Ban to design a six-story building in Osaka for its showroom and offices. The architect employed a Vierendeel truss system for the structure so that every other floor, beginning with the ground level, has a clear span of 22 meters. These column-free floors, totaling more than 2,100 square meters, are dedicated to showrooms, offices, and meeting rooms. The glass skin of the building allows views of the city; and an exterior courtyard, which contains an ivy privacy screen, is reminiscent of Ban's House for a Dentist and his Ivy Structures 1 and 2.

One particularly innovative element of this office building is the wood cladding on the steel structure. The wood acts as both an interior finishing material and fireproofing, since it does not transfer heat to the steel once it reaches a charcoal state. After testing both particleboard and plywood for the cladding, Ban chose to use a double layer of 25-mm-thick particleboard. This combined 50 mm thickness, providing one hour of fire protection, was determined by the standard specifications for flammable barrier design, which is calculated from the height of the building and the time necessary to evacuate the building.

Ban had begun experimenting with wood as a potential fireproof material several years earlier, in Tazawako Station. There he had clad the steel beams in wood, which functioned not only as a lateral support but also as insulation and to prevent condensation. However, it was not until the GC Building that he received permission to use this unlikely material as fireproofing.

GC Osaka Building, Chuo, Osaka,
Japan, 2000
LEFT: Ground floor showroom
BELOW LEFT: Section, 1:500
BELOW RIGHT: Detail of beam, 1:20
BOTTOM (left to right): First floor plan,
second floor plan, third floor plan, 1:500

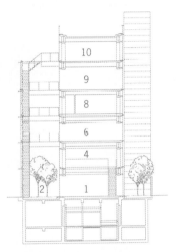

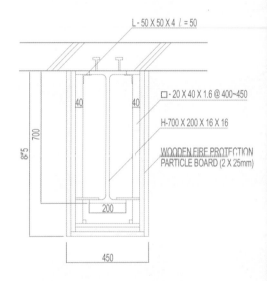

1 Showroom
2 Courtyard
3 X ray room
4 Library/information corner
5 Dining room
6 Office
7 Reception room
8 Training room
9 Meeting room
10 Resources room

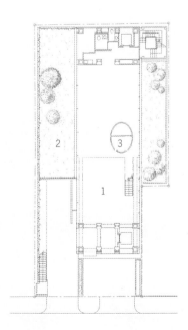

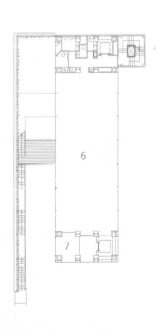

GC Osaka Building, Chuo, Osaka,
Japan, 2000
BELOW: Isometric view
OPPOSITE: Side courtyard and
south facade

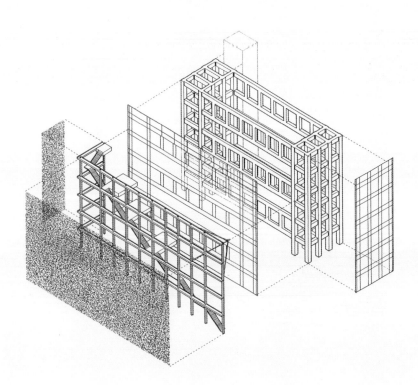

IMAI HOSPITAL DAYCARE CENTER

COMPLETION DATE: May 2001
LOCATION: Odate, Akita, Japan
STRUCTURAL ENGINEERS:
TIS & Partners —
Norihide Imagawa, Koh Sakata

OPPOSITE: South entrance

The roof in traditional Japanese architecture has frequently been described as the most important and expressive element of a building. Proportion, curve, and texture define its beauty and reveal the architect's sensitivity, especially in buildings of monumental size. Ban's daycare center is all roof. In fact, it could be considered a double roof system, with each roof distinct and serving a specific function. For the inner roof, which defines the overall interior space, Ban chose an engineered wood called laminated veneer lumber (LVL). He originally designed this inner roof to be a woven, netlike structure that would act as a compressive member to form an arch-shaped tunnel. However, at 30 mm the LVL was too thick to weave. Ban instead arrived at a solution inspired by a famous craft in the Odate region called *magewappa*. Basically a bentwood technique, it has been used for generations to make items such as *bento bako* (lunch boxes) and steaming baskets. Ban interpreted it on a much larger scale, bending nineteen sheets of 10.6 m x 60 cm x 9 cm LVL to enclose a 19.8 x 5.2-meter interior. The open spaces formed by the overlapping of the bentwood and thirteen sheets of LVL are glazed.

The exterior roof, made of fiberglass and folded steel plates, is angled at 45 degrees to allow snow to slide off. Translucent polycarbonate panels admit filtered sunlight inside, while an air pocket between the inner and outer roofs acts as insulation. This space also contains three-dimensional configurations of thin steel rods that reinforce the LVL. Ventilation caps near the roof and a grille at the base can be opened or closed depending upon the season.

Just as Ban discovered a way for paper to function structurally, with the Daycare Center he found a way to use thin sheets of LVL to span a large area. Ultimately, the center uses less wood than a typical design while at the same time creating a warm, womblike environment for the children and their care providers.

Imai Hospital Daycare Center, Odate, Akita,
Japan, 2001
BELOW (top to bottom): Plan, 1:250;
sections, 1:250; detail section, 1:100
BOTTOM CENTER: South and west
facades under construction
OPPOSITE: South entrance at night

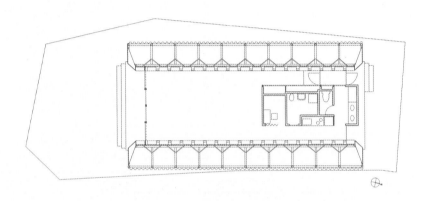

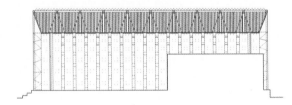

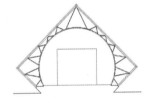

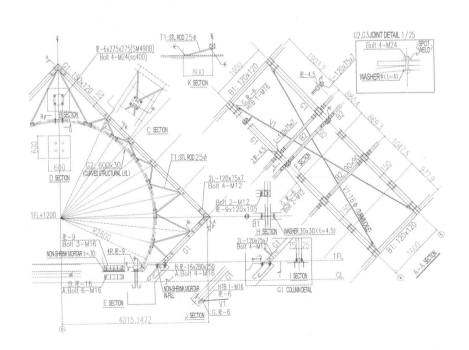

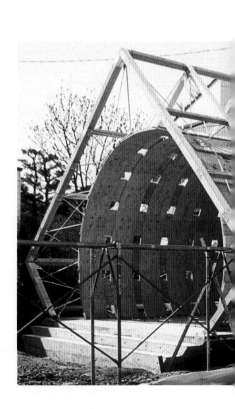

Imai Hospital Daycare Center, Odate,
Akita, Japan, 2001
OPPOSITE LEFT: Completed interior
LEFT: Detail of south entrance
BELOW: Axonometric view

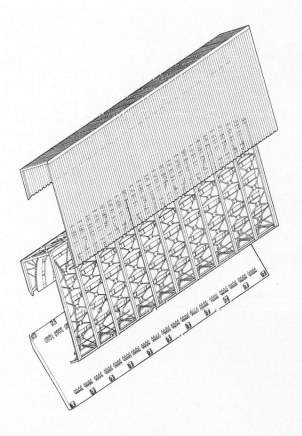

ATSUSHI IMAI MEMORIAL GYMNASIUM

COMPLETION DATE: August 2002
LOCATION: Odate, Akita, Japan
STRUCTURAL ENGINEERS:
TIS & Partners —
Norihide Imagawa, Yuuki Ozawa

OPPOSITE: Interior of main arena showing
laminated strand lumber (LSL) dome
BELOW: Site plan, 1:600

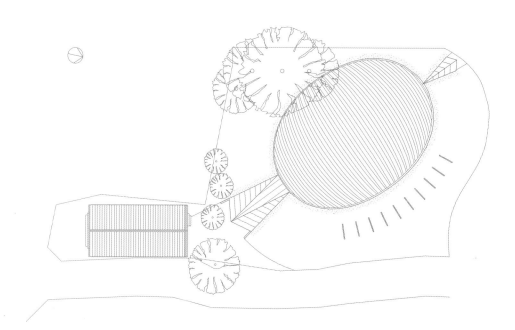

This gymnasium is situated in a small enclave of private houses, a two-story regional hospital, and a daycare center—the latter also designed by Ban one year earlier. Commissioned by the same client, the daycare center and gymnasium maintain the relatively modest scale of the surrounding buildings. For the 980-square-meter gym, which also functions as a small concert hall, this was achieved by placing the majority of the architectural program underground; only the roofs of the main space and entrance are visible. The main volume—an elliptical space inspired by the seventeenth-century architecture of Giovanni Lorenzo Bernini—contains a standard-size basketball arena. Annex spaces off the ellipse contain a swimming pool, changing rooms, and a piano room.

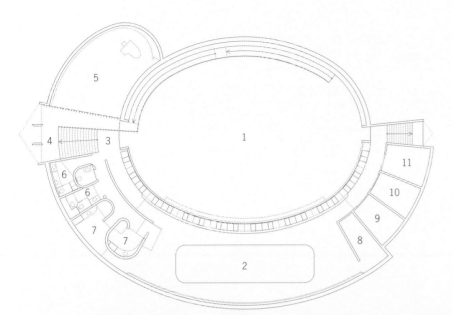

Atsushi Imai Memorial Gymnasium, Odate,
Akita, Japan, 2002
LEFT: Plan, 1:400
OPPOSITE AND BELOW (left to right):
Entrance viewed from below, arena
interior, view toward pool; swimming pool

1 Arena
2 Pool
3 Entrance hall
4 Entrance
5 Piano room
6 Washroom
7 Changing room
8 Pool storage
9 Water treatment room
10 Boiler room
11 Water tank room

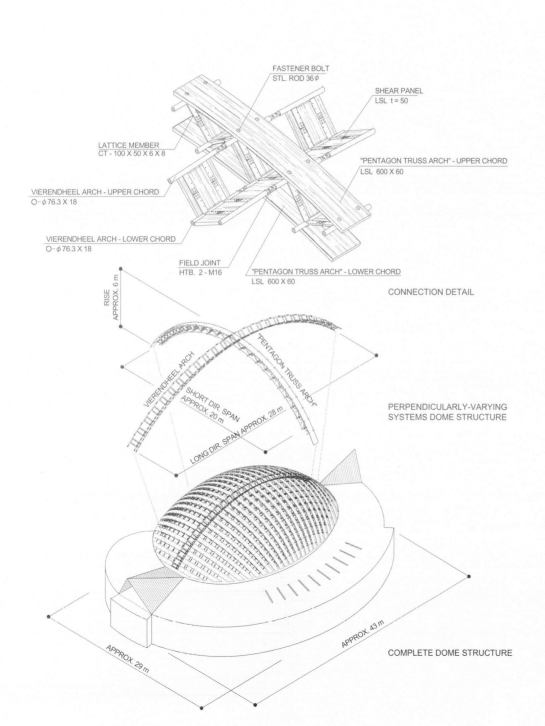

FASTENER BOLT
STL. ROD 36φ

SHEAR PANEL
LSL t = 50

LATTICE MEMBER
CT - 100 X 50 X 6 X 8

"PENTAGON TRUSS ARCH" - UPPER CHORD
LSL 600 X 60

VIERENDHEEL ARCH - UPPER CHORD
O - φ 76.3 X 18

VIERENDHEEL ARCH - LOWER CHORD
O - φ 76.3 X 18

FIELD JOINT
HTB. 2 - M16

"PENTAGON TRUSS ARCH" - LOWER CHORD
LSL 600 X 60

CONNECTION DETAIL

RISE APPROX. 6 m

VIERENDHEEL ARCH

"PENTAGON TRUSS ARCH"

SHORT DIR. SPAN APPROX. 20 m

LONG DIR. SPAN APPROX. 28 m

PERPENDICULARLY-VARYING
SYSTEMS DOME STRUCTURE

APPROX. 43 m

APPROX. 29 m

COMPLETE DOME STRUCTURE

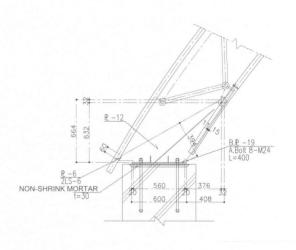

32
664
632
60
15
30°
PL - 12
PL - 6
2LS - 6
NON-SHRINK MORTAR
t = 30
B.PL - 19
A.Bolt 8 - M24
L = 400
70   560   20   376   32
600   408

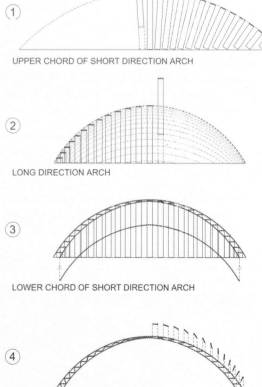

① UPPER CHORD OF SHORT DIRECTION ARCH

② LONG DIRECTION ARCH

③ LOWER CHORD OF SHORT DIRECTION ARCH

④ SHORT DIRECTION LATTICE MEMBER

Atsushi Imai Memorial Gymnasium, Odate,
Akita, Japan, 2002
OPPOSITE LEFT: Detail of roof truss
OPPOSITE RIGHT (top to bottom):
Detail at truss footing, 1:40; schematic
diagram of dome organization, 1:400
BELOW LEFT: Detail views of dome
construction with laminated strand lumber
BELOW: Cross section and longitudinal
section, 1:400

1 Arena
2 Pool
3 Entrance hall
4 Entrance

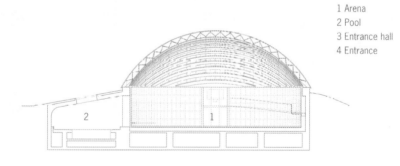

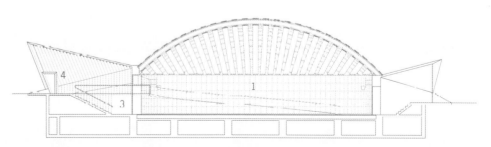

Atsushi Imai Memorial Gymnasium, Odate,
Akita, Japan, 2002
LEFT: East facade

Ban chose laminated strand lumber (LSL) as the structural material for the 20 x 28-meter dome that spans the sports arena. Like the laminated veneer lumber used in the daycare center, LSL is an engineered wood. However, it uses lower-grade logs, such as aspen, which are unsuitable for conventional lumber products. The material can be made in lengths of more than 14 meters and widths of 2.5 meters.

For the gymnasium's dome, Ban created a series of arches spanning 28 meters, and twenty-five 20-meter truss arches organized radially. This three-dimensional framework allows the LSL to act as the primary structural material with only a minimal use of steel structure, which runs on the long direction (north-south). Translucent polycarbonate roof panels admit natural light into the central arena and create checkerboard shadows on the floor.

The outer ring of the gymnasium, which is primarily underground, is constructed of reinforced concrete with double-glazed polycarbonate panels and metal roofing. Some parts of the ring will eventually disappear as grass and other plants begin to cover areas of the roof.

WICKERWORK HOUSE

DESIGN DATES:
June 2001 – September 2002
LOCATION: Chino, Nagano, Japan
STRUCTURAL ENGINEERS: Arup Japan
— Arata Oguri, Tatsuo Kiuchi

BELOW LEFT: Axometric view
BOTTOM: Demonstrating the construction
technique for woven plywood ceiling
OPPOSITE TOP: Model showing wickerwork
ceiling at left and final roof covering
at right

OPPOSITE BOTTOM LEFT: Model detail,
underside of ceiling; square portals
between woven plywood admit light
OPPOSITE BOTTOM RIGHT: Plan and
elevation, 1:400

This weekend house for a couple, surrounded by forest in a summer resort area in Nagano prefecture, is a glass box surmounted by a large woven-plywood dome. The 5.2-meter-high dome spans 12.6 meters, enclosing some 158 square meters of living space, including a terrace.

To create the Wickerwork House, Ban used the same structural principles he helped to develop for the Forest Park Pavilion, with a few minor alterations. Like the Pavilion, the woven plywood ceiling is broken down into interlocking units. Each unit, composed of four 1.6 m x 30 cm structural plywood (larch) boards, was prefabricated and then connected on site to create the woven ceiling. As the individual units are interlocked, they create a natural curve due to the length and thickness of the plywood. An insulating layer of urethane foam is sprayed on top of the ceiling, followed by an outer layer of glass-fiber reinforced plastic (GFRP) for weatherproofing.

The main difference between the house and the Pavilion is the addition of insulation and the use of wider strips of plywood. It was not crucial to have natural light permeate the roof, as at the Pavilion, and insulation was an obvious requirement for the house. In addition, the woven structure is not revealed on the exterior of the house, which is in keeping with woven ceilings prevalent in traditional Japanese houses—a source of inspiration for this innovative structure.

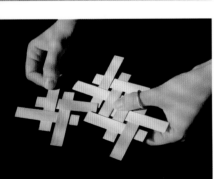

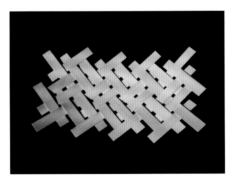
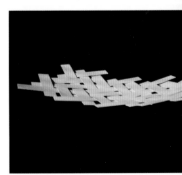

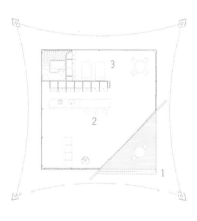

1 Entrance
2 Living/dining/kitchen
3 Sleeping

■GC OSAKA BUILDING

Experiment date _____ October 19 – 22 1999

Location _____ Central R & D Laboratory, Japan Testing
Center for Construction Materials

Performed by _____ Mr. Hiroshi Tanaike, Superintendent
Mr. Tokuaki Shibasawa, Test Leader
Mr. Katsuyuki Kitajima, Test Engineer
Mr. Harushige Saito, Test Engineer
Mr. Hidetake Shigenaga, Test Engineer
Mr. Toshiyuki Sekiguchi, Test Engineer
(Fire Protection & Fireproof Group)

Test Report Profile

Steel has greater strength compared to timber or concrete at normal temperatures. However, it is only half its strength at 500°C due to its physical characteristics. Nevertheless, steel structures must continue to bear structural loads throughout a fire, and so they are required to be protected by fire-resistant materials. Mainly, heavy materials such as concrete, mortar, and/or brick have been used. Lightweight asbestos has been used, but has been discovered to be harmful to humans. In constructing the GC Osaka Building, wood-based particleboard was applied as a fire-resistant material. Tests were conducted to see whether particleboard would pass as a fire-resistant material and prove to protect the structure for at least one hour in a fire.

Particleboard is a flat board made by bonding and hot pressing wood chips. Usually these boards are greater than 10mm thick and have a specific gravity of 0.5 – 0.7.

Fire-resistance tests were conducted to prove one hour of fire protection.

Particleboard Fire-Resistance Test

1-1 _____ Test Specimens

As shown in Figure 1, a steel frame (□20x40x1.6@425) was attached to an SS400 standard rolled structural steel section, H-400x200x8x13 (yield strength: 316N/mm², tensile strength: 457N/mm², elongation 30%). A double layer of pre-bonded, 25mm-thick particleboard, aged for 60 days after production and for 2 days after bonding (density: 640kg/m³ after 7 days of drying at 105°C, water content: 8.8%, adhesive: polyvinyl acetate resin emulsion 225g/m²) was screwed to the steel frame as the fire-resistant material. The inner layer of particleboard was fixed to the frame using tapping screws (ø = 3.5, l = 40) and the inner and outer layers of particleboard were fixed using wood screws (ø= 3.8, l = 38) after they had been bonded together. The rolled structural steel was 5.5m in length and the particleboard covered the entire surface except for 350mm on both ends that were left exposed. Two test specimens were prepared for this test.

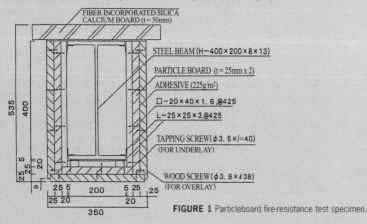

FIBER INCORPORATED SILICA CALCIUM BOARD (t = 50mm)
STEEL BEAM (H-400×200×8×13)
PARTICLE BOARD (t = 25mm x 2)
ADHESIVE (225g/m²)
□-20×40×1.6,@425
L-25×25×3,@425
TAPPING SCREW(ø3.5×l=40) (FOR UNDERLAY)
WOOD SCREW(ø3.8×l38) (FOR OVERLAY)

FIGURE 1 Particleboard fire-resistance test specimen.

Particleboard Fire-Resistance Test

1-2 _____ Test Procedures

The test procedure was carried out in compliance with ISO/FDIS 834-1 (1997). As shown in Figure 2, a bending test was performed by applying two linear loads at two points, equal distances apart across a span of 5100mm. After the constant load was applied, the specimen was heated for 60 minutes by burners running on gas oil fuel. The still-loaded specimen was observed for a further 120 minutes. The displacement and the temperature transition of the specimens were measured.

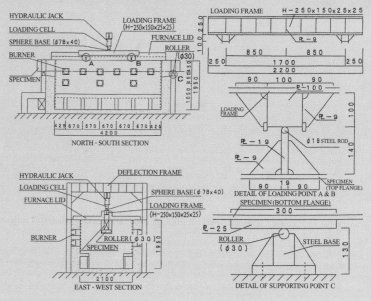

NORTH - SOUTH SECTION

EAST - WEST SECTION

DETAIL OF LOADING POINT A & B

DETAIL OF SUPPORTING POINT C

FIGURE 2 Procedures for constant loading.

Determination of a constant load value:

The steel beam's weight per unit length was 1.31kgf/cm. A constant load was determined on the condition that maximum bending stress (consisting of the beam's own weight, the jig's weight, and the constant linear loads) did not exceed the long-term allowable stress of 1.6tf/cm². P was the value of the constant load on a loading point before subtracting the jig's weight. P was computed using the following formula, and the total load (2P) was 211kN. Consequently, the loading weight was determined to be 208kN, deducting the jig's weight from P.

$$P = \left(\frac{3}{l} \cdot \sigma \cdot Z\right) - \frac{3wl}{8}$$

l : Span of the two supporting points, 510cm.
Z : Section modulus, 1170cm³
w : Steel beam weight per unit length 1.31kgf/cm
σ : Long-term allowable stress of SS41, 1600kgf/cm²

Specimens were heated for the first 60 minutes, then observed for a further 120 minutes.

Points for recording heating temperature, steel beam displacement, and temperature transition:

Figure 3 shows the ten points where heating temperature was recorded and the twelve points where the steel beam displacement was recorded. The temperature readings were located at the center of the span (2 points), 700mm away from the center (4 points), and 1400mm away from the center (4 points). Readings for the displacement of the steel beam were recorded at the center of the span (DG1, DG2), along the two linear loading lines (DG3/DG4, and DG5/DG6), at the two supporting points (DG7/DG8, and DG9/DG10) and at both edges (DG11/DG12). DG11 and DG12 were used to measure the elongation of the beam. The pressure in the fire pit was maintained at 10Pa throughout the test.

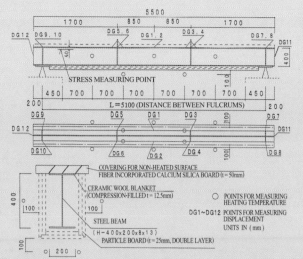

FIGURE 3 Points for heating temperature readings and beam displacement readings.

Points for temperature readings of the steel beam are shown in Figure 4. The 24 locations were fixed in the zone of the largest bending moment (area of the span center). At three locations along the beam (at the center of the span, and 740mm on either side of the center), temperature reading locations were distributed to two points on the upper flange, two points at the center of the web, and four points on the lower flange.

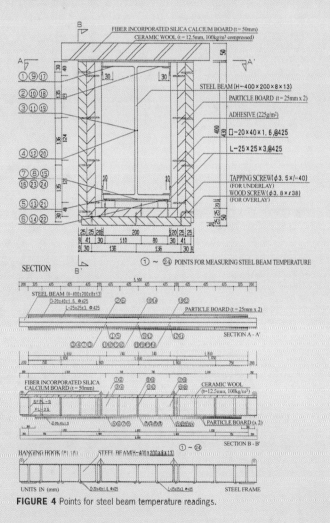

FIGURE 4 Points for steel beam temperature readings.

Figure 5 shows a view of the fire pit interior with the specimen suspended in place at the top and burners shown on either side.

FIGURE 5 View of interior of fire pit.

Particleboard Fire-Resistance Test

1-3 _____ Test Results

The results of the heating temperatures for specimens A and B are shown in Figure 6. With heat applied for 60 minutes, the temperature for both specimens rose between 900 and 1000°C. Thirty minutes after the heating had ended, the temperature of specimen A was between 400 and 500°C and of specimen B between 450 and 550°C. After that, the downward curve became gentle and the temperature in the fire pit at the end of the test (180 minutes) was between 200 and 300°C for specimen A and between 300 and 400°C for specimen B.

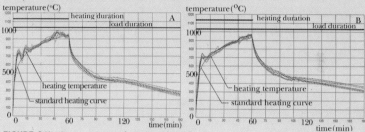

FIGURE 6 Heating temperature of specimen A and B.

Figures 7a and 7b show the deflection, elongation, and load variations of specimens A and B, respectively, through the passage of time. The initial deflection value of each specimen before heating was 10mm at the center (δ_1), 8mm at loading point (δ_2), and 9mm at loading point (δ_3). Both figures reflect this condition before heat was applied as deflection value zero in order to read the variations of deflection after heating. Consequently, there was no variation of the maximum deflection between specimens A and B after 60 minutes of heating. The maximum deflection rate was 0mm/min. for specimen A and 1mm/min. for specimen B after 2 minutes of heating. Within 60 minutes of applied heat, the elongation for specimen A was 1mm after 49 minutes, and for specimen B, 2mm after 53 minutes. The maximum deflection of both specimens after heating was terminated was between 24 and 25mm (162.6mm=L^2/400d, L=5100mm d=400mm) at 120 minutes. The maximum deflection speed of both specimens was 2mm/min. (A: after 98 min., B: after 104 min. 30 sec.), and the maximum elongation for both specimens was between 25 and 26mm occurring at 130 minutes.

Upon heating for 60 minutes, maximum deflection was 24–25mm (at 120 min.), maximum deflection speed was 2mm/min., and maximum elongation was 25–26mm (at 130minutes)

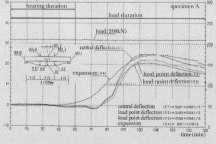

FIGURE 7a Deflection, elongation, and load variation due to the effects of time: specimen A.

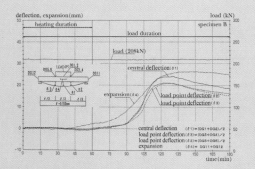

deflection, expansion(mm)   load (kN)

FIGURE 7b Deflection, elongation and load variation due to the effects of time: specimen B.

Table 1 shows the temperature variations of the steel beams for Specimens A and B. Figures in parentheses indicate the elapsed time after heat was applied. The maximum temperature of the beam for specimen A was 75°C and the highest temperature of the average value among the three cross section locations was 68°C. Respectively, those figures for specimen B were 87°C and 83°C. After the applied heat was terminated, the maximum temperature and the highest average temperature at any cross section were 477°C (at 123 min. 30 sec.) and 440°C (at 126 min. 30 sec.) for beam A, and 486°C (at 132 min. 30 sec.) and 460°C (at 137min. 30 sec.) for beam B.

TABLE 1 Maximum temperatures of steel beams.

Specimen		A			B		
Test time		60 min. *1	120 min.	180 min.	60 min. *1	120 min.	180 min.
Max. Temperature		75 (60 min.)	472 (120 min.)	477 (123 min. 30sec.)	87 (60 min.)	474 (120 min.)	486 (125 min 30 sec.)
Average	*3 Cross Section Mark	I	64 (60 min.)		431 (120 min.)	83 (60 min.)	443 (120 min.)	446 (125 min. 30 sec.)
		II	68 (60 min.)	434 (120 min.)	440 (126 min. 30 sec.)	82 (59 min. 30 sec.)	428 (120 min.)	460 (137 min. 30 sec.)
		III	64 (60 min.)	418 (120 min.)	430 (129 min.)	78 (60 min.)	390 (120 min.)	423 (134 min. 30 sec.)
	Upper Flange		71 (60 min.)	370 (120 min.)	390 (133 min.)	83 (60 min.)	351 (120 min.)	417 (148 min. 30 sec.)
	Web		67 (60 min.)		429 (120 min.)	84 (60 min.)	434 (120 min.)	442 (128 min. 30 sec.)
	Lower Flange		62 (60 min.)	459 (120 min.)	462 (122 min. 30 sec.)	79 (60 min.)	449 (120 min.)	466 (128 min. 30 sec.)

Temperatures in degrees Celsius

Notes:
*1 Heating time was 60 minutes.
*2 Average temperature of each cross section represents the average value of the four points shown below.

Calculation of Average:
Cross section I: (1+3+6+7) / 4
Cross section II: (10+12+13+15) / 4
Cross section III: (17+19+22+23) / 4

Table 2 explains how specimens A and B transformed throughout the duration of the tests. The outer particleboards of both specimens had almost entirely crumbled away after 60 minutes of heating. However, the inner particleboards had not fallen off although their surfaces were burning. The inner particleboards fell away at around 150 minutes for both specimens A and B, and the steel beams were exposed, but the beams continued to bear the load throughout the entire 180 minutes of the test.

TABLE 2 Transformation of the specimens over time.

Specimens		Time	A — Visual observations
Test Duration	Heating with load	2min 30sec	Particleboards began to burn and whole specimen was brazed 30 sec.
		30 min.	Picture 3 shows specimen's condition at 30 min. time heating.
		43 min.	Part of outer particleboard on lower flange began peeling.
		43min 50sec	Part of outer particleboard on lower flange began to fall away.
		47 min.	Part of outer particleboard on both side faces (web faces) began to fall away.
		60 min.	No notable change of bearing power against load was observed at 60 minutes time. Almost entire outer particleboards had fallen away after heating finished. But no inner particleboards fell off or away, although they already began burning at the time.
	Sustaining load	95 min.	Particleboards on both ends still burning, other flames blown out. Hot ashes partially remaining.
		105 min.	Inner particleboard on lower flange began to burn. Web catching on fire due to burning particles (particles burned for about 15 mins.)
		120 min.	Inner particleboard of lower flange began to fall away.
		150 min.	Almost all outer and inner particleboards except for both ends fell away and exposed steel beam.
		180 min.	Test was completed. Specimen sustained ability to bear constant load.
After test			Almost all outer and inner particleboards except for both ends fell away and steel beam was exposed.

Specimens		Time	B — Visual observations
Test Duration	Heating with load	3 min.	Particleboards began to burn and whole specimen was brazed 30 sec.
		30 min.	Picture 5 shows specimen's condition at 30 min. time heating.
		43 min.	Part of outer particleboard on lower flange began peeling.
		45min 50sec	Part of outer particleboard on lower flange began to fall away.
		53min 30sec	Part of outer particleboard on both side faces (web faces) began to fall away.
		60 min.	No notable change of bearing power against load was observed at 60 minutes time. Almost entire outer particleboards had fallen away after heating finished. But no inner particleboards fell off or away, although they already began burning at the time.
		90 min.	Particleboards on both ends still burning, other flames blown out. Hot ashes partially remaining.
		100 min.	Inner particleboard of lower flange began to burn.
		150 min.	Almost all outer and inner particleboards except for both ends fell away and exposed steel beam.
		180 min.	Test was completed. Specimen sustained ability to bear constant load.
After test			Almost all outer and inner particleboards except for both ends fell away and steel beam was exposed.

At around 150 minutes the particleboards had fallen, exposing the beams, but the beams continued to bear the load for the 180 minutes of testing.

FIGURE 8a View of specimen A before test.

FIGURE 8b View of specimen A after test.

APPENDIX 1 Sample of beam section with particleboard fire protection.
APPENDIX 2 Flames being applied to a fire-protected mock-up.
Note: Appendix images show mock-ups that were not actually used in this experiment.

■ IMAI HOSPITAL DAYCARE CENTER

Experiment date _____ July – September 2000

Location _____ Chiba Polytechnic College
Housing Environment Department
Chiba, Japan

Performed by _____ Assistant Prof. Dr. Minoru Tezuka

Test Report Profile

In this building, LVL (laminated veneer lumber) curved at a radius of 2600mm was used, and so bending tests were done on both curved LVL and straight LVL to confirm Young's modulus and changes in strength of the material.

LVL: It is a wooden material produced by laminating layers of relatively thick lamina. The veneer is peeled from logs in the natural circular direction of the rings of wood so that the fibers of the veneer are mostly parallel. LVL is made by laminating many layers of lamina in parallel, whereas in plywood, every other layer of lamina runs perpendicular.

LVL is made by laminating many layers of lamina in parallel.

LVL Bending Test
1-1_____Test Specimens

For this experiment, two types of wood lamina, Douglas fir and Lodgepole pine, were used to produce LVL. For both types of wood, four specimens of straight LVL and four specimens of curved LVL (of radius 2600mm) were prepared for a total of 16 specimens. In manufacturing the two types of LVL specimens, extra attention was taken to ensure that the curved LVL and straight LVL were composed of the same lamina. The dimensions of each specimen were 30mm (D) x 90mm (W) x 690mm (L). Since it was not possible to shape LVL of 30mm depth into a curve, it was divided into three separate lamina layers that were individually curved and then relaminated.

LVL Bending Test
1-2_____Test Procedures

As shown in Figure 1, bending tests for all experiments were carried out by applying loads at two points equal distances apart across a span of 630mm. There were three types of tests: Type I, Type II, Type III, testing straight LVL, curved LVL with bow facing up, and curved LVL with bow facing down, respectively. Loading was applied at a constant rate of 0.16kN/min., and the displacement was measured vertically at the center of the span.

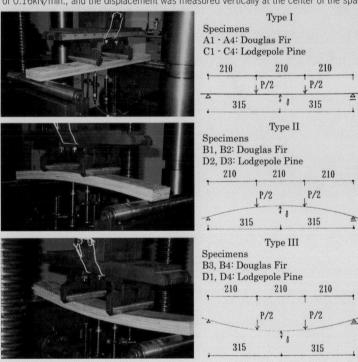

Type I
Specimens
A1 - A4: Douglas Fir
C1 - C4: Lodgepole Pine

Type II
Specimens
B1, B2: Douglas Fir
D2, D3: Lodgepole Pine

Type III
Specimens
B3, B4: Douglas Fir
D1, D4: Lodgepole Pine

FIGURE 1 Test procedure.

LVL Bending Test
1-3_____Test Results

The relationship between load and displacement and the failure conditions for each test type are shown in Figure 2 through Figure 4. From the slope and maximum load (Pmax) shown in the graphs, the Young's modulus and bending strengths are calculated according to the formula below.

$$E_b = \frac{23 \times \Delta P \times L^3}{1296 \times I \times \delta}$$

L= 63cm, Δ: The difference of the maximum load and minimum load (kgf) in proportional zone
δ: Displacement corresponding to ΔP (cm)
I: Moment of inertia of area (cm⁴)

$$\sigma_b = \frac{Pmax \times L}{6\,Z}$$

L= 63cm
Pmax: Maximum load (kgf)
Z= section modulus (cm³)

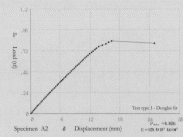

FIGURE 2 (left) Load-displacement relationship (Type I, Douglas fir, A2). (right) Failure condition.

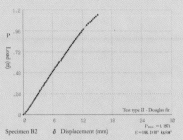
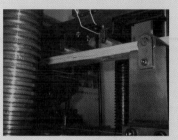

FIGURE 3 (left) Load-displacement relationship (Type II, Douglas fir, B2). (right) Failure condition.

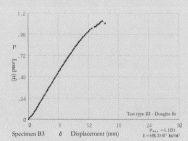

FIGURE 4 (left) Load-displacement relationship (Type III, Douglas fir, B3). (right) Failure condition.

The failure conditions for all tests are shown in Figure 5. All specimens failed (broke) at the center of the span. The resulting data for each test type and wood species are shown in Table 1, and the resulting Young's modulus and bending strength are respectively illustrated in Figure 6 and Figure 7. According to the data obtained, there is a difference in the results between the two species of wood, but there is almost no difference in the results between straight and curved LVL.

TABLE 1 Bending test results of LVL.

	Avg. Width	Avg. Thickness	Z	I	Pmax	σb	ρ	w.c.	R	Eb	L	Test Type
A1	8.911	2.979	13.18	19.63	1098.5	875.2	0.582	7.87	-	161.2	689.5	I
A2	8.918	2.98	13.36	20.03	857.82	674.2	0.542	7.84	-	129.4	690	I
A3	8.94	3.004	13.45	20.20	894.54	698.5	0.56	7.9	-	135.5	689	I
A4	8.896	3.003	13.37	20.08	910.86	715.3	0.566	7.94	-	155.4	689.5	I
B1	8.893	3.217	15.34	24.67	1204.6	824.6	0.612	8.21	2560	139.4	679	II
B2	8.912	3.237	15.50	25.19	1197.5	807.9	0.624	8.3	2070	140.1	670.5	III
B3	8.894	3.188	15.07	24.01	1127.1	785.6	0.647	8.35	2292	168.2	678	II
B4	8.875	3.24	15.53	25.16	1051.6	711.1	0.64	8.22	2666	147	680.5	II
C1	8.857	2.995	13.24	19.83	979.2	776.5	0.568	8.4	-	118.3	690.5	I
C2	8.828	2.971	12.99	19.29	908.82	734.8	0.57	8.31	-	119.8	690	I
C3	8.827	2.00	13.16	10.66	886.38	707.6	0.56	8.58	-	118.5	689.5	I
C4	8.838	2.986	13.13	19.61	753.78	602.6	0.549	8.26	-	110.9	690	I
D1	8.776	3.033	13.46	20.41	685.44	534.9	0.599	8.39	2576	131.3	688	III
D2	8.761	2.987	13.03	19.46	857.82	691.4	0.606	8.79	2497	109.7	688	II
D3	8.735	3.188	14.8	23.59	913.92	648.6	0.582	8.64	2567	98.9	688.5	II
D4	8.776	2.938	12.63	18.55	886.38	737.1	0.62	8.37	2592	136.4	686	III

Z: section modulus (cm³); I: moment of inertia of area (cm⁴); Pmax: maximum load (kgf)
σb: bending strength (kgf/cm³); ρ: density (g/cm³); w.c.: water content (%)
R: radius of curvature (mm); Eb: Young's Modulus (x10³kgf/cm²); L: span length (mm)

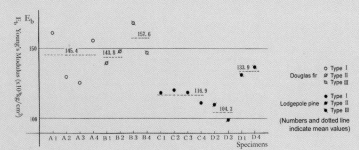

FIGURE 5 Dispersion of Young's modulus.

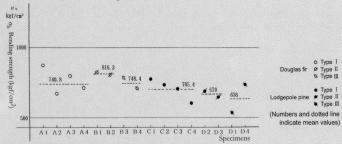

FIGURE 6 Dispersion of bending strength.

There is almost no difference in the results between straight and curved LVL.

■ ATSUSHI IMAI MEMORIAL GYMNASIUM

Experiment date	July – September 2001
Location	Tohoku Polytechnic College, Applied Course Department of Advanced Architectural Technology for Construction Systems, Miyagi, Japan
Performed by	Dr. Minoru Tezuka Prof. Nobumichi Yamada

Test Report Profile

The plan of the dome in this gymnasium is elliptical and the dome was supported by trussed arches and Vierendeel arches. The trussed arches were organized parallel to the minor axis of the ellipse and the Vierendeel arches parallel to the major axis. The trussed arch was composed of laminated strand lumber (LSL) chord members and steel diagonal members. On the other hand, the Vierendeel arch was composed of steel pipe horizontal members, steel vertical members, and LSL shear panels. The loads of the roof were distributed in the directions parallel to the major and minor axes and transferred down to the reinforced concrete ring beam on the perimeter of the dome.

LSL chords of the trussed arch parallel to the minor axis were bent and tested to examine a decrease of Young's modulus and bending strength. Joint connecting diagonal members and the chord, and the lag screw single-shear LSL-to-LSL connection in field joint of chords, were tested to examine their strength.

LSL is a structural material made of poplar and aspen, or aspen, white birch, and red maple. These timbers are peeled and cut into strand pieces 25mm wide by 305mm long, and 0.7mm thick. After these strand pieces are dried, they are glued by laying their grains in the same direction.

The dome of the gymnasium was supported by LSL trussed arches (minor axis) and Vierendeel arches (major axis).

Component Material Experiments

1	LSL Bending Test
2	Drift pin (36Ø) Single Shear LSL-to-Steel Connection Test (parallel to grain)
3	Drift pin (36Ø) Single Shear LSL-to-Steel Connection Test (perpendicular to grain)
4	Drift pin (36Ø) Single Shear LSL-to-LSL Field-Joint Connection Tension Test (parallel to the grain)
5	Lag Screw (12Ø) Single Shear LSL-to-LSL Field-Joint Connection (Parallel to the grain)
6	Shear Stiffness Test of LSL Panel

Component Material Experiments

	LSL Bending Test
1-1	Test Specimens

On the trussed arch, curved LSL was used. Since it was not possible to shape 60mm-thick LSL into a curve, it was divided into three laminas, each 20mm thick, that were individually curved and then relaminated. Ten specimens of straight LSL and twenty specimens of curved LSL were prepared. Laminas made from the same lot were used on both straight and curved LSL and all laminas were glued with the grain of the material aligned in the same direction. Specimens were kept at 20±2°C and 65±5% relative humidity. Their weight was stabilized and confirmed before testing.

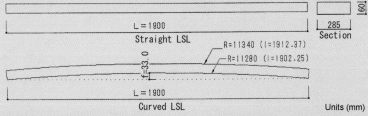

FIGURE 1 LSL Bending test specimens.

	LSL Bending Test
1-2	Test Procedures

The test was conducted with the loading speed set to 4kN/min. Loads were applied at two points, each 150mm away from the center of the span (span=1740mm). The displacement was measured at the center of the span, at the loading points, and at the support points as shown in Figure 2.

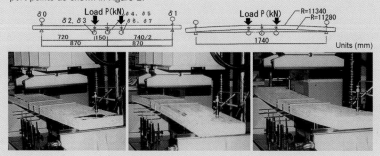

FIGURE 2 LSL bending test procedures (units: mm).

LSL Bending Test

1-3_____Test Results

Examples of the load-displacement relationship for each type of specimen are shown in Figure 3. Based on the slope and maximum load shown here, Young's modulus and bending strength were calculated using the formula below.

$$E_b = \frac{\Delta P \times 72 \times 30^2}{16 \times \Delta \delta \times I}$$

ΔP: Difference of load between the max. and min. proportional limit (kgf)

$\Delta \delta$: Difference of corresponding displacement ΔP (cm)

I: moment of inertia of area (cm⁴)

P_{max}: Maximum load (kgf)

$$\sigma_b = \frac{P_{max} \times 72}{2 \times Z}$$

Z: Section modulus (cm³)

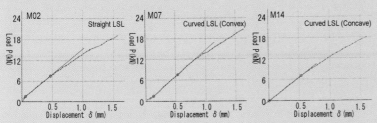

FIGURE 3 Load-displacement relationship.

Figure 4 shows the failure condition caused by the bending moment at the center of the span. Table 1 displays the test results. In spite of the small difference in the average strength, it is difficult to conclude that the strength decreases when the LSL is curved. Young's modulus exceeded 100×10^3 kgf/cm² regardless of the shape of the specimen. Therefore, the strength and Young's modulus were not dependent on the curvature of the LSL.

FIGURE 4 Failure conditions of bending tests.

TABLE 1 Results of the LSL bending tests.

Shape	Curved LSL (Convex)											Curved LSL (Concave)										
Specimen	M24	M29	M30	M22	M23	M26	M9	M7	M8	M28	Avg.	M13	M15	M10	M12	M6	M14	M1	M3	M18	M11	Avg.
Water Content (%)	7.1	7.2	7.0	7.2	7.1	6.9	6.9	7.2	7.3	6.9	7.1	7.0	7.2	7.1	7.0	7.1	7.3	6.9	6.9	6.7	6.9	7.0
Density (kgf/cm³)	0.72	0.71	0.71	0.71	0.70	0.70	0.70	0.70	0.68	0.67	0.70	0.72	0.71	0.71	0.71	0.70	0.70	0.70	0.70	0.69	0.68	0.70
Bending Strength (kgf/cm²)	543	502	547	533	503	497	496	477	477	555	513	496	474	488	468	441	439	511	549	452	432	475
Young's modulus (x10³kgf/cm²)	101	115	119	140 (0.26)	103	104	95	104	107	100	109 (0.07)	106	107	108	99	94	105	108	97	99	103	103

Shape	Straight LSL										
Specimen	M20	M27	M21	M2	M4	M16	M5	M17	M25	M19	Avg.
Water Content (%)	7.1	7.2	7.0	7.4	7.5	7.2	7.1	7.1	7.1	7.1	7.2
Density (kgf/cm³)	0.72	0.71	0.71	0.71	0.70	0.70	0.69	0.69	0.68	0.68	0.70
Bending Strength (kgf/cm²)	553	526	533	463	449	526	422	503	452	460	489
Young's modulus (x10³kgf/cm²)	116	111	125	114	105	107	90	118	100	112	110

Manufacturer data:
Average bending strength   494 kgf/cm²
Average Young's Modulus   106 x 10³ kgf/cm²
Average water content   7%

The average bending strength of LSL was 494kgf/cm². The strength and Young's modulus were not dependent on the curvature of the LSL.

Drift pin (36Ø) Single Shear LSL-to-Steel Connection

A steel bar, 36mm in diameter, was used for the connection between the diagonal member (web) and upper and lower chords of the trussed arches parallel to the minor axis of the ellipse. This steel bar was welded to the top and bottom steel pipes acting as the chord members of the Vierendeel arch. The shortest distance between the steel pipe and LSL was 36.4mm and the gap between the pin and hole was filled with epoxy. Drift pin (36Ø) single shear tests were carried out in the directions parallel and perpendicular to the grain.

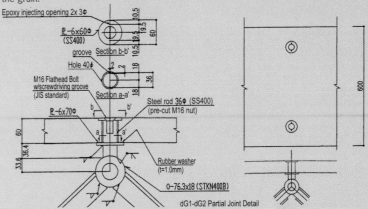

FIGURE 5 Connection between diagonal member (web) and top and bottom chords.

In the trussed arch, a drift pin (36Ø) was used to connect the diagonal members to the upper and lower chords.

Drift pin (36Ø) Single Shear LSL-to-Steel Connection Test (parallel to grain)

2-1_____Test Specimens

The specimen with a drift pin for double shear connection was composed of the main member steel and LSL side members, as shown in Figure 6. The loading plate was welded at the center of the pin. The LSL side member was 60mm thick and 108mm wide ($\doteqdot$3Xd) perpendicular to the grain of the LSL and 395mm ($\doteqdot$11Xd) in length parallel to the grain. The drift pin was inserted into the hole of the LSL side members and the gap (=44–36) between the pin and hole was filled with epoxy on the condition that the shortest distance between the loading plate and the LSL side members was kept to 36.4mm. The loaded end distance was 250mm ($\doteqdot$7Xd) and the unloaded end distance was 145mm ($\doteqdot$4Xd). The shear test was carried out with the disadvantaged condition that the washers were removed and the holes for the washers were cut in the side members. Twelve specimens were prepared and kept at $20\pm2°C$ and $65\pm5\%$ relative humidity. Their weight was stabilized and confirmed before testing.

Drift pin (36Ø) Single Shear LSL-to-Steel Connection Test (parallel to grain)

2-2_____Test Procedures

As shown in Figure 6, shear tests were carried out by inserting a 16mm plate into the loading plate. The loading speed was 30kN/min. To prevent the plate from toppling, wooden blocks painted with silicon grease were placed between the LSL and the plate. The displacement was measured at a rectangular bar fixed to the loading plate, and at the top of the side members. Relative displacement was calculated by subtracting the displacement of the side members from the displacement of the rectangular bar.

The failure condition shows yields of drift pin (36Ø).

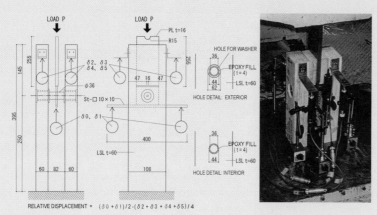

RELATIVE DISPLACEMENT = $(\delta 0 + \delta 1)/2 - (\delta 2 + \delta 3 + \delta 4 + \delta 5)/4$

FIGURE 6 Shearing test procedures.

Drift pin (36Ø) Single Shear LSL-to-Steel Connection Test (parallel to grain)

2-3 _____ Test Results

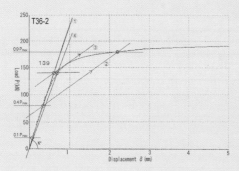

FIGURE 7 Load-displacement relationship.

One example of the load-relative displacement relationship is shown in Figure 7. The yield load and stiffness of all specimens led to standard allowable load and standard stiffness as written below.

A. Standard Allowable Load

i) From the load-displacement curve produced by the test, a straight line can be drawn from the points at 1/10 maximum load to 4/10 maximum load (line 1 in Figure 7).

ii) Another line can be drawn from the point 9/10 maximum load to the point 4/10 maximum load (line 2 in Figure 7). Using the same slope of line 2, a third line (line 3) can be drawn tangent to the load-displacement curve. The load at the intersection of line 1 and line 3 is the yield load in the test.

iii) Reading from the yield load gathered from each specimen, the lower yield load is obtained by the following formula:

$$TL = \bar{x} - Ks$$
$$\bar{x} = \sum_{i=1}^{n} (x_i/n)$$
$$s^2 = \sum_{i=1}^{n} (x_i - x)^2/(n-1)$$

TL: lower yield load
$\bar{x}$: average from experiment
s: standard deviation
K: constant obtained from the table below

TABLE 2 K factors for one-sided tolerance limits for normal distribution content of 95% and confidence of 75%*.

NUMBER OF SPECIMENS	K	NUMBER OF SPECIMENS	K	NUMBER OF SPECIMENS	K
3	3.152	11	2.074	50	1.811
4	2.681	12	2.048	100	1.758
5	2.464	15	1.991	200	1.732
6	2.336	20	1.932	500	1.693
7	2.251	25	1.895	1000	1.679
8	2.189	30	1.869	1500	1.672
9	2.142	35	1.849	2000	1.669
10	2.104	40	1.834	3000	1.664

* From Guttman and Irwin. *Statistical Tolerance Regions Classical and Bayesian.* No. 26, Griffin's Statistical Monographs & Courses (London: Griffin, 1970), pp. 90–93.

iv) Standard allowable load of the joint is defined by 2/3 of the value obtained in iii).

B. Standard Stiffness

i) The slope of the line from the origin to a point on the load–displacement curve corresponding to the yield load in the test leads to stiffness.

ii) The average stiffness of each specimen will be the standard stiffness of the joint.

The failure condition of a specimen in Figure 8 shows remarkable curvature of the pin caused by bending. The yield load and stiffness of other specimens are listed in Table 3. Standard allowable stress, standard stiffness, and allowable strength are listed below the table. Young's modulus and yield strength of the drift pin were $2.1 \times 10^6 \text{kgf/cm}^2$ and 3095kgf/cm^2.

FIGURE 8 Failure condition of specimen after shearing test.

TABLE 3 Test results of drift pin (36Ø) single shear LSL-to-steel connection test (parallel to the grain).

SPECIMEN No.		WATER CONTENT (%)	DENSITY (g/cm³)	P max (kN)	YIELD LOAD (kN)	STANDARD STIFFNESS (kg/cm)
T36-1	A	6.9	0.69	203.5	137	202800
	B	6.9	0.68			
T36-2	A	7.4	0.72	199.0	139	207100
	B	7.1	0.71			
T36-3	A	7.1	0.70	199.0	143	204300
	B	7.1	0.70			
T36-4	A	7.3	0.71	195.0	149	201200
	B	7.1	0.70			
T36-5	A	7.3	0.71	205.0	149	206600
	B	7.1	0.70			
T36-6	A	7.1	0.69	193.5	133	191600
	B	7.1	0.70			
AVERAGE		7.1	0.70	199.2	141.7	202300

S = 6.53
TL = 141.7 - (6.53 x 2.336) =126.4
Standard Allowable Load = (2/3) 126.4 = 84.27 kN (8595kgf)
84.27 / 2 = 42.13 kN/piece (4298kgf/piece)

Standard Stiffness 202300 kgf/cm
202300 / 2 = 101150 kgf/cm/piece

Allowable Shear Strength
for temporary loading: 4298 kgf/piece
for sustained loading: 2149 kgf/piece

Young's modulus and yield strength of the drift pin were 2.1X10⁶kgf/cm² and 3095kgf/cm², respectively.

Drift pin (36Ø) Single Shear LSL-to-Steel Connection Test (perpendicular to grain)

3-1 _____ Test Specimens

A drift pin (36Ø) with a loading plate was inserted into the center of LSL and filled with epoxy. The loaded edge distance was 100mm. At 252.5mm (≒7Xd) from both edges and in the center of its depth, a 37mm-diameter hole was drilled and a 36mm steel rod was inserted as a supporting point. Twelve specimens were prepared and kept at 20±2˚C and 65±5% relative humidity. Their weight was stabilized and confirmed before testing. Figure 9 shows the dimensions of the specimens.

Drift pin (36Ø) Single Shear LSL-to-Steel Connection Test (perpendicular to grain)

3-2 _____ Test Procedures

As shown in Figure 9, the shearing test was carried out by inserting a 16mm-thick steel plate into the loading plate and applying load. The loading speed was 30kN/min. The displacement was measured at both the loading plate and the center of the span of the side members.

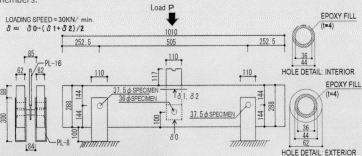

FIGURE 9 Shearing test procedures.
FIGURE 10 View of shearing test.

Drift pin (36Ø) Single Shear LSL-to-Steel Connection Test (perpendicular to grain)

3-3 _____ Test Results

FIGURE 11 Load-displacement relationship.

Figure 11 shows an example of the relationship between load and displacement from the shearing test. Yield load and stiffness were determined in the same way (force applied in the direction of the fiber) as in the shearing test for the 36mm drift pin. Figure 12 shows the failure condition of the specimen. In the layer of the steel rod and epoxy surface destruction was visible. Table 4 shows yield load and stiffness of another specimen. Standard allowable load, standard yield load, standard stiffness, and allowable strength are noted beside the table.

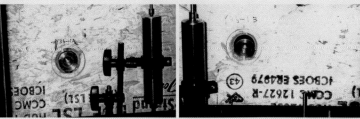

FIGURE 12 Failure condition of specimens after shearing test.

TABLE 4 Results of drift pin (36Ø) single shear LSL-to-steel connection test (perpendicular to the grain).

SPECIMEN No.	DENSITY (g/cm³)	P max (kN)	YIELD LOAD (kN)	STANDARD STIFFNESS (kg/cm)
Y36-1	0.70	147.10	90.0	93700
Y36-2	0.69	126.60	80.0	111000
Y36-3	0.68	136.80	100.0	80300
Y36-4	0.69	129.40	—	—
Y36-5	0.67	126.00	—	—
Y36-6	0.68	142.40	103.0	70700
AVERAGE	0.69	134.70	93.3	88900

Water content = 7.3%
S = 10.44
TL = 93.25 (10.44 x 2.681) = 65.26 kN
Standard Allowable Load = (2/3) 65.26 = 43.51 kN (4438kgf)
43.51 / 2 = 21.75 kN/piece (2219kgf/piece)

Standard Stiffness 88900 kgf/cm
88900 / 2 = 44500 kgf/cm/piece

Allowable Shear Strength
for temporary loading: 2219 kgf/piece
for sustained loading: 1110 kgf/piece

The yield load and stiffness perpendicular to grain were nearly half those of specimens parallel to the grain.

Single Shear LSL-to-LSL Field-Joint Connection

The chord members of the trussed arch parallel to the minor axis of the ellipse required field joints on occasion during construction. A halving joint with drift pins and lag screws was projected. The intention was that compressive force would be transferred by touching both ends of the members with epoxy, and tensile force would be transferred by drift pins (36Ø) and lag screws (12Ø).

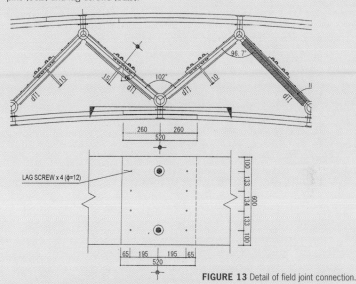

FIGURE 13 Detail of field joint connection.

The chord members of the trussed arches required field joints in the LSL-to-LSL connection. The LSL used a halving joint technique with drift pin and lag screw connections, and so shearing tests and tension tests were carried out to obtain shear strengths.

Drift pin (36Ø) Single Shear LSL-to-LSL Field-Joint Connection Tension Test (parallel to the grain)

4-1 _____ Test Specimens

The LSL members were prepared, 60mm thick, 133mm wide (perpendicular to the grain), and 780mm in length (parallel to the grain). The specimens were notched off 560mm from the edge at a depth of 30mm. The specimens were layed together to leave a distance of 40mm between their ends, a drift pin (36Ø) was inserted through both members, and epoxy was filled in the gap between the pin and the LSL (Figure 13). The end distance of 260mm was based on the structural design. Specimens were controlled at 20±2°C and 65±5% relative humidity. Their weight was stabilized and confirmed before testing.

A drift pin (36Ø) was inserted through both members and epoxy was filled in the gap between the pin and the LSL.

Drift pin (36Ø) Single Shear LSL-to-LSL
Field-Joint Connection Tension Test
(parallel to the grain)

4-2 Test Procedures

As shown in Figure 14, tensions tests were carried out by clamping the two steel bars (screwed into steel blocks as universal joints) using the chucks of the testing apparatus, and pulling them apart at a loading speed of 5kN/min. The average of the displacements at the notches of the specimens was the relative displacement.

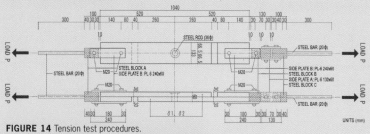

FIGURE 14 Tension test procedures.

FIGURE 15 View of tension test apparatus and specimen.

Drift pin (36Ø) Single Shear LSL-to-LSL
Field-Joint Connection Tension Test
(parallel to the grain)

4-3 Test Results

Figure 16 shows an example of the load-displacement relationship. The yield load and stiffness were decided in the same way as in the drift pin (36Ø) single shear LSL-to-steel connection test (parallel to the grain). The failure conditions of the specimens are shown in Figure 17. The inclined drift pin and separation of jointed surfaces can be seen. Table 5 shows the yield load and stiffness that were obtained for all specimens.

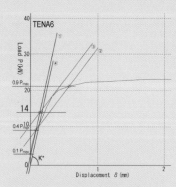

FIGURE 16 Load-displacement relationship.
FIGURE 17 Failure conditions of tension test.

The inclined drift pin and separation of jointed surfaces can be seen.

TABLE 5 Results of drift pin (36Ø) Single Shear LSL-to-LSL Field-Joint Connection Tension Test (parallel to the grain).

SPECIMEN No.	WATER CONTENT (%)	DENSITY (g/cm³)	P max (kN)	YIELD LOAD (kN)	STANDARD STIFFNESS (kg/cm)
TEN A1	7.1 / 7.2	0.71 / 0.70	27.35	16.0	51000
TEN A2	7.0 / 7.3	0.72 / 0.71	26.80	13.0	265200*
TEN A3	7.2 / 7.5	0.71 / 0.70	26.70	13.0	33150
TEN A4	7.4 / 7.1	0.69 / 0.70	29.55	16.0	21760
TEN A5	7.3 / 7.5	0.73 / 0.71	29.55	16.0	326400*
TEN A6	7.3 / 7.1	0.69 / 0.71	23.15	14.0	79330
TEN A7	7.4 / 7.3	0.72 / 0.71	23.20	12.0	94150
Average	7.3	0.71	26.67	14.3	124400 (55880)**

S = 1.70
TL = 14.3 - (1.70 x 2.251) = 10.46
Standard Allowable Load = (2/3) 10.46 = 6.97 kN (711kgf/pin)

Standard Stiffness: 55880 kgf/cm/piece

Allowable Shear Strength
for temporary loading: 711 kgf/piece
for sustained loading: 356 kgf/piece

**average value omitting values of *

Lag Screw (12Ø) Single Shear LSL-to-LSL Field-Joint Connection (parallel to the grain)

5-1 Test Specimens

Two LSL members were prepared, 60mm in thickness, 60mm in width (perpendicular to the grain), and 780mm in length (parallel to the grain). The specimens were notched off 560mm from the edge at a depth of 30mm. The specimens were layed together to leave a distance of 40mm between their ends, and a lag screw (12Ø) was inserted through both members. The end distance was 85mm (≒7Xd). Specimens were controlled at 20±2°C and 65±5% relative humidity. Their weight was stabilized and confirmed before testing.

Lag screws (12Ø) were inserted through both members with their end distance being 85mm (≒7×d).

Lag Screw (12Ø) Single Shear LSL-to-LSL Field-Joint Connection (parallel to the grain)

5-2 Test Procedures

As in the tension test of the drift pin (36Ø), tension tests under a constantly increasing load of 3kN/min. were carried out using universal joints, as shown in Figure 18, The average of the displacements at the notches of the specimens was the relative displacement.

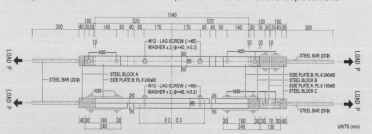

FIGURE 18 Tension test procedures.

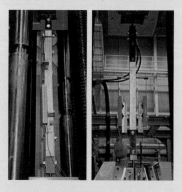

FIGURE 19 View of tension test apparatus and specimen.

Lag Screw (12Ø) Single Shear LSL-to-
LSL Field-Joint Connection (parallel to
the grain)

5-3_____Test Results

Figure 20 shows an example of the load-displacement relationship. The yield load and stiffness were decided in the same way as in the drift pin shear connection. The failure condition of the specimens is shown in Figure 21. The gap around the lag screw and the split at the base of the notch can be seen. Yield load and stiffness are shown in Table 6.

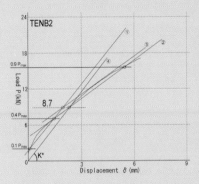

FIGURE 20 (left) Load-displacement relationship.
FIGURE 21 (right) Failure conditions of tension test.

The gap around the lag screw and the split at the base of the notch can be seen.

TABLE 6 Results of lag screw (12Ø) Single Shear LSL-to-LSL Field-Joint Connection Tension Test (Parallel to the grain).

SPECIMEN No.	WATER CONTENT (%)	DENSITY (g/cm³)	Pmax (kN)	YIELD LOAD (kN)	STANDARD STIFFNESS (kg/cm)	FAILURE CONDITIONS
TEN B1	7.8	0.68	18.10	8.7	3910	split at the base of the notch (101kgf/cm²)*
	7.6	0.72				
TEN B2	7.7	0.70	17.45	8.7	4050	split at the base of the notch (98.3kgf/cm²)*
	7.2	0.70				
TEN B3	7.2	0.66	17.20	8.2	5560	
	7.9	0.68				
TEN B4	7.2	0.66	18.10	9.9	3280	
	7.7	0.72				
TEN B5	7.2	0.70	16.10	8.9	3680	
	7.8	0.67				
TEN B6	7.5	0.68	17.50	8.7	3550	split at the base of the notch (97.7kgf/cm²)*
	7.5	0.68				
TEN B7	7.4	0.69	16.90	9.4	6580	
	7.8	0.69				
Average	7.5	0.69	17.34	8.93	4370	

S = 0.555
TL = 8.93 - (0.555 x 2.251) = 7.68 kN
Standard Allowable Load = (2/3) 7.68
= 5.12kN/pin (522 kgf)
Standard Stiffness: 4370 kgf/cm

Allowable Shear Strength
for temporary loading: 261 kgf/piece
for sustained loading: 131 kgf/piece

_____Shear Stiffness of the LSL panel

The upper and lower chord members of the Vierendeel arches parallel to the major axis of the elliptical roof are composed of steel pipe (Ø=76.3, t=18). Welded to the chords are steel "Cut-Tees" (CT) (50 x 100 x 6 x 8) where a 50mm-thick LSL panel is affixed by lag screws (Ø=9). The LSL panel's shear stiffness or rigidity was tested in order to analyze the Vierendeel arch structure.

Welded to the chords are steel "Cut-Tees" (CT) (50 x 100 x 6 x 8) where a 50mm-thick LSL panel is affixed by lag screws (Ø=9). The LSL panel's shear stiffness or rigidity was tested in order to model the Vierendeel arch structure.

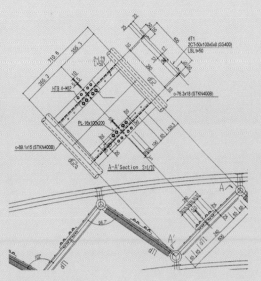

FIGURE 22 Detail of LSL shear panel connection.

_____Shear Stiffness Test of LSL Panel
6-1_____Test Specimens

As shown in Figure 23, three 838.6mm-long CT and four 380mm-long steel flat bars (FB) are connected with M16 bolts at each node. The two LSL panels are fixed to this composition. Each CT-to-LSL panel connection was fixed using four lag screws (Ø=9, l=50). The diameter of the holes in the CT was 10mm, and those in the LSL panels were 7mm. The LSL panels were controlled at 20±2°C and 65±5% relative humidity. Their weight was stabilized and confirmed before testing and pairs of LSL panels of similar weight were chosen to make up each specimen for each test.

_____Shear Stiffness Test of LSL Panel
6-2_____Test Procedures

As shown at Figure 23, a concentrated load was applied to the CT in the center while the other two outside CTs were supported. This shear test was carried out at a constantly increasing load of 15kN/min., and the displacements ($\delta=(\delta2+\delta3)/2$) were measured. The center of each panel fundamentally required two notches, but the specimens were delivered to the testing facility with only one notch, so in order to simulate the actual condition of the panel, a total of three 40mm deep slits were provided.

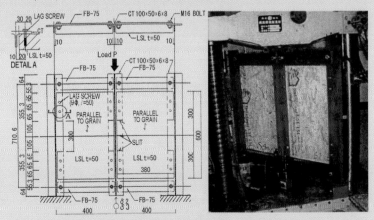

FIGURE 23 Shear test procedures.

Shear Stiffness Test of LSL Panel

6-3   Test Results

An example of the load-displacement relationship from the shear test is shown in Figure 24. The short-term allowable strength of eight lag screws is known to be approximately 20kN from the previous test. Therefore, the slope from the origin to the point at 20kN is determined as the shear stiffness or rigidity. Destruction is concentrated at the lag screw points as shown in Figure 25. Table 7 shows the stiffness mentioned above for the other specimens. The shear stiffness of the panel was calculated beside the table.

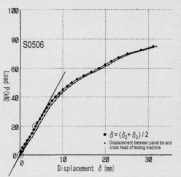

FIGURE 24 Load-displacement relationship.
FIGURE 25 Failure conditions of tension test.

TABLE 7 Results of shear stiffness test of LSL panel.

SPECIMEN No.	DENSITY (g/cm³)	Pmax (kN)	STIFFNESS (P/δ)(kgf/cm)
S 0312	0.69	79.20	9980
S 0506	0.68	77.10	5750
S 0810	0.67	80.00	8700
S 0911	0.66	83.45	8990
S 0207	0.65	81.93	5980
S 0104	0.72	80.00	8330
AVERAGE	0.68	80.28	7960

Pmax: The load when the LSL comes in contact with the frame.

Shear stiffness of a panel (Q<1020kgf)
7960/2 = 3980 kgf/cm

Water content: 6.7%

Destruction was concentrated at the lag screws. The shear stiffness of a panel was 3980kgf/cm.

Experiment date   September – October 2001

Location   Tokyo Denki University, Chiba Newtown Campus, Chiba, Japan

Performed by   Prof. Norihide Imagawa

Full-Scale Loading Test

The site of the gymnasium was in an area of heavy snowfall, recording over 150cm in the winter. The elliptical dome, which spans 20m as the minor axis, 30m as the major axis, with a rise of 6m, is required to bear 450kg/m² (3kg/m²/cm x 150cm) of uniformly distributed snow load and unevenly distributed load for snowdrifts. Two trussed arches of the minor axis were prepared and loaded in this test, to investigate the behavior of uniformly and unevenly distributed load.

The gymnasium is located in an area of heavy snowfall, so two full-scale trussed arches were constructed and loaded to simulate normal snow accumulation (uniformly distributed load) and snow drifts (unevenly distributed load).

Full-scale Loading Test

7-1   Test Specimens

Two trussed arches were constructed (the two which were to be located at the minor axis). The trussed arch was composed of LSL (600mm wide X 60mm thick) as the top and bottom chords; and steel CT (100X50X6X8 SS400) made up the diagonal members. The Young's modulus of each material is shown in Table 8.

TABLE 8 Young's modulus of trussed arch material.

MATERIALS	YOUNG'S MODULUS (kgf/cm²)
WOODEN BOARD (LSL) 600 x 60	Avg. E=92296
CT - 100 x 50 x 6 x 8 SS400)	E = 2.1 x 10⁶
○ - 76.3 x 18 (STKM400B)	E = 2.1 x 10⁶

Full-Scale Loading Test

7-2   Test Procedures

As shown in Figure 26, snow load will be transferred from the LSL (t=60mm) to a steel rod (36Ø) and through a steel tube (Ø=78.5, t=18), which is the top chord in the direction of the major axis, down to the diagonal member. Loads equivalent to the snow loads were applied as concentrated loads to the top chord. The standard area is determined to be 0.558m x 1.17m from the top part dimension, therefore each load (=P) applied to the steel tube referring to the variation in snowfall 75cm, 150cm, 225cm, is 147kg, 294kg, (=0.558 x 1.17 x150 x 3) 441kg, respectively.

The specimen's loading points and loading schedule is shown in Figure 26.

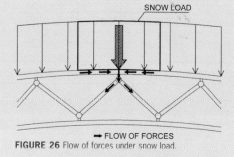

→ FLOW OF FORCES
FIGURE 26 Flow of forces under snow load.

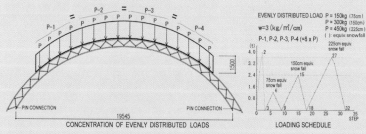

FIGURE 27 Loading diagram and schedule of evenly distributed loads.

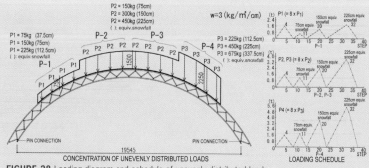

FIGURE 28 Loading diagram and schedule of unevenly distributed loads.

Loading method

Steel plates were placed on the ground to create a horizontal surface for the test, due to the outdoor testing location. The two pairs of trussed arches were aligned parallel and pin-supported on H-400x400x13x21, which were placed on the steel plate. H-shaped steel beams were subjected to the reaction forces of the supporting points and reaction forces of the concentrated loads acting at the nodes. As shown in Figure 29, concentrated loads were applied in succession by four oil pressure jacks, at 32 points, by transferring the reaction forces of the simply supported beams.

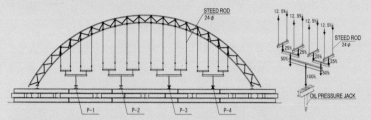

FIGURE 29 Loading method by transferring reaction forces of the simply supported beams.

Concentrated loads were applied in succession by four oil pressure jacks, at 32 points, by transferring the reaction forces of the simply supported beams.

Measuring displacement

To measure displacement, the pin supports at both ends of the trussed arch were fixed and another arch was adjacent to the truss arch, as the specimen was used as a measuring tool. The displacement gauges were set up at three points (DM in Figure 31) and eye measurements were set up at sixteen points (D in Figure 31). The measuring points are indicated in Figure 30 and Figure 31.

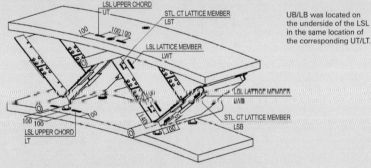

UB/LB was located on the underside of the LSL in the same location of the corresponding UT/LT.

FIGURE 30 Points of strain measurements by using strain gauges

Measuring strain

The strain was measured by strain gauges on the upper and lower chords of the LSL and the lattice members (LSL, steel CT). It was also measured at the center of the span of the LSL supported by 36Østeel rods on the upper and lower chords. The strain of 24Ø steel rods was measured at 32 points to confirm applied loads. Sixty-seven points were measured on the upper and lower chords (UT, UB, LT, LB), 44 points on the lattice members, and 44 points on steel CT(LST, LSB). The main measuring points are shown with the test results in figures 30 and 31.

The strain of 24Ø steel rods was measured at 32 points to confirm applied loads. 67 points were measured on the

upper and lower chords, 44 points on the lattice members, and 44 points on steel CT.

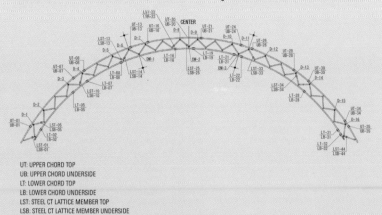

UT: UPPER CHORD TOP
UB: UPPER CHORD UNDERSIDE
LT: LOWER CHORD TOP
LB: LOWER CHORD UNDERSIDE
LST: STEEL CT LATTICE MEMBER TOP
LSB: STEEL CT LATTICE MEMBER UNDERSIDE

FIGURE 31 Measuring points of displacements and strains.

7-3 Full-Scale Loading Test
Test Results

The test data and analytical values regarding the displacements of the uniformly distributed load are shown in Table 9 and 10. The maximum value of the horizontal displacement from the test data was –6.6mm at D-2-X, as shown in Figure 31 and Table 9. This displacement value was 108.2% (=6.6/6.1x100) of the analytical value, when the displacements of the measured values and those of the analysis were compared under 225cm snow load. The maximum value of the vertical displacement was –15.1mm at D-9-Y and its value was 94.9% (=15.1/15.9x100) of the analytical value, as shown in Figure 31 and Table 10.

The test data and analytical values regarding the displacements of the unevenly distributed load are shown in Table 11 and 12. The maximum value of the horizontal displacement from the test data was –13.3mm at D-4-X, as shown in Figure 31 and Table 11. Its value was 85.3% (=13.3/15.6x100) of the displacement of the analysis, when the displacement of measured values and those of the analysis were compared under 225cm snow load. The maximum value of the vertical displacement from the test was –16.9mm at D-11-Y, and this value is 90.4% (=16.9/18.7x100) of the analytical value, as shown in Figure 31 and Table 12.

The test data and analytical values regarding the maximum stress on each member of the uniformly distributed load are shown on Figure 31 and Table 13 through 15. The maximum stress on the upper chord was –28.8kg/cm² at UT-21. It was 86% (=28.8/33.5x100) of the analytical value shown in Table 13, when the maximum stress of the measured value and those of the analysis were compared under the 225 cm snow load. The maximum stress on the lower chord was –57.7kg/cm² at LB-02 and was 87.7% (=57.7/65.8x100) of the analytical value shown in Table 14. The maximum stress on the steel CT lattice was –867.3kg/cm² at LSB-10 and was 137.6% (=867.3/630.5x100) of the analytical value shown in Table 15.

The test data and analytical values regarding the maximum stress on each member of the unevenly distributed load are shown in Table 16 through 18. The maximum stress on the upper chord was –36.8kg/cm² at UB-20. Its value was 117% (=36.8/31.4x100) of the analytical value shown in Table 16, when the measured values and analytical values were compared under 225cm snow load. The maximum stress on the lower chord was –73.8kg/cm² at LB-32, and it was 152.5% (=73.8/48.4x100) of the analytical value shown in Table 17. The maximum stress on the steel CT lattice was -1047.9kg/cm² at LSB-13, and its value was 125.1% of the analytical value shown in Table 18.

According to the result, the truss arch is strong enough to bear 1.5 times more snow load than was expected. The behavior can be assumed from the analysis because the displacements and stress from the measured values were close to those of the analysis.

The results of the test data and analytical values for the stress of the LSL lattice member were omitted because of the low importance in this test. The LSL lattice members were not intended for structural purposes in the trussed arch of the minor axis.

The truss arch is strong enough to bear 1.5 times more snow load than was expected.

TABLE 9 Horizontal displacement (x) evenly distributed loads.

Snow fall (cm)	1		2		3		4		5	
	D-1	D-16	D-2	D-15	D-3	D-14	D-4	D-13	D-5	D-12
50	-1.9	0.0	-2.1	0.0	-1.2	0.1	-0.9	1.4	0.0	-1.8
	-1.2	1.2	-2.0	2.0	-1.8	1.8	-1.3	1.3	-0.4	0.4
100	-2.6	1.3	-2.9	1.0	-1.5	1.0	-0.9	1.9	0.0	-1.7
	-1.6	1.6	-2.7	2.7	-2.5	2.5	-1.8	1.8	-0.5	0.5
150	-3.3	2.7	-4.4	2.2	-2.0	1.9	-2.6	2.9	0.0	-1.5
	-2.5	2.5	-4.0	4.0	-3.7	3.7	-2.8	2.8	-0.7	0.7
200	-4.5	2.9	-5.8	3.1	-3.5	2.8	-2.2	3.6	-0.3	-1.4
	-3.3	3.3	-5.4	5.4	-5.0	5.0	-3.7	3.7	-1.0	1.0
225	-4.8	2.9	-6.6	3.9	-4.5	3.4	-3.8	3.9	-0.6	-1.4
	-3.7	3.7	-6.1	6.1	-5.6	5.6	-4.1	4.1	-1.1	1.1

Snow fall (cm)	6		7		8		1'		2'
	D-6	D-11	D-7	D-10	D-8	D-9	DM-1	DM-3	DM-2
50	-1.0	-1.3	-1.0	-0.5	0.0	-0.5	-3.66	-1.10	-1.71
	0.0	0.0	0.1	-0.1	0.1	-0.1	-0.30	0.30	0.00
100	-1.0	-0.8	-0.7	-0.5	0.0	0.1	-3.87	-0.97	-1.51
	0.0	0.0	0.2	-0.2	0.1	-0.1	-0.40	0.40	0.00
150	-1.0	-0.6	-0.6	-0.5	0.0	-0.5	-4.06	-0.79	-1.46
	0.0	0.0	0.3	-0.3	0.1	-0.1	-0.61	0.61	0.00
200	-1.0	-0.3	-0.3	-0.5	-0.4	-0.5	-4.46	-0.53	-1.33
	-0.1	0.1	0.3	-0.3	0.2	-0.2	-0.32	0.32	0.00
225	-1.0	-0.3	-0.2	-0.5	0.6	-0.5	-4.75	-0.61	-1.38
	-0.1	0.1	0.4	-0.4	0.2	-0.2	-0.92	0.92	0.00

TABLE 10 Vertical displacement (y) evenly distributed loads.

Snow fall (cm)	1		2		3		4		5	
	D-1	D-16	D-2	D-15	D-3	D-14	D-4	D-13	D-5	D-12
50	0.0	-1.8	0.0	-2.3	-0.5	-1.5	-0.8	-2.0	-3.0	-3.1
	-0.3		0.4		0.3		-0.3		-2.3	
100	0.0	-1.8	0.0	-1.8	-0.5	-1.5	-0.8	-1.5	-4.1	-4.3
	-0.3		0.6		0.5		-0.4		-3.0	
150	0.0	-1.8	0.0	-1.6	-0.5	-1.5	-2.0	-1.3	-5.5	-5.7
	-0.5		0.9		0.8		-0.6		-4.5	
200	0.0	-1.8	0.7	-1.0	-0.5	-1.5	-2.1	-0.9	-7.1	-6.9
	-0.6		1.3		1.0		-0.7		-6.0	
225	0.0	-1.8	0.7	-1.0	-0.5	-1.5	-2.4	-0.7	-7.6	-7.8
	-0.7		1.4		1.1		-0.8		-6.7	

Snow fall (cm)	6		7		8		1'		2'
	D-6	D-11	D-7	D-10	D-8	D-9	DM-1	DM-3	DM-2
50	-2.9	-3.1	-4.2	-4.2	-4.0	-4.8	-3.70	-5.79	-7.08
	-3.3		-4.2		-5.3		-3.90		-5.32
100	-4.8	-5.0	-6.2	-6.7	-6.6	-7.4	-5.66	-7.64	-9.12
	-4.4		-5.7		-7.1		-5.24		-7.17
150	-6.7	-6.8	-8.2	-7.4	-9.5	-10.1	-7.87	-9.52	-11.95
	-6.6		-8.5		-9.1		-7.86		-10.76
200	-8.5	-8.6	-10.4	-10.9	-12.6	-13.3	-9.99	-11.25	-14.71
	-8.8		-11.3		-14.2		-10.49		-14.35
225	-9.7	-9.5	-11.7	-12.2	-13.8	-15.1	-10.93	-12.20	-16.04
	-9.9		-12.7		-15.9		-11.80		-16.14

TABLE 11 Horizontal displacement (x) unevenly distributed loads.

UPPER ROW: MEASURED VALUE (mm) LOWER ROW: ANALYTICAL VALUE (mm)

Snow fall (cm)	D-1	D-2	D-3	D-4	D-5	D-6	D-7	D-8	D-9	D-10
50	-1.6	-3.4	-2.7	-4.8	-1.6	-2.2	-5.6	-2.0	-1.7	-3.2
	-1.9	-2.6	-3.5	-3.5	-2.8	-2.4	-2.2	-2.0	-2.1	-2.3
100	-2.6	-5.0	-4.8	-7.0	-3.8	-4.0	-7.2	-3.5	-3.2	-4.8
	-2.7	-5.1	-7.0	-6.9	-5.6	-4.9	-4.3	-4.0	-4.2	-4.7
150	-3.8	-6.8	-7.0	-9.4	-5.3	-5.5	-8.5	-4.8	-4.7	-6.2
	-4.0	-7.7	-10.6	-10.4	-8.4	-7.3	-6.5	-6.1	-6.3	-7
200	-5.1	-8.8	-9.8	-11.8	-7.5	-7.5	-10	-6.4	-6.4	-7.6
	-5.4	-10.2	-14.1	-13.8	-11.2	-9.7	-8.7	-8.1	-8.4	-9.3
225	-5.9	-10.1	-11.4	-13.3	-8.7	-8.4	-11.1	-7.6	-6.9	-8.3
	-6.1	-11.5	-15.8	-15.63	-12.6	-10.9	-9.7	-9.1	-9.4	-10.5
250	-6.6	-10.9	-12.9	-14.9	-9.9	-9.4	-11.9	8.4	-8.2	-9.6
	-6.7	-12.8	-17.6	-17.3	-14.0	-12.1	-10.8	-10.1	-10.5	-11.7

Snow fall (cm)	D-11	D-12	D-13	D-14	D-15	D-16	DM-1	DM-2	DM-3
50	-4.0	-3.6	-3.1	-1.0	1.0	1.7	-2.63	-2.42	-1.95
	-2.4	-2.3	-1.6	-1.0	0.1	0.3	-2.71	-2.32	-2.30
100	-5.4	-3.8	-3.9	-1.7	1.1	1.9	-4.45	-3.89	-3.37
	-4.7	-4.6	-3.2	-2.0	0.3	0.6	-5.42	-4.64	-4.61
150	-7.6	-5.2	-4.9	-2.3	1.4	2.3	-6.12	-5.20	-4.61
	-7.1	-6.9	-6.2	-3.1	0.4	0.9	-8.13	-6.96	-6.91
200	-8.9	-7.0	-5.9	-2.9	1.8	3.0	-8.27	-6.93	-6.18
	-9.5	-9.2	-6.5	-4.1	0.6	1.2	-10.85	-9.28	-9.22
225	-11.7	-7.9	-6.5	-3.3	2.0	3.3	-9.32	-7.78	-7.03
	-10.7	-10.4	-7.3	-4.6	0.7	1.3	-12.20	-10.44	-10.37
250	-11.0	-8.9	-7.0	-4.8	2.0	3.9	-10.47	-8.77	-7.88
	-11.9	-11.5	-8.1	-5.1	0.7	1.5	-13.56	-11.60	-11.52

TABLE 12 Vertical displacement (y) unevenly distributed loads.

UPPER ROW: MEASURED VALUE (mm) LOWER ROW: ANALYTICAL VALUE (mm)

Snow fall (cm)	D-1	D-2	D-3	D-4	D-5	D-6	D-7	D-8	D-9	D-10
50	-2.1	0.0	0.7	1.9	-1.0	-1.0	-2.4	-2.7	-4.9	-4.3
	-0.2	0.7	1.8	1.8	0.7	-0.2	-1.3	-3.2	-3.9	-4.3
100	-2.2	0.5	1.5	3.0	-0.4	-1.4	-3.2	-4.9	-7.1	-7.4
	-0.5	1.5	3.7	3.7	1.5	-0.5	-2.6	-6.4	-7.7	-8.9
150	-2.4	0.8	2.6	3.5	-0.2	-2.0	-4.4	-7.2	-10.4	-10.5
	-0.7	2.2	5.5	5.5	2.2	-0.7	-3.9	-9.6	-11.6	-13.0
200	-2.6	1.2	3.7	4.7	-0.2	-2.6	-6.2	-10.1	-13.7	-14.3
	-1.0	3	7.3	7.3	3.0	-1.0	-5.3	-12.8	-15.5	-17.4
225	-2.6	1.4	4.4	5.2	-0.2	-3.1	-7.1	-11.9	-15.6	-16.2
	-1.1	3.3	8.2	8.3	3.4	-1.1	-5.9	-14.5	-17.4	-19.5
250	-2.7	1.8	4.9	5.5	0.0	-3.6	-8.0	-13.4	-17.6	-18.9
	-1.2	3.7	9.2	9.1	3.7	-1.2	-6.6	-16.1	-19.3	21.7

Snow fall (cm)	D-11	D-12	D-13	D-14	D-15	D-16	DM-1	DM-2	DM-3
50	-5.7	-4	-3.2	-2.5	-1.0	-1.0	-1.53	-3.53	-4.77
	-4.2	-3.7	-2.2	-1.3	-0.1	-0.1	-0.92	-3.59	-4.32
100	-8.4	-6.8	-4.3	-3.5	-1.1	-1.0	-2.18	-4.62	-7.74
	-8.3	-7.5	-4.4	-2.6	-0.2	-0.1	-1.84	-7.18	-8.65
150	-11.6	-9.7	-6.3	-4.9	-1.1	-1.0	-2.99	-7.15	-10.70
	-12.5	-11.2	-9.2	-4.0	-0.3	-0.2	-2.76	-10.76	-12.97
200	-14.9	-13.4	-8.8	-6.0	-1.6	-1.3	-4.49	-10.18	-14.47
	-16.7	-15.0	-8.8	-5.3	-0.4	-0.2	-3.69	-14.35	-17.29
225	-16.9	-14.6	-9.8	-7.6	-2.1	-1.7	-4.63	-11.95	-16.49
	-18.7	16.8	-9.9	-5.9	-0.5	-0.2	-4.41	-16.14	-19.45
250	-19.2	-17.3	-11.5	-8.7	-2.4	-1.9	-5.50	-13.87	-18.58
	-20.8	-18.7	-11.0	-6.6	-0.6	-0.3	-4.60	-17.94	-21.62

TABLE 13 Stress of upper chord: evenly distributed loads.

UPPER ROW: MEASURED VALUE (kgf/cm²)   LOWER ROW: ANALYTICAL VALUE (kgf/cm²)

Snow fall (cm)	01		08		16		21		26		30		34	
	UT	UB	UT	UB	UT	UB	UT	UB	UT	UB	UT	UB	UT	UB
50	2.0	-4.0	0.9	-2.5	-4.3	-4.3	-6.1	-1.9	-4.0	1.2	0.4	-1.8	1.8	5.1
	2.5	-1.0	0.6	-1.1	-6.0	-5.3	-6.9	-2.1	-5.9	-1.8	2.0	-0.6	2.7	-1.0
100	3.4	-9.1	0.6	-5.7	-9.0	-8.9	-12.6	-4.2	-8.6	2.8	0.9	-4.2	2.3	8.9
	5.4	-2.0	1.3	-2.2	-12.8	-10.6	-14.9	-3.3	-12.8	-3.2	4.2	-1.4	5.3	-2.6
150	4.3	-12.8	-0.2	-9	-14.1	-13.5	-19.4	-6.7	-13.2	4.0	1.0	-6.1	4.2	10.6
	8.1	-2.9	2.0	-3.3	-19.3	-16.0	-22.4	-4.9	-19.2	-4.8	6.3	-2.1	8.0	-3.9
200	4.8	-14.2	-1.1	-12.2	-18.9	-17.6	-25.6	-9.0	-17.4	5.1	0.9	-7.6	6.8	10.9
	10.8	-3.9	2.6	-4.3	-21.3	-21.3	-29.8	-6.5	-25.6	-6.4	8.4	-2.9	10.7	-5.2
225	5.1	-14.8	-1.2	-13.6	-21.3	-19.8	-28.8	-10.1	-19.5	5.5	0.7	-8.1	8.0	11.4
	12.2	-4.4	3.0	-4.9	-28.9	-23.9	-33.5	-7.3	-28.8	-7.2	9.4	-3.2	12.0	-5.8

TABLE 14 Stress of lower chord: evenly distributed loads.

Snow fall (cm)	UPPER ROW: MEASURED VALUE (kgf/cm²)								LOWER ROW: ANALYTICAL VALUE (kgf/cm²)					
	02		05		08		16		22		28		31	
	LT	LB	LT	LB	LT	LB	LT	LB	LT	LB	LT	LB	LT	LB
50	-2.0	-11.9	-2.4	-9.3	-7.9	0.7	2.2	1.8	-5.4	1.5	-1.9	6.6	0.9	0.0
	-1.7	-14.6	-1.9	-10.8	-3.4	-1.7	-1.8	1.1	-2.1	0.6	-1.9	-10.8	-1.7	-14.6
100	-4.7	-24.2	-5.4	-18.6	-16.3	1.0	4.1	2.6	-11.2	3.2	-4.3	-13.5	-1.8	-17.4
	-3.5	-29.2	-3.8	-21.5	-7.3	-2.9	-4.4	2.1	-4.5	1.9	-3.8	-21.5	-3.5	-29.2
150	-7.4	-37.5	-8.6	-28.6	-24.8	1.1	5.5	3.3	-17.3	4.7	-6.9	-20.9	-2.3	-28.3
	-5.2	-43.9	-5.8	-32.3	-11.0	-4.3	-6.6	3.2	-6.7	2.9	-5.7	-32.3	-5.2	-43.9
200	-9.4	-50.9	-11.3	-38.3	-31.8	0.9	7.0	4.2	-23.3	5.9	-9.5	-28.3	-3.0	-40.4
	-6.9	-58.5	-7.7	-43.0	-14.6	-5.7	-8.7	4.2	-9.0	3.9	-7.6	-43.0	-6.9	-58.5
225	-10.2	-57.7	-12.3	-43.2	-35.3	0.8	7.8	4.5	-25.8	6.6	-10.5	-31.7	-3.4	-46.5
	-7.8	-65.8	-8.6	-48.4	-16.5	-6.4	-9.8	4.8	-10.1	4.4	-8.6	-48.4	-7.8	-65.8

TABLE 15 Stress of lattice member (steel CT only): evenly distributed loads.

Snow fall (cm)	UPPER ROW: MEASURED VALUE (kgf/cm²)								LOWER ROW: ANALYTICAL VALUE (kgf/cm²)					
	01		10		14		25		33		34		44	
	LST	LSB	LST	LSB	LST	LSB	LST	LSB	LST	LSB	LST	LSB	LST	LSB
50	-46.2	144.9	33.6	-199.5	33.6	-189.0	0.0	23.1	27.3	-149.1	-48.3	--	-46.2	172.2
	-1.0	3.4	26.2	-140.1	22.0	-109.0	-8.2	21.1	22	-109.0	47.0	-42.6	-1.0	3.4
100	-96.6	289.8	54.6	-371.7	60.9	-359.1	-4.2	50.4	48.3	-285.6	-92.4	--	-98.7	352.8
	-2.0	6.9	52.4	-280.2	43.9	-218.0	-16.3	42.1	43.9	-218.0	94.0	-85.3	-2.0	6.9
150	-153.3	441.0	79.8	-567.0	90.3	-546.0	-6.3	67.2	69.3	-426.3	-140.7	--	-153.3	533.4
	-3.0	10.3	78.6	-420.3	65.9	-327.1	-24.5	63.2	65.9	-327.1	141.0	-127.9	-3.0	10.3
200	-203.7	577.5	109.2	-774.9	121.8	-716.1	-8.4	86.1	92.4	-569.1	-184.8	--	-201.6	699.3
	-4.1	13.7	104.7	-560.4	87.9	-436.1	-32.6	84.2	87.9	-436.1	188.1	-170.6	-4.1	13.7
225	-231.0	644.7	123.9	-867.3	136.5	-808.5	-10.5	100.8	105.0	-638.4	-207.9	--	-224.7	772.8
	-4.6	15.5	117.8	-630.5	98.9	-490.6	-36.7	94.8	98.9	-490.6	211.6	-191.9	-4.6	15.5

TABLE 16 Stress of upper chord: unevenly distributed loads.

Snow fall (cm)	UPPER ROW: MEASURED VALUE (kgf/cm²)								LOWER ROW: ANALYTICAL VALUE (kgf/cm²)					
	01		07		13		20		24		28		35	
	UT	UB	UT	UB	UT	UB	UT	UB	UT	UB	UT	UB	UT	UB
50	2.6	-4.3	0.0	4.6	-1.8	-6.6	-1.1	-10.1	-4.7	-9.6	-8.4	-7.4	2.3	-4.2
	3	-1.4	2.2	4.2	-1.9	-1.3	-2.3	-7.0	-2.6	-8.1	-5.4	-2.4	2.1	-1.4
100	4.5	-10.9	2.1	8.5	-3.3	-13.1	-2.1	-17.4	-8.5	-16.9	-13.2	-13.5	4.1	-6.5
	6.1	-2.8	4.4	8.3	-3.7	-2.7	-4.6	-14.0	-5.1	-16.2	-10.9	-4.8	4.2	-2.9
150	6.5	-17.2	4.2	12.2	-5.2	-19.5	-3.0	-25.0	-12.1	-24.0	-16.9	-19.4	5.9	-9.1
	9.1	-4.2	6.7	12.5	-5.6	-4.0	-6.9	-21.0	-7.7	-24.3	-16.3	-7.1	6.3	-4.3
200	7.6	-21.1	6.6	16.4	-6.6	-25.9	-3.6	-32.8	-15.9	-31.7	-22.3	-26.1	8.8	-11.1
	12.2	-5.6	8.9	16.7	-7.5	-5.3	-9.2	-27.9	-10.2	-32.4	-21.7	-9.5	8.4	-5.8
225	7.9	-22.9	8.1	18.8	-7.2	-29.4	-3.9	-36.8	-17.8	-35.8	-25.5	-29.6	9.9	-12.1
	13.7	-6.3	10.0	18.7	-8.4	-6.0	-10.4	-31.4	-11.5	-36.5	-24.4	-10.7	9.5	-6.5
250	8.1	-24.0	9.7	21.1	-7.8	-32.9	-4.1	-41.1	-19.9	-39.9	-29.2	-33.0	11.4	-13.1
	15.2	-7.0	11.1	20.8	-9.4	-6.7	-11.5	-34.9	-12.8	-40.6	-27.1	-11.9	10.5	-7.2

TABLE 17 Stress of lower chord: unevenly distributed loads.

Snow fall (cm)	UPPER ROW: MEASURED VALUE (kgf/cm²)								LOWER ROW: ANALYTICAL VALUE (kgf/cm²)					
	02		07		08		19		21		28		32	
	LT	LB	LT	LB	LT	LB	LT	LB	LT	LB	LT	LB	LT	LB
50	1.8	-9.0	-3.4	-10.1	-9.8	-2.1	4.4	2.2	5.4	0.3	-3.0	-7.8	-1.8	-28.9
	-1.8	-13.9	-2.0	-13.6	-6.7	-4.2	0.4	1.5	0.9	1.6	-1.8	-6.8	-6.2	-10.7
100	0.1	-18.3	-7.9	-21.1	-19.5	-4.1	7.4	3.1	8.3	1.2	-5.2	-13.7	-3.8	-39.4
	-3.6	-27.8	-4.0	-27.1	-13.4	-8.5	0.8	2.9	1.8	3.1	-3.6	-13.6	-12.5	-21.5
150	-0.9	-27.5	-12.1	-31.7	-28.9	-5.6	8.5	5.2	12.2	1.8	-7.5	-20.3	-5.8	-49.3
	-5.4	-41.6	-6.0	-40.7	-20.0	-12.7	1.3	4.4	2.8	4.7	-5.4	-20.3	-18.7	-32.2
200	-0.4	-37.1	-15.6	-42.4	-38.1	-7.4	8.3	8.4	15.3	2.9	-10.1	-27.0	-7.8	-65.4
	-7.2	-55.5	-8.1	-54.3	-26.7	-16.9	1.7	5.9	3.7	6.3	-7.2	-27.1	-25.0	-43.0
225	-0.1	-42.2	-17.3	-48.3	-42.8	-8.5	9.0	9.9	17.3	3.3	-11.2	-30.5	-8.4	-73.8
	-8.1	-62.5	-9.1	-61.1	-30.1	-19.0	1.9	6.6	4.2	7.1	-8.1	-30.5	-28.1	-48.4
250	0.2	-47.6	-18.9	-54.0	-47.3	-9.7	8.2	12	19.0	3.9	-12.2	-34.0	-8.3	-81.1
	-9.0	-69.4	-10.1	-67.9	-33.4	-21.1	2.1	7.3	4.6	7.8	-9.1	-33.9	-31.2	-53.7

TABLE 18 Stress of lattice member (steel CT only): unevenly distributed loads.

Snow fall (cm)	UPPER ROW: MEASURED VALUE (kgf/cm²)								LOWER ROW: ANALYTICAL VALUE (kgf/cm²)					
	05		10		13		22		33		34		44	
	LST	LSB	LST	LSB	LST	LSB	LST	LSB	LST	LSB	LST	LSB	LST	LSB
50	42.0	-195.3	10.5	-161.7	-69.3	279.3	21.0	-88.2	27.3	-107.1	-73.5	--	-29.4	25.2
	36.4	-94.6	7.9	-92.2	-54.0	186.1	17.1	-85.6	7.1	-36.4	-65.4	72.6	-6.8	17.6
100	71.4	-399.0	16.8	-262.5	-113.4	483.0	37.8	-189.0	31.5	-136.5	-126.0	--	-65.1	155.4
	72.7	-189.3	15.8	-184.4	-107.9	372.2	34.1	-171.2	14.2	-72.9	-130.8	145.3	-13.7	35.2
150	100.8	-598.5	21.0	-367.5	-157.5	697.2	56.7	-294.0	42.0	-199.5	-174.3	--	-98.7	281.4
	109.1	-283.9	23.7	-276.6	-161.9	558.4	51.2	-256.7	21.2	-109.3	-196.2	217.9	-20.5	52.7
200	136.5	-816.9	31.5	-487.2	-203.7	919.8	90.3	-434.7	50.4	-249.9	-233.1	--	-132.3	344.4
	145.5	-378.6	31.6	-368.8	-215.8	744.5	68.2	-342.3	28.3	-145.8	-261.6	290.6	-27.3	70.3
225	157.5	-936.6	37.8	-550.2	-231.0	1047.9	105.0	-508.2	60.9	-291.9	-266.7	--	-151.2	373.8
	163.7	-425.9	35.5	-414.9	-242.8	837.6	76.8	-385.1	31.9	-164.0	-294.3	326.9	-30.8	79.1
250	178.5	-1060	44.1	-615.3	-260.4	1190.7	123.9	-588.0	69.3	-331.8	-298.2	--	-176.4	264.6
	181.9	-473.2	39.5	-461.0	-269.8	930.6	85.3	-427.9	35.4	-182.2	-326.9	363.2	-34.2	87.9

APPENDIX 1 Full-scale loading test: A section of the trussed arch being lifted.

APPENDIX 2 Full-scale loading test: Detail of LSL-to-lattice connection with strain gauges attached.

APPENDIX 3 Full-scale loading test: Center section of trussed arch being lifted into place. Note the field-joint connection.

APPENDIX 4 Full-scale loading test: Overall view of test.

BAMBOO

BAMBOO

Bamboo has been used as a material in Asia, Africa, and South America for many centuries, beginning in the second century AD when it replaced papyrus and parchment. Since then it has had a wide variety of applications, from forming objects for tea ceremonies to scaffolding for multistory buildings. Today it is being rediscovered as a building material by architects and designers searching for regional sustainable technologies.

There are many reasons for bamboo's appeal: It is inexpensive; it is intensely renewable (growing up to fifteen meters in its first year); its cultivation can prevent soil erosion; and it converts more carbon dioxide to oxygen than many other plants. The plant is suitable for construction use within five to eight years, and it has a yield twenty-five times higher than timber. Unlike timber, it regenerates after being harvested. It is very sturdy because of its hollow interior, which is light and elastic. And there is no waste with bamboo, since it does not have to be stripped of bark and its leaves can be used as fodder.

Ban has been aware of the potential of bamboo for some years; in many ways it is a natural extension of his work with paper tubes. Both materials are hollow and have a positive effect on the environment. He is also conscious of architects who have preceded him in experimenting with bamboo; they include Buckminster Fuller, Frei Otto, and Renzo Piano. The one person who has promoted the use of bamboo in construction most intensively is Colombian architect Simón Vélez. His work with bamboo is primarily in South America, but his influence has been international. He shares with Ban the ethical and civic responsibilities of his profession and combines creative and pragmatic approaches in his work. His first bamboo building in Europe was commissioned by the Zero Emissions Research Initiative (ZERI) for Expo 2000 in Hannover, Germany; it was located across from Ban's paper-tube Japan Pavilion.

In 1995, when Ban was proposing the temporary shelters in Rwanda, he also recommended building permanent housing for Rwandans using bamboo, since the material is abundant in the region. Specifically, by substituting bamboo for timber, he hoped to prevent further deforestation. More recently Ban has experimented with bamboo laminates for a house in China. When he searched for regional building materials, he found that the lumber types were

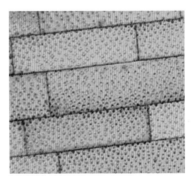

limited; even structural plywood was unavailable. What caught his attention was a plywood the color of blood. This was a laminate of thin strips of bamboo woven with the surface layer into a sheet. The inner layers are oriented perpendicular like plywood, and the laminate was typically used for concrete framework. Ban thought that if bamboo strips could be made into plywood, it might be possible to laminate them into building lumber.

Until this point, his interest in bamboo had been limited. Except for the work of Vélez, there had been little advancement in the structural use of the material because of its nature: It has a tendency to split when dry, it is susceptible to insects and mold, and its diameter varies. However, by laminating the material with a certain type of glue and in a controlled environment, it was possible to make a stable building material from bamboo strips. With the help of a local factory, Ban made a sample of laminated bamboo lumber that was subjected to the standard boiling and bending tests required by Japan's Ministry of Agriculture, Forestry, and Fisheries. The tests showed that laminated bamboo had a structural strength between that of steel and timber.

Ban continued to use bamboo laminates in other projects in the United States: the Schwartz Residence in Connecticut, where he uses bamboo in the box beam, and the bamboo grid structures in Houston and St. Louis. In the latter project the technique is based on a traditional Japanese wickerwork pattern known as *ajiro*, although it is altered slightly to accommodate the recommendations of the structural engineers.

As with all of the materials that Ban has used, the apparently humble bamboo has been transformed into a viable, sturdy, and versatile structural material. Through a combination of ingenuity, extensive research, and testing by architects such as Ban and Vélez, the true potential of bamboo has finally been revealed.

OPPOSITE LEFT: Bamboo stalks
OPPOSITE RIGHT: Cross-section of laminated bamboo
BELOW LEFT: Dining area, Bamboo Furniture House, Great Wall at Shui Guan, China, 2002
BELOW RIGHT: Surface detail of laminated bamboo plywood

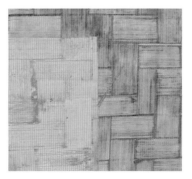

BAMBOO FURNITURE HOUSE

COMPLETION DATE: June 2002
LOCATION: Great Wall
at Shui Guan, China
STRUCTURAL ENGINEER: Minoru Tezuka

BELOW: Living area
RIGHT: Entrance facade

Situated on a mountain overlooking the Great Wall of China, Ban's fourth Furniture House—
a prefabricated modular building system where furniture units also function as the primary structural
component—is part of the Commune by the Great Wall, a group of twelve houses each designed
by a different Asian architect. Ban's one-story courtyard house for a wealthy family of four combines
local vernacular elements with modernist aesthetics and uses his newest material interest—bamboo.

Ban initially tried to find building materials particular to China, but was dissatisfied with the limited
types of lumber available. Instead, he discovered a plywood comprised of laminated, woven strips
of bamboo that was normally used for concrete framework. Ban thought that if bamboo could be made
into plywood, then it could also be laminated into strips for building lumber. With the assistance
of a local bamboo factory, Ban made a sample of laminated bamboo lumber and conducted the boiling
and bending tests mandated by Japan's Ministry of Agriculture, Forestry, and Fisheries.

Ban chose the Furniture House system for pragmatic reasons. Because of the remote site and limited
budget, administration was to be handled by the client, so Ban wanted to minimize the amount
of factory and on-site supervision necessary. The architect also tried to simplify the material palette

Bamboo Furniture House, Great Wall at
Shui Guan, China, 2002
OPPOSITE LEFT: Dining area
OPPOSITE RIGHT: Interior hall, view toward
living area
BELOW LEFT (top to bottom): Elevation,
section, plan, 1:300
BELOW RIGHT: Detail of furniture unit, 1:30

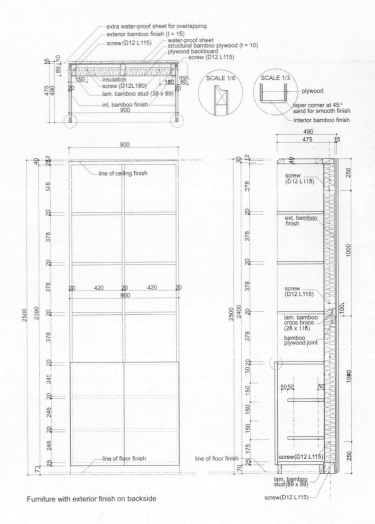

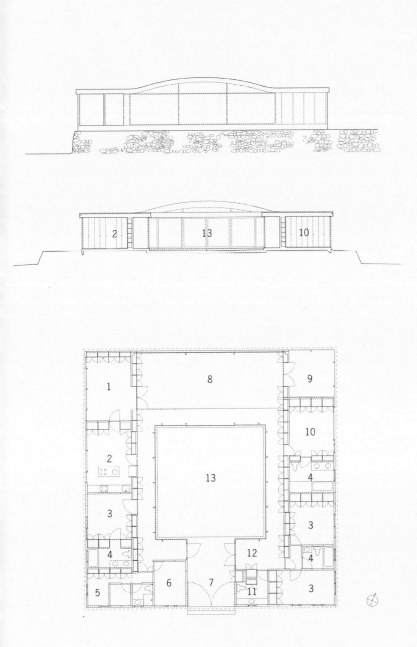

1 Dining room	8 Living room
2 Kitchen	9 Terrace
3 Bedroom	10 Master bedroom
4 Bathroom	11 Powder room
5 Maid/driver's room	12 Foyer
6 Storage	13 Courtyard
7 Entrance	

Bamboo Furniture House, Great Wall at
Shui Guan, China, 2002
LEFT: Axonometric view, 1:600
CENTER: Interior courtyard
OPPOSITE: View of terrace and north facade

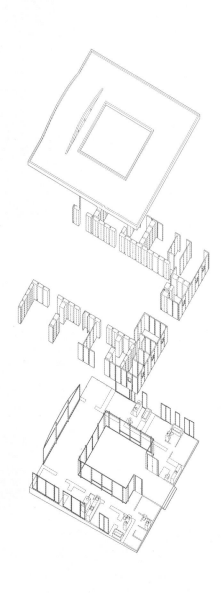

by using laminated bamboo lumber for the framing units and beams as well as the interior and exterior finish. Ultimately, it was difficult to control not only the quality of the overall construction but also the fabrication of the furniture units; these issues led to multiple delays. Still, the project allowed Ban to explore the potential for building in China and to develop laminated bamboo into a new building material.

SCHWARTZ RESIDENCE

DESIGN DATES: February 2001–
September 2002
LOCATION: Sharon, Connecticut,
United States
ASSOICATE ARCHITECTS:
Dean Maltz Architect — Dean Maltz,
Justin Shaulis, Andrew Lefkowitz,
Mara Dorkin, Hirosugi Mizutani
STRUCTURAL ENGINEERS:
Buro Happold — Craig Schwitter,
J. Cohen, Cristobal Correa

OPPOSITE TOP LEFT: Aerial view of model
OPPOSITE TOP RIGHT: Model, view of living
area in foreground and car barn gallery
in background (top); aerial view of living, dining,
and kitchen areas
CENTER LEFT: Site plan, 1:5000 (1"=400')
CENTER RIGHT: First floor plan, 1:1000 (1"=80')
BOTTOM: Roof detail, 1:75 (5/32"=1')

This house for a family of four is nestled on top of a forested ridge that offers spectacular views of the
Berkshire Mountains. The clients, who are avid collectors of both modern art and antique cars, wanted this
house for both short- and long-term retreats from their New York City residence.

Ban took his design cue from the 100-acre site—its setting in the forest, its rocky landscape, its location
in the heart of New England. He determined that the 1500-square-meter house (16,000 square feet)
should be an integral part of the landscape rather than an object in it. He reinterpreted the indigenous
elements of the area—a farm compound and stone wall   and designed a complex of four
pavilions connected by a 2.4-meter-high (8 feet), U-shaped stone wall that serves as the spine of the house.

The four pavilions are distinguished by function. An antique car pavilion at the south end of the complex
serves as a gallery and maintenance area for the owners' cars. The athletic and guest pavilion adjacent to
the pool includes a squash court, exercise room, guest room, and home office. The public pavilion contains
the living room, dining room, library, and kitchen and faces out toward the landscape. Next to the public
pavilion is the family quarter; of all of the pavilions, this has the most open view of the mountains.
The family pavilion includes three bedrooms and a studio, each with a bathroom.

The two primary support systems for the roof are the bearing wall that inscribes the inner part of the U-shaped
house, and the glass curtain wall along its northern edge. Slender steel mullions placed every 3 meters
(10 feet) support the glass. The house's primary structural innovation occurs with the use of 1.27 cm (1/2 inch)
bamboo plywood in the box beam, which spans a maximum of 11.3 meters (37 feet) between the bearing
and glass walls. Ban first used bamboo plywood in this way in the Bamboo Furniture House in China.
In the Schwartz house, it sheathes 60 x 15-cm pieces of lumber (2 feet by 6 inches) to form the box beam.
The box beams are supported on the bearing wall and along the glass wall by the steel columns. By using these
types of post-and-beam and bearing wall systems, Ban created a residence with a very flexible interior and
a focus on panoramic views.

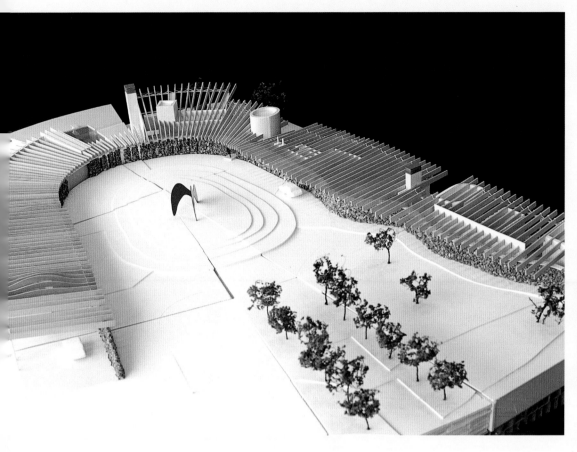

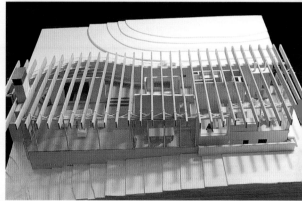

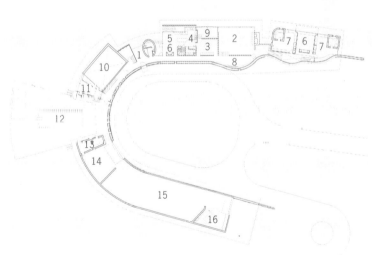

1 Entrance
2 Living room
3 Dining room
4 Kitchen
5 Breakfast room
6 Family room
7 Bedroom
8 Library
9 Screened porch
10 Squash court below
11 Exercise room
12 Pool
13 Storage
14 Garage
15 Car barn gallery
16 Lift/wash

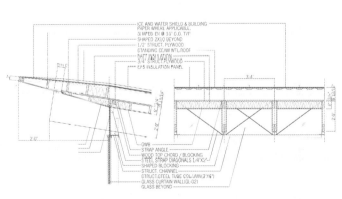

BAMBOO GRID SHELL STRUCTURES

FOREST PARK PAVILION

PROJECTED COMPLETION: 2004
LOCATION: St. Louis, Missouri,
United States
ASSOCIATE ARCHITECTS:
Dean Maltz Architect — Dean Maltz,
Justin Shaulis, Andrew Lefkowitz
STRUCTURAL ENGINEERS:
Arup, London — Cecil Balmond,
Charles Walker, Martin Self, Tristan
Simmons, Benedikt Schleicher

BAMBOO ROOF

COMPLETION DATE: November 2002
LOCATION: Rice University Art Gallery,
Houston, Texas, United States
STRUCTURAL ENGINEERS:
Arup, London — Cecil Balmond,
Charles Walker, Martin Self, Tristan
Simmons, Benedikt Schleicher

Forest Park Pavilion, St. Louis, Missouri,
projected completion 2004
BELOW LEFT (top to bottom): Section and
plan, 1:1000 (1"=80')
BELOW RIGHT (top to bottom): Mock-up of
grid-shell pinwheel connection, sketches
of connection details
OPPOSITE (left to right): Preliminary study
for pavilion roof and column, computer-
generated image of whole grid shell

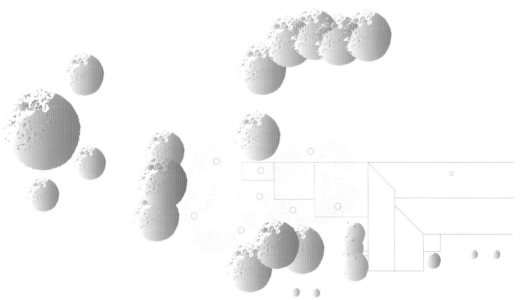

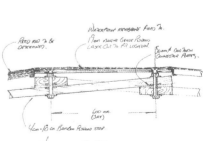

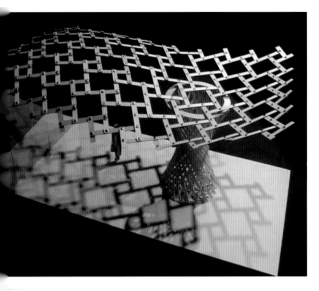
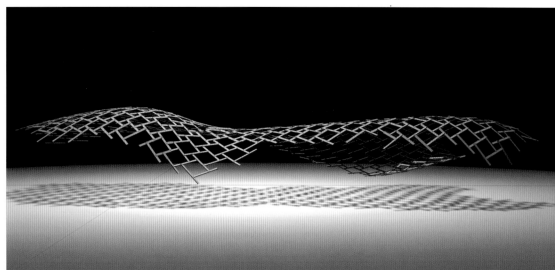

FOREST PARK PAVILION

Ban was commissioned by Forest Park Forever—a private, non-profit organization dedicated to making St Louis's Forest Park the premier national urban park—to design an outdoor pavilion as part of a new master plan. In collaboration with Cecil Balmond of Arup London, he incorporated ideas from several former projects to create a graceful, gossamerlike 45.7-meter-long woven canopy (150 feet).

Ban utilized several precedents in his design concept, most important the wickerwork idea from Uno Chiyo Memorial Museum, an unbuilt project designed in collaboration with Frei Otto in 2000. The memorial's distinctive woven roof used a wickerwork pattern called *ajiro*, which is most often seen in the ceilings of traditional Japanese houses. Ban and Otto, however, used this pattern as inspiration for the primary structure using thin, woven sheets of laminated veneer lumber (LVL). Since these sheets can be manufactured in long lengths and in any thickness, they were ideal for realizing a timber-tension structure like the memorial or the park pavilion.

One of the primary changes in the pavilion was the use of laminated bamboo, which Ban had pioneered at the Bamboo Furniture House (China) and planned to use in the Sagaponac House (New York). In China, Ban circumvented bamboo's flaws, including inconsistent thicknesses, by creating a bamboo laminate. When Ban presented the Forest Park project to Balmond, he was searching for the most efficient way to make a pavilion using laminated bamboo and the *ajiro* wickerwork technique. Balmond's solution was to eliminate the inner part of the woven base unit and to use shorter pieces of laminated bamboo to create each unit. Since the maximum length of laminated bamboo is currently 2.4 meters (8 feet), this became the pavilion's basic measurement. At the point where the units intersect, the system acts like a cardboard box when folded closed, so that the thickness of the bamboo begins to have a convex or curved form. Eight columns, or "trunks" of laminated bamboo support this woven bamboo blanket. A layer of PVC membrane offers protection from rain while admitting adequate natural light.

Bamboo Roof, Houston, Texas, 2002
TOP ROW (left to right): Assembling bamboo members, students and professors completing assembly, complete grid shell being raised by crane, steel pipes of columns being fixed to grid shell

ABOVE LEFT: Detail of column connections to grid shell
ABOVE RIGHT: Completed grid shell and projected shadow on plaza floor
BELOW LEFT: Column connection detail, 1:5
BELOW RIGHT: Site plan, 1:500 (1"=40')
OPPOSITE: Bamboo Roof seen from southeast

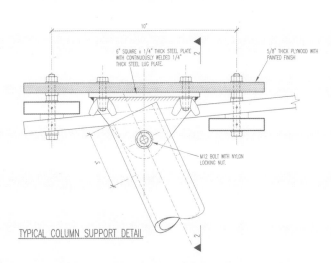

TYPICAL COLUMN SUPPORT DETAIL

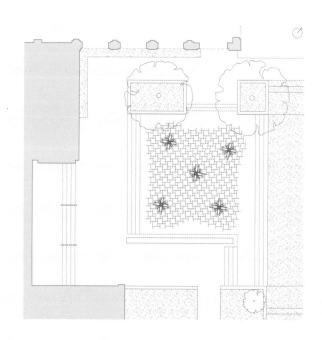

BAMBOO ROOF

Rice University Art Gallery commissioned this site-specific installation, an open-weave canopy of bamboo boards measuring 11 x 11 meters (36' x 36') and weighing more than 1.2 tons. A representative from Ban's office, along with an engineer from Arup and a team of fifty students, professors, and other volunteers from Rice University and the University of Houston, constructed the roof in sections in the gallery plaza. The installation is a half-scale prototype of the pavilion at St. Louis; at both scales, the effect is and will be poetic, conjuring up images of gossamer nets or lace-like canopies.

■ BAMBOO FURNITURE HOUSE

Experiment date _____ December 2000 – January 2001

Location _____ Chiba Polytechnic College Housing Environment Department Chiba, Japan

Performed by _____ Asst. Prof. Dr. Minoru Tezuka

Test Report Profile

Furniture units were the main structure in this building. Structural plywood was used as the backboard in these furniture units in order to resist lateral forces; the frame was fixed to this backboard. The space within the furniture unit is produced by fixing the sideboards, to the vertical member of the frame, which supports the vertical loads acting on the shelves, and allows doors to be installed. The backboard is subjected to shear force due to the lateral force. Vertical loads and bending moment due to these lateral forces caused axial forces on the vertical members. The upper member serves to transfer shear force to the backboard and the lower member serves to transfer shear force from the backboard to the footing beam.

Instead of using structural plywood for the backboard, in this building the architect used laminated bamboo boards made by bonding layers of lamina in the same direction. The thin bamboo boards were woven in the orthogonal direction into the lamina. Compression tests and dowel bearing strength tests were performed on the laminated bamboo board; the first was designed to obtain the shear modulus and the latter to assume the bolted connection strength.

Laminated bamboo boards were made by bonding thin layers of orthogonally woven laminas.

1 _____ Laminated Bamboo Compression Test
2 _____ Dowel Bearing Strength Test

Laminated Bamboo Compression Test
1-1 _____ Test Specimens

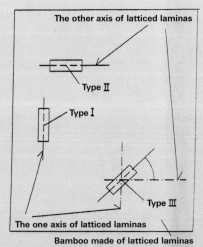

FIGURE 1 Method for test specimens cut from laminated bamboo boards.

Three kinds of specimens (Type I, Type II, and Type III) were produced. Type I was cut so the direction of the fibers coincides with one axis of the latticed laminas. Type II was cut to coincide with the axis perpendicular to that of Type I. Type III was cut so its axis is at a 45-degree angle to the axis of the latticed laminas. Type I specimens were named CTG2, CTG3, CTG4. Type II specimens were CYG2, CYG3, CYG4, and Type III specimens, CNG2, CNG3, CNG4. Four strain gauges were attached to each specimen, in the long direction and short direction. The water content of the specimens was 9%. Figure 1 shows how the different specimens were cut from the laminated bamboo plywood (bamboo made of latticed laminas).

Laminated Bamboo Compression Test
1-2 _____ Test Procedures

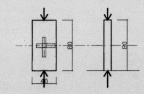

The compression test was carried out as shown in Figure 2, and the vertical strain and lateral strain was measured. The loading speed was set at 102kgf/min.

FIGURE 2 Test procedures for compression tests.

Laminated Bamboo Compression Test
1-3 _____ Test Results

Figure 3 shows the relationship between load and vertical strain for one example of each type. The slope of lateral strain divided by the slope of vertical strain in proportional limit was Poisson's ratio. (=v). The results of the compression test is shown in Table 1. When it was considered that the bamboo was an orthotropic plate, the v/E of Type C-1 and that of C-2 must be equal. Since there was little difference in (v/E) between Type I and Type II, the shear modulus was calculated by the following Jenkin's formula:

$$\frac{1}{G_{xy}} = \frac{1}{E_{45}} - \left(\frac{1}{E_x} + \frac{1}{E_y} - \frac{2v_{xy}}{E_x} \right)$$

E_x: Young's modulus from Type I test.
v_{xy}: Poisson's ratio from Type I test.
E_y: Young's modulus from Type II test.
E_{45}: Young's modulus from Type III test.
G_{xy}: Shear modulus

The details of the calculation of the shear modulus are shown after Table 1.

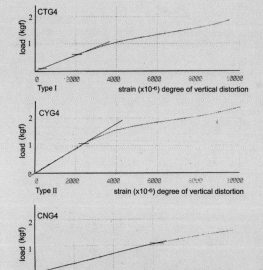

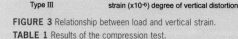

FIGURE 3 Relationship between load and vertical strain.
TABLE 1 Results of the compression test.

Type	specimen (NO.)	width (mm)	thickness (mm)	strength (kgf/cm²)	E (×10³kgf/cm²)	v	v/E
I	CTG2	40.18	10.84	592	109.7	0.109	
	CTG3	39.35	11.57	278	73.9	0.036	
	CTG4	39.58	10.96	453	67.9	0.083	
	Average			**441**	83.8	0.076	9.07×10⁻⁷
II	CYG2	39.60	10.78	663	119.0	0.106	
	CYG3	40.20	11.74	554	93.1	0.071	
	CYG4	39.29	11.44	550	99.3	0.097	
	Average			**589**	103.8	0.091	8.77×10⁻⁷
III	CNG2	38.80	11.04	261	40.2	—	
	CNG3	38.56	11.28	416	43.2	—	Average specific gravity 0.89
	CNG4	39.89	10.83	462	40.1	—	
	Average			**380**	41.2	—	

$$(9.07 \times 10^7 + 8.77 \times 10^7) / 2 = 8.92 \times 10^7$$

$$\frac{1}{G_{xy}} = \frac{1}{41.2 \times 10^3} - \left(\frac{1}{83.8 \times 10^3} + \frac{1}{103.8 \times 10^3} - 8.92 \times 10^7 \times 2\right)$$

$$G_{xy} = 12.9 \times 10^3 \, kgf/cm^2$$

Young's modulus of Type I and Type II averaged 83.8–103.8X10³kgf/cm².

Dowel Bearing Strength Test

2-1 _____ Test Specimens

Specimens of 48mm x 176mm were cut as shown in Figure 4. The cutting orientation of the specimens was the same as in the compression test. A hole of 18mm diameter was made in the specimen as shown. The water content of the specimens was 9%.

Specimens:

Type I: CTB4, CTB5, CTB6
Type II: CYB4, CYB5, CYB6
Type III: CNB3, CNB5, CNB6

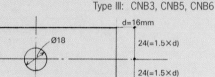

FIGURE 4 Test specimens for dowel bearing strength tests.

Dowel Bearing Strength Test

2-2 _____ Test Procedures

A steel bar, 16mm in diameter, was passed through the 18mm diameter hole of the specimen, and the load was applied to the short side of the specimen, as shown in Figure 5. The load was transmitted to the V-block through the steel bar. Jigs were attached at the lower part of the specimen where the compressive stress was 0. The displacement between the test bed and the jigs (δ_1,δ_2) were measured. The relative displacement was set at ($\delta_1+\delta_2$) /2. The loading speed was set at 15kgf/min.

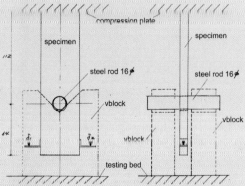

FIGURE 5 Test procedures for dowel bearing strength tests.

Dowel Bearing Strength Test

2-3 _____ Test Results

Figure 6 shows one example of the relationship between load and relative displacement for each of the specimen types. The slope of the straight line in Figure 6 divided by the thickness of the specimen was the bearing stiffness, shown in Table 2 as S. S of Douglas fir is known to be around 7800kgf/cm², and the average values for Type I, II, III, were about twice the value of 7800kgf/cm². Also, there was little difference in S among the three

types. For each type, average maximum load (=Pmax) divided by the sum of the thickness of the specimen (=t) multiplied by the diameter of the steel bar (=16mm) was compared to the average compressive strengths from Table 1. Pmax/(t x d) far exceeded the compressive strength of the specimen (1.44 – 2.01 times greater).

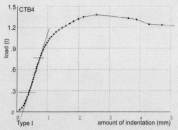
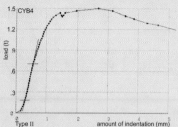
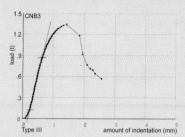

FIGURE 6 Relationship between load and relative displacement.

TABLE 2 Results of the dowel bearing strength tests.

Type	specimen (NO.)	thickness (mm)	Pmax. (kgf)	Pmax/(t·d) (kgf/cm²)	S (kgf/cm²)
I	CTB4	10.56	1380	817	13250
	CTB5	10.51	1580	940	17130
	CTB6	10.23	1068	652	11810
	Average			**803**	14060
II	CYB4	11.24	1499	834	17800
	CYB5	10.80	1519	879	20313
	CYB6	10.25	1353	825	18300
	Average			**846**	18800
III	CNB3	11.25	1354	752	16660
	CNB5	10.14	1486	916	17660
	CNB6	10.04	995	620	11640
	Average			**763**	15320
					16060

The bearing stiffness of Douglas fir is known to be around 7800kgf/cm², and the average of Type I, II, and III was about twice that figure.

■ FOREST PARK PAVILION

Experiment date _____ April 2002

Location _____ Tokyo National University of Fine Arts and Music, Department of Architecture, Faculty of Fine Arts, Tokyo, Japan

Performed by _____ Dr. Minoru Tezuka
Prof. Yoshiaki Tsuboi

Test Report Profile

In this building, laminated bamboo lumber is used in a structure that is exposed to wind and rain, thus delamination tests and bending tests were carried out. Upon confirmation of the bamboo's ability to withstand the weather, compression tests and shearing tests were performed to complete the data required.

Laminated bamboo lumber consists of long strips of bamboo cut in the direction of the fiber. First, the strips of bamboo are laminated together horizontally to create a thin flat layer of bamboo. Then, many of these flat layers of bamboo are laminated together to achieve the desired thickness of the lumber, with all of the fibers running parallel to each other.

Laminated bamboo lumber consists of long strips of bamboo cut in the direction of the fiber and laminated in flat horizontal layers to achieve the desired thickness. All fibers run parallel to each other.

1 _____ Laminated Bamboo Boiling Delamination Test
2 _____ Laminated Bamboo Bending Test

1 _____ Laminated Bamboo Boiling Delamination Test

Boiling delamination testing of laminated materials for structural use is prescribed by the Japanese Agricultural Standard (JAS) as follows:

a) Test specimens:

Two test pieces in the shape of a square whose sides are 75mm shall be made from each sample material. For sample materials less than 75mm wide, the length shall equal 75mm, and the width shall be the dimension of the relevant building material.

b) Testing procedures:

Steep the specified testing pieces in boiling water for 5 hours, then steep at room temperature water for another hour. After steeping the pieces, place them in a constant temperature dryer (=60±3°C) to let dry for 24 hours.

c) Standard requirements of test results:

Percentage of delamination is to be less than 10%. Total length of delamination within one adhesive layer is to be less than 1/3 of the total length of four sides of the adhesive layer (delamination less than 3mm long is to be omitted).

$$\text{Percentage of Delamination (\%)} = \frac{\text{Total length of delamination along four sides of testing piece}}{\text{Total length of adhesive layers along four sides of testing piece}} \times 100$$

1-1 _____ Laminated Bamboo Boiling Delamination Test
Test Specimens

From each of two laminated bamboo lumbers (90mm x 1000mm x 15mm) made with water-soluble vinyl urethane adhesive, one specimen 75mm x 75mm (specimen A and B) was cut out. Also, from each of two laminated bamboo lumbers (150mm x 1000mm x 30mm) made with Resorcinol adhesive, two specimens 75mm x 75mm (specimen C-1, C-2, D-1, D-2) were cut out.

1-2 _____ Laminated Bamboo Boiling Delamination Test
Test Procedures

The prescribed JAS standard was followed. Figure 1 shows the testing conditions.

FIGURE 1
Testing conditions of the specimens.

1-3 _____ Laminated Bamboo Boiling Delamination Test
Test Results

An example of the test results for a specimen made with water-soluble vinyl urethane adhesive (specimen A) is shown in Figure 2, and an example of the test results for a specimen made with Resorcinol adhesive is shown in Figure 3 (specimen C-1). From the resulting data, the laminated bamboo with water soluble vinyl urethane did not pass the JAS standard, while all specimens with Resorcinol adhesive passed the JAS standard.

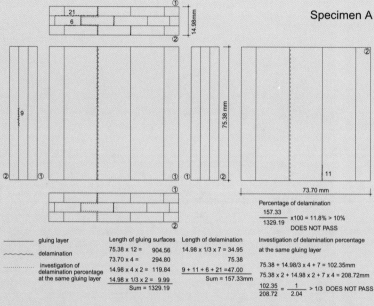

FIGURE 2 Test results of specimen made with water-soluble vinyl urethane adhesive (specimen A).

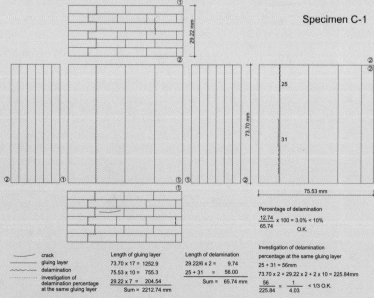

FIGURE 3 Test results of specimen made with Resorcinol adhesive (specimen C-1).

All specimens made with Resorcinol adhesive passed the JAS standard.

Laminated Bamboo Bending Test

2-1 _____ Test Specimens

A total of four specimens were cut. Two specimens (No. 14412A, 14412B) 90mm x 700mm were cut from each of two samples of 15mm-thick laminated bamboo lumber made with water-soluble vinyl urethane. Two specimens (No. 14412C, 14412D) 150mm x 700mm were cut from each of two samples of 30mm-thick laminated bamboo made with Resorcinol adhesive.

Laminated Bamboo Bending Test

2-2 _____ Test Procedures

As shown in Figure 4, the tests were carried out by applying a concentrated load at the center of a 600mm span. The load was applied at a constant rate of 20kgf/min. to specimens No. 14412A and 14412B, and at a constant rate of 100kgf/min. to specimens No. 14412C and 14412D. The displacement was measured directly under the loading point.

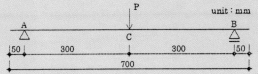

FIGURE 4 Laminated bamboo bending test procedures.

Laminated Bamboo Bending Test

2-3 _____ Test Results

The relationship between load and displacement is shown in Figure 5. Young's modulus was calculated using a proportional limit load and its displacement from this. The bending strength and Young's modulus were calculated using the following formulas, and the test results are shown in Table 1.

$$\sigma_b = \frac{1/4 P_{max}l}{Z}$$

$$E = \frac{P^* l^3}{48 I \delta}$$

P_{max}: maximum load (kgf)
l: span (=60cm)
Z: section modulus (=$bt^3/6$) cm^3
b: width (cm)
t: thickness (cm)

σ_b: bending strength (kgf/cm^2)
P^*: proportional limit load (kgf)
I: moment of inertia of area (=$bt^3/12$)cm^4
δ: displacement at the time of P^*(cm)
E: Young's modulus (kgf/cm^2)

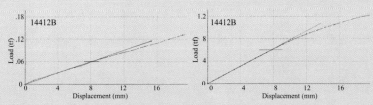

FIGURE 5 Relationship between load and displacement.

TABLE 1 Test results of laminated bamboo bending tests.

NO.	b* mm	t* mm	z* cm³	I** cm⁴	Bending strength kgf/cm²		Young's modulus x 10³ kgf/cm²		Water content percentage (%)
14412A	89.95	14.90	3.328	2.460	1020	1155	121.9	123.8	10.52
14412B	89.80	14.88	3.314	2.471	1286		125.7		10.65
14412C	149.95	29.83	22.24	33.00	1249	1270	105.7	111.1	11.50
14412D	150.00	29.80	22.20	33.07	1291		116.4		11.14

*b,t,z, at point C
** average section I

Because the raw bamboo was Moso bamboo, Young's modulus and bending strength of the composite materials were close to the data for the raw material (125x10³ kgf/cm², 1440 kgf/cm²).

Young's modulus and bending strength (111.1X10³kgf/cm², 1270kgf/cm²) were

close to but less than that of raw Moso bamboo (125x10³kgf/cm², 1440kgf/cm²)

Experiment Date _____ October – November 2002

Location _____ Kanto Polytechnic College, Applied Course, Department of Advanced Architectural Technology for Construction Systems, Tochigi, Japan

Performed by _____ Dr. Minoru Tezuka
Prof. Nobumichi Yamada

3 _____ **Laminated Bamboo Compression Test**
4 _____ **Laminated Bamboo Shearing Test**

Laminated Bamboo Compression Test

3-1 _____ Test Specimens

Specimens of 40mm x 80mm were cut from three different sheets of 12mm-thick laminated bamboo (Resorcinol adhesive). Three specimens of each of three types were produced from each of the three sheets of laminated bamboo for a total of 27 specimens. Type C-1: the fiber of the bamboo runs parallel to the long dimension of the specimen. Type C-2: the fiber runs perpendicular to the long direction. Type C-3: the fiber runs at 45 degrees to the long direction of the specimen. The numbering system for the specimens was type number of originating laminated bamboo sample - number of test (ie. C-1-2-1: Type C-1, made from laminated bamboo sample #2, and #1 of three test specimens).

Laminated Bamboo Compression Test

3-2 _____ Test Procedures

As shown in Figure 6, a total of four strain gauges were attached to each specimen for Types C-1 and C-2. Two gauges were positioned on either side, precisely in the center of the specimen, oriented in both the short and long direction. A total of two strain gauges were attached to Type C-3 specimens, centered on either side of the specimen, oriented in only the long direction. Then, compression tests were carried out by loading the specimens at a constant rate of 30kgf/cm²/min.

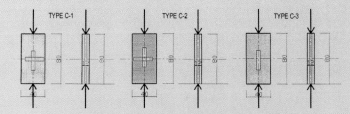

FIGURE 6 Compression test procedures and positions of strain gauges.

Laminated Bamboo Compression Test

3-3 _____ Test Results

The relationship between stress and strain for one specimen of each type is shown in Figure 7. E (Young's modulus) was calculated from the slope of the stress-vertical strain relationship. Poisson's ratio was calculated by dividing the slope of the stress-vertical strain relationship by the slope of the stress-horizontal strain relationship. The results from the tests are shown in Table 2. Because the bamboo was an orthotropic plate, the v/E of Type C-1 and that of C-2 must be equal. The average v/E value of C-1 was 3.59×10^{-6}cm²/kgf and that of C-2 was 2.48×10^{-6}cm²/kgf. The v/E of C-1 was 1.45 times that of C-2, but they were considered to be of the same order. Under the assumption that $(v/E)_{C-1} = (v/E)_{C-2}$, the shear modulus G on boards 1 through 3 was calculated using the following Jenkin's formula. The resulting data is shown in Table 2.

Because bamboo was an orthotropic plate, the ν/E of Type C-1 and that of C-2 must be equal.

$$\frac{1}{G_{xy}} = \frac{4}{E_{45}} - \left(\frac{1}{E_x} + \frac{1}{E_y} - \frac{2\nu_{xy}}{E_x} \right)$$

E_x: Young's modulus obtained from the compressive tests of Type C-1.
ν_{xy}: Poisson's ratio obtained from the compressive tests of Type C-1.
E_y: Young's modulus obtained from the compressive tests of Type C-2.
E_{45}: Young's modulus obtained from the compressive tests of Type C-3.

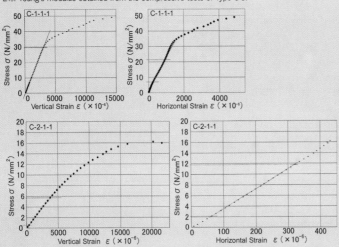

FIGURE 7 Relationship between stress and strain.

TABLE 2 Shear modulus (derived from compression tests).

C-1	E	ν	ν/E	E (AVG.)	ν (AVG.)	ν/E (AVG.)
C-1-1-1	101.2	0.480	4.74			
C-1-1-2	87.34	0.300	3.43	89.48	0.400	4.48
C-1-1-3	79.90	0.421	5.27			
C-1-2-1	100.7	0.312	3.10			
C-1-2-2	112.5	0.274	2.44	103.4	0.290	2.82
C-1-2-3	96.93	0.283	2.92			
C-1-3-1	91.76	0.305	3.32			
C-1-3-2	104.7	0.324	3.09	98.30	0.341	3.46
C-1-3-3	98.44	0.392	3.98			
AVERAGE	97.05	0.344	3.59			

C-1 $E_x= 89.48\times10^3$ $E_y= 13.09\times10^3$
$\nu_{xy}/E_x = \nu_{yx}/E_y$
$= 3.475\times10^{-6}(=(4.48+2.47)/2)$
$E_{45} = 21.59\times10^3$
$1/G_{xy}=4/E_{45}-(1/E_x+1/E_y-2\nu_{xy}/E_x)$
$G_{xy}=9.56\times10^3$

C-2 $E_x=103.4\times10^3$ $E_y=15.86\times10^3$
$\nu_{xy}/E_x = \nu_{yx}/E_y$
$= 2.72\times10^{-6}(=(2.82+2.62)/2)$
$E_{45} = 27.14\times10^3$
$1/G_{xy}=4/E_{45}-(1/E_x+1/E_y-2\nu_{xy}/E_x)$
$G_{xy}=12.48\times10^3$

C-3 $E_x=98.3\times10^3$ $E_y=13.19\times10^3$
$\nu_{xy}/E_x = \nu_{yx}/E_y$
$= 2.905\times10^{-6}(=(3.46+2.35)/2)$
$E_{45} = 21.36\times10^3$
$1/G_{xy}=4/E_{45}-(1/E_x+1/E_y-2\nu_{xy}/E_x)$
$G_{xy}=9.34\times10^3$

C-2	E	ν	ν/E	E (AVG.)	ν (AVG.)	ν/E (AVG.)
C-2-1-1	15.49	0.0405	2.61			
C-2-1-2	11.94	0.0267	2.24	13.09	0.0325	2.47
C-2-1-3	11.83	0.0302	2.55			
C-2-2-1	15.96	0.0444	2.78			
C-2-2-2	13.70	0.0349	2.55	15.86	0.0451	2.62
C-2-2-3	22.05	0.0561	2.54			
C-2-3-1	10.48	0.0227	2.17			
C-2-3-2	13.08	0.0329	2.52	13.19	0.0311	2.35
C-2-3-3	16.01	0.0377	2.35			
AVERAGE	14.50	0.0362	2.48			

C-3	E45	E (AVG.)
C-3-1-1	21.89	
C-3-1-2	23.28	21.59
C-3-1-3	19.60	
C-3-2-1	22.52	
C-3-2-2	25.89	27.14
C-3-2-3	33.02	
C-3-3-1	18.32	
C-3-3-2	22.94	21.36
C-3-3-3	22.82	
AVERAGE	23.36	

Sectional dimensions, strengths, and water content are shown in Table 3. Failure conditions of the specimens are shown in Figure 8. Average values for compressive strength and Young's modulus of raw Moso bamboo (in the direction of the fiber) are 780kgf/cm² and 125x10³kgf/cm² respectively. Existing minimum values are 55x10³kgf/cm² and 440kgf/cm² respectively. The test values 532kgf/cm² (compressive strength) and 97.05x10³kgf/cm² (Young's modulus) were less than average, but exceeded the minimum values.

TABLE 3 Results of laminated bamboo compression test — strength

SPECIMEN NO.	AVERAGE THICKNESS (mm)	AVERAGE WIDTH (mm)	AVERAGE HEIGHT (mm)	AREA (mm²)	Pmax (kN)	COMPRESSION STRENGTH (N/mm²)	M.C. (%)
C-1-1-1	12.10	40.53	80.33	490.35	24.48	49.92	10.1
C-1-1-2	12.18	40.10	80.78	488.22	22.44	45.96	10.1
C-1-1-3	12.23	40.08	80.80	489.92	23.24	47.44	9.7
C-1-2-1	12.13	40.35	81.03	489.24	25.78	52.69	9.7
C-1-2-2	12.10	40.70	80.58	492.47	27.42	55.68	9.7
C-1-2-3	12.08	40.30	80.30	486.62	24.64	50.63	9.7
C-1-3-1	12.05	41.20	80.35	496.46	24.88	50.11	9.5
C-1-3-2	12.20	39.95	80.00	487.39	30.02	61.59	9.5
C-1-3-3	12.20	38.75	78.13	472.75	26.30	55.63	9.5
C-2-1-1	12.13	40.55	80.23	491.67	8.00	16.27	9.9
C-2-1-2	12.15	40.78	80.43	495.42	7.40	14.94	9.9
C-2-1-3	12.23	40.60	79.90	496.34	6.46	13.02	9.9
C-2-2-1	12.10	39.35	78.95	476.14	7.50	15.75	9.9
C-2-2-2	12.13	40.35	79.78	489.24	8.66	17.70	9.9
C-2-2-3	12.05	40.35	80.80	486.22	9.56	19.66	9.7
C-2-3-1	12.13	40.25	80.88	488.03	7.40	15.16	9.3
C-2-3-2	12.20	39.63	80.08	483.43	7.88	16.30	9.3
C-2-3-3	12.15	40.23	80.05	488.73	9.32	19.07	9.3
C-3-1-1	12.18	40.78	80.80	496.44	12.22	24.62	10.2
C-3-1-2	12.15	40.48	80.35	491.77	12.48	25.38	10.2
C-3-1-3	12.25	35.53	74.95	435.18	11.14	25.60	10.2
C-3-2-1	12.13	38.68	78.43	468.93	13.72	29.26	9.9
C-3-2-2	12.10	39.88	79.60	482.49	16.54	34.28	9.6
C-3-2-3	12.05	40.65	80.58	489.83	19.14	39.07	9.6
C-3-3-1	12.18	38.18	76.58	464.78	12.22	26.29	9.6
C-3-3-2	12.20	39.50	79.80	481.90	13.80	28.64	9.6
C-3-3-3	12.20	38.68	79.38	471.84	14.28	30.26	9.6

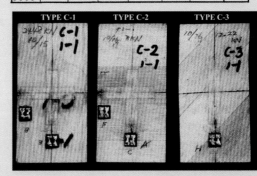

FIGURE 8 Failure conditions of the laminated bamboo compression test.

Compressive strength of 532kgf/cm² and Young's modulus of 97.05x10³kgf/cm² were less than average, but exceeded the minimum existing values.

Shearing Test

4-1 _____ Test Specimens

To obtain the shear strength in plane and through the thickness of the laminated bamboo lumber, Type A-1 specimens notched in the plane, and Type B-1 specimens notched in the thickness, were made from three 12mm-thick sheets of laminated bamboo lumber made with Resorcinol adhesive. The Type B-1 specimens were made by gluing together notched and unnotched pieces of 12mm-thick laminated lumber using Epoxy resin adhesive and then screwing the combined pieces together. The notched pieces of Type B-1 specimens were made so that the corner of the notch was as close as possible to the glued surface. Figure 9 shows the Type A-1 and Type B-1 specimens.

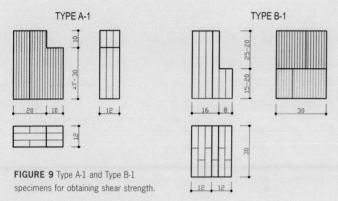

FIGURE 9 Type A-1 and Type B-1 specimens for obtaining shear strength.

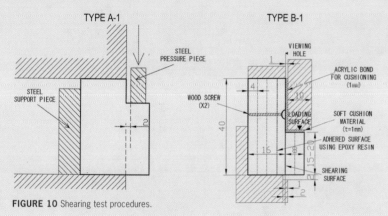

FIGURE 10 Shearing test procedures.

Shearing Test
4-2 _____ Test Procedures

As shown in Figure 10, shearing tests were carried out by applying load to a steel block that transmitted the load to the test specimen. The test method for type A-1 is used to obtain the shear strength in plane, and the test method for type B-1 is used to obtain the shear strength in thickness. Although both are, in principle, the same method, trial-and-error adjustments were made in type B-1 in order to produce proper results. The load was applied at a constant rate of 30 to 45 kgf/cm²/min. at the average shear stress.

Shearing Test
4-3 _____ Test Results

The shear strength following Japan Industrial Standard (JIS) was calculated from the following formula:

$$\text{Shear strength} = \frac{P_{max}}{A}$$

P_{max}: maximum load (kN)
A: shear area (mm²)

The results for shear strength in plane (Type A-1) are shown in Table 4, and the shear strength in thickness (Type B-1) are shown in Table 5. There were many differences in the results of Type A-1 and Type B-1, and the average values of shear strength were 17.12N/mm² and 14.4N/mm², respectively. The numbering of the specimens in Tables 4 and 5 are grouped to distinguish similar specimens and conditions. The failure conditions

of the two types of specimens are shown in Figure 11. Although all of the specimens for the shear tests in plane failed through the main material, some specimens for shear tests in thickness failed through the adhesive surface and not the main body of the material.

TABLE 4 Results of shear strength in plane.

SPECIMEN NO.	AVERAGE WIDTH (mm)	AVERAGE HEIGHT (mm)	AREA (mm²)	Pmax (kN)	SHEAR STRENGTH (N/mm²)	M.C. (%)
A-1-1-1	12.15	30.45	369.97	5.66	15.29	11.0
A-1-1-2	12.23	30.40	371.64	5.70	15.33	11.0
A-1-1-3	12.20	30.25	369.05	5.15	13.95	11.0
A-1-2-10	25.70	11.95	307.12	5.40	17.58	8.9
A-1-2-11	25.50	11.98	305.36	6.22	20.36	8.9
A-1-2-12	25.45	12.00	305.40	5.06	16.56	8.9
A-1-2-13	25.73	11.98	308.06	5.98	19.41	8.9
A-1-2-14	24.90	11.98	298.18	5.12	17.17	8.9
A-1-3-1	12.08	29.55	356.82	6.34	17.76	9.5
A-1-3-2	12.23	28.55	349.02	6.82	19.54	9.5
A-1-3-3	12.30	29.90	367.77	6.46	17.56	9.5

TABLE 5 Results of shear strength in thickness.

SPECIMEN NO.	AVERAGE HEIGHT (mm)	AVERAGE WIDTH (mm)	AREA (mm²)	Pmax (kN)	SHEAR STRENGTH (N/mm²)	M.C. (%)
B-1-1-10	20.25	29.88	604.97	8.38	13.852	9.3
B-1-1-11	20.25	30.43	616.11	9.84	15.971	9.3
B-1-1-12	20.25	29.95	606.49	10.04	16.554	9.3
B-1-1-13	20.28	29.78	603.69	10.20	16.896	9.3
B-1-1-14	20.25	29.68	600.92	6.42	10.684	9.3
B-1-1-15	20.28	21.43	434.39	5.12	11.787	9.3
B-1-1-16	20.20	20.30	410.06	5.52	13.461	9.3
B-1-2-25	16.23	29.38	476.61	6.22	13.051	8.9
B-1-2-26	16.65	30.00	499.50	8.62	17.257	8.9
B-1-2-27	15.58	22.38	348.49	4.62	13.257	8.9
B-1-2-28	15.30	20.90	319.77	5.66	17.700	8.9
B-1-2-29	20.00	29.90	598.00	10.14	16.957	8.9
B-1-2-30	15.90	29.70	472.23	7.08	14.993	8.9
B-1-3-10	20.28	30.05	609.26	5.04	8.272	9.3
B-1-3-11	20.30	28.80	584.64	8.12	13.889	9.3
B-1-3-12	17.03	29.28	498.41	8.40	16.854	9.3
B-1-3-13	17.68	30.03	530.69	6.72	12.663	9.3
B-1-3-14	20.05	29.73	595.99	7.22	12.114	9.3
B-1-3-15	20.25	22.00	445.50	6.28	14.097	9.3
B-1-3-16	20.25	20.75	420.19	7.32	17.421	9.3

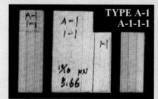
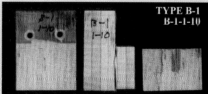

FIGURE 11 Failure conditions of shearing test specimens.

The average shear strength in plane and in thickness was 17.12N/mm² and 14.4N/mm² respectively.

PREFAB-
RICATION

TRIU596405 0
NYKU602281 3
NYKU610156 9
TRLU 635922 7
RLU 4095803
tex
TEXU 73105 9
NYKU604274 3
TRIU 5937898
TRLU 4423498
TRLU 4283159
NYKU659734 0
TRLU 6185017
TRIU 998035 7
GATU 437080 4
TRIU 926138 9
CUTION 9" HIGH CTAINER
CUTION 9" HIGH CTAINER

PREFABRICATION

Like papermaking, prefabrication's roots lie in ancient Egypt, where boat makers attempted to standardize their craft. However, experimentation by architects and engineers in designing prefabricated housing systems did not begin until the late nineteenth century and only began to gain momentum after Henry Ford's mass production of the Model T in the early twentieth century. Ford's unification of production and assembly helped define "prefabrication" as the manufacturing and assembly of standardized parts in advance for transport to and placement at a specific site. Also around this time, companies began to experiment with "kit-of-parts" houses. Some of these included precut lumber pieces, while others, like Sears & Roebuck's houses-by-mail kit, sold between 1908 and 1940, included everything from precut lumber to house paint.

It was not until after World War II that prefabrication was envisioned less as a cookie-cutter solution and more as an opportunity to create building systems with promise for mass-customization. The Case Study House program, begun in California in 1945 by John Entenza, editor of *Arts & Architecture* magazine, gave physical presence to ideas about prefabrication and industrialized building as they related to modern architecture. The program was designed to allow architects an opportunity to respond creatively to the rising need for single-family homes in the United States by experimenting with materials and form. As Craig Ellwood, one of the Case Study House architects, said, "Ideas have become important buildings that otherwise might never have existed. This has been the program's prime function, its foremost achievement." (Quoted in Esther McCoy, *Case Study Houses: 1945–1962*.)

Influenced by the program, in 1991 Ban used the title "Case Study House" followed by sequential numbers to refer to his experimental houses. He has completed nine "case study houses" to date and has explored other thematic series—each characterized by innovative techniques or use of materials.

Prefabrication is one of many ideas that Ban has explored in these series. In Case Study House 02, also known as the PC Pile House, he used precast concrete pile to avoid extensive excavation at the relatively remote and hilly site. The hollow form of the pile is similar to a paper tube and shares certain structural applications, albeit in different conditions and circumstances. Several years later, Ban used the same precast pile system at Tazawako Station to keep the construction period very short and the costs low. The result was a grand peristyle that defines the entrance to the station and the terminus of the street.

Ban has also experimented with prefabricated furniture units. During Japan's 1995 earthquakes, falling furniture was the cause of many deaths, and as an architect, Ban felt partially responsible for the lost lives. He began to explore the possibility of utilizing furniture as primary structural component due to its extraordinary durability and strength. Ban's initial attempt took place in the Library of a Poet—a hybrid paper-tube structure with floor-to-ceiling bookshelves on the east and west facades to strengthen against lateral forces. This project introduced the possibility of producing a pure structural system using prefabricated and built-in bookcases, shelves, and closets.

Ban's first Furniture House was completed in 1996 and overlooks his Weekend House. Taking inspiration from Ludwig Mies van der Rohe's architecture, especially the German Pavilion and the Farnsworth House, Ban substituted prefabricated structural shelving units for walls and columns. Once the units were on-site, several workers could install them in one day, reducing labor, time, and construction costs.

Ban has completed four Furniture Houses, including one near the Great Wall of China that is made primarily of bamboo. He is also in the final design phase of a fifth, in Sagaponack, Long Island. In both the Great Wall and Sagaponack projects, Ban used the Furniture House idea because the remote locations would prevent him from supervising the houses' on-site construction. By concentrating his efforts on maintaining quality at the factory, he gained more control over the entire project. Each Furniture House is different in terms of program and form, demonstrating that prefabrication does not mean generic and identical outcomes.

Further refinement and experimentation within the Furniture House system has produced several versions, including the Nine-Square Grid House and the Institute at the Centre d'Interpretation du Canal de Bourgogne. Using the idea of balloon-frame construction but substituting steel studs for wood, Ban created furniture units out of steel and wood panels. For the institute, Ban is also constructing the exhibition system, using readily available steel shelf angles that can be arranged flexibly along a proscribed grid.

By combining primary structure and furniture components with variations of material, form, and program, Ban has created his own thematic experiment independent from historic achievements such as the *Arts & Architecture* Case Study Houses. In essence, he has created a pure architecture where structure and interior program are intrinsically united.

LEFT: View of PC piles, Complex by Railroad, Shibuya, Tokyo, Japan, 1992.
RIGHT: Installation of prefabricated furniture, Furniture House 1, Lake Yamanaka, Yamanashi, Japan, 1995.

PC PILE HOUSE

COMPLETION DATE: May 1992
LOCATION: Susono, Shizuoka, Japan
STRUCTURAL ENGINEERS: Matsui Gengo,
Hoshino Architect & Engineer —
Shuichi Hoshino

BELOW: Site plan, 1:1000
OPPOSITE: View from southeast

This studio and weekend house, located in central Japan near Mt. Fuji, was commissioned by a photographer with a limited budget. He wanted a weekend house with a maximum degree of openness that also took advantage of the various topographical aspects of the site. Most essential was capturing the panoramic views of the landscape while also finding an appropriate structural system to build on areas with slopes of up to 45 degrees.

With these conditions in mind, Ban chose to use six precast concrete piles 30 cm in diameter to support the roof and floor slab directly. The nature of this type of prefabricated system minimized the time spent on site and also avoided extensive excavation for pile construction, which can require complex framework for casting concrete. The concrete piles penetrate the building and support the floor slab, which is 7 to 8 meters above ground. The slab itself is made from 10-meter lengths of engineered wood, resting on pairs of girders that connect the front and rear concrete piles. For the roof, steel I-beams are set on top of the piles and corrugated steel sheets are set above them.

With this house, Ban used a new type of insulating skin on the north and west elevations: two layers of translucent polycarbonate panels attached on either side of the 2 x 4 studs, with infill insulation of small Styrofoam balls commonly used as packaging material. This idea resurfaced in later houses, such as the House for a Dentist and, in modified form, the Naked House. By contrast, the south and east facades are completely glazed to open up to the view. The only interior walls, which define the bathroom and darkroom, are made of oriented strand board and provide a contrasting color palette for the house without competing with the primary focus of the surrounding landscape.

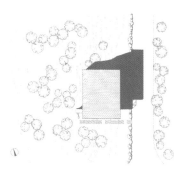

PC Pile House, Susono, Shizuoka, Japan, 1992
BELOW LEFT (top to bottom):
Plan and section, 1:200
BELOW CENTER: Balcony along south facade
BELOW RIGHT: Detail of precast
pile and translucent wall in bathroom
OPPOSITE TOP LEFT: Detail of translucent wall
OPPOSITE TOP RIGHT: Axonometric of
translucent wall
OPPOSITE BOTTOM: Dining area, view to the
southeast

1 Living/Dining
2 Darkroom

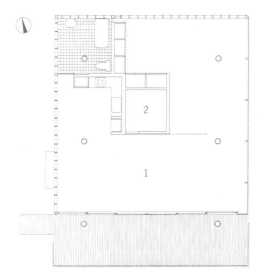

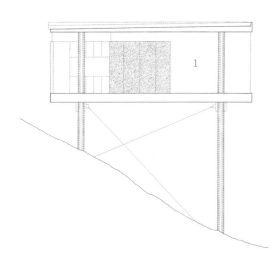

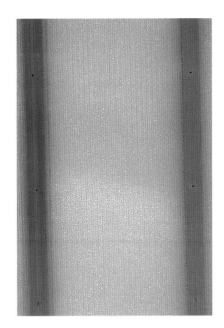

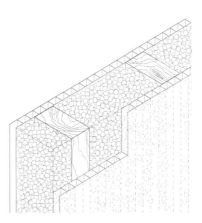

TAZAWAKO STATION

COMPLETION DATE: March 1997
LOCATION: Tazawako, Akita, Japan
STRUCTURAL ENGINEERS:
Gengo Matsui, Sadakazu Yoda

BELOW: Station plaza façade at night

Tazawako Station, Tazawako, Akita, Japan, 1997
BELOW LEFT (top to bottom): Section,
second floor plan, first floor plan, 1:500
BELOW RIGHT (top to bottom):
Cross-section 1:500, axonometric view
OPPOSITE LEFT: Detail of steel and wood
beams with supporting PC piles behind glass.
OPPOSITE RIGHT: Main concourse and
stairway to community hall

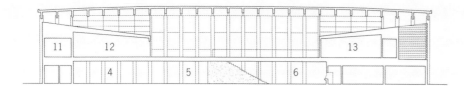

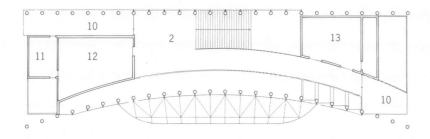

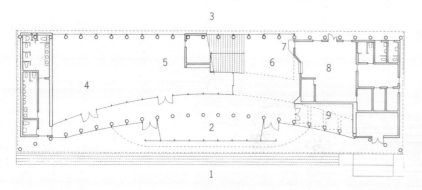

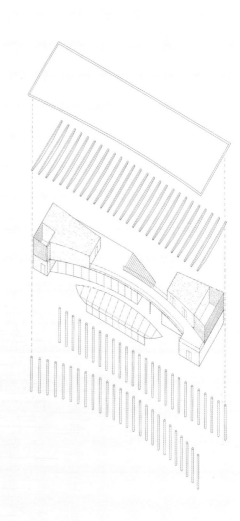

1 Station plaza
2 Community hall
3 Platform
4 Tazawako information
5 Information bureau
6 Concourse
7 Tickets

8 Office
9 Waiting room
10 Roof
11 Storage
12 Pavilion for Forest and Water
13 Cinema club

For this new *Shinkansen* ("Bullet Train") station in a town famous for its hot springs and skiing, Ban had two clients with different requirements. The Japan Railway company (JR) mandated two things: the use of steel or concrete as the main structural material, and a flat roof so snow would not accumulate on the ground, reducing the daily maintenance during the winter. The second client, the town of Akita, wanted a station with monumentality, since it served as a gateway to this resort area, but at the same time one that would not obstruct the extraordinary views of the mountains from the station plaza. The time frame for completing the construction was seven months.

Although Ban acknowledged his clients' requirements and integrated them into the station's structure, he did not want them to dictate the design. Ban chose to use precast concrete piles, which he had employed in the PC Pile House. This structural system was not only cheaper and stronger than normal pile construction, it also saved a great deal of time.

Fifty-two precast columns of the same size were divided equally into two rows, one slightly curved facing the plaza, and the second parallel to the train tracks. These columns dispersed the station's vertical loads and supported its huge pitched roof. Columns were fixed to the foundation and to the main beams at the top by pin joints. Ban had originally wanted to make the beams out of laminated timber, but JR prohibited the use of structural timber. Instead, the architect contrived a composite beam system that used 16-mm-thick steel plates to take the structural load, sandwiched between laminated timber panels to provide stiffness and withstand lateral forces. The wood cladding also insulated the steel and prevented condensation in the building. It was only later that Ban discovered that the wood also had a fireproofing capability, and he used it to this effect for the first time two years later in his GC Osaka Building.

The rectangular roof sitting on top of the arc of columns creates a large canopy and an enveloping, grand entrance. The cantilever of the roof beams increases farther into the station, as does the beam depth at the column heads. This deepening of the beams creates the natural and subtle pitch that was initially requested for the prevention of snow accumulation on the ground, while maintaining a sense of monumentality.

The station interior, which primarily uses oriented strand board as a surface material, is comprised of independent boxes serving various functions, including the JR offices and a convenience store. They are inserted beneath the great roof and separated from the main structure of precast columns and beams. Only these interior boxes are heated, making the station more energy efficient while maintaining a sufficient comfort level for visitors.

Tazawako Station, Tazawako, Akita, Japan, 1997
OPPOSITE: Mezzanine level, view toward plaza
BELOW: Station plaza facade

FURNITURE HOUSE 1

COMPLETION DATEe: April 1995
LOCATION: Lake Yamanaka,
Yamanashi, Japan
STRUCTURAL ENGINEERS: Gengo Matsui,
Minoru Tezuka, Shuichi Hoshino

BELOW: Living/kitchen area
OPPOSITE: East facade at night

Module (sizes)
Standard closets are 90 cm wide, 70 cm deep and 240 cm tall, and bookshelves are 90 cm wide, 45 cm deep and 240 cm tall. Several other widths and depths of furniture are available to accommodate various furniture uses and space planning. Walls that do not function as furniture are also available.

Construction of the furniture
a. Finished backboard: Any exterior and interior finish can be selected and applied. The application method for exterior finishes is adjusted according to requirements (i.e. to prevent spreading flames).
b. Water barrier membrane: Necessary if a. (above) is used for exterior.
c. Structural plywood board: 12mm thick.
d. Insulation: Necessary if a. (above) is used for exterior.
e. Timber frame: 2 x 4 lumber (water content: 15%).
f. Backboard of interior storage
g. Interior storage: Varies according to unit.
h. Door: Any finish can be selected and applied.

Resistance to earthquakes
In all units, complete synthesis is assured by 12mm-thick structural plywood boards. These units are carefully placed considering the space planning and earthquake load. For structural calculations, only the backboards are taken into account; the side boards add extra support in addition to the required structural strength. Therefore, the system is highly resistant to earthquake loads.

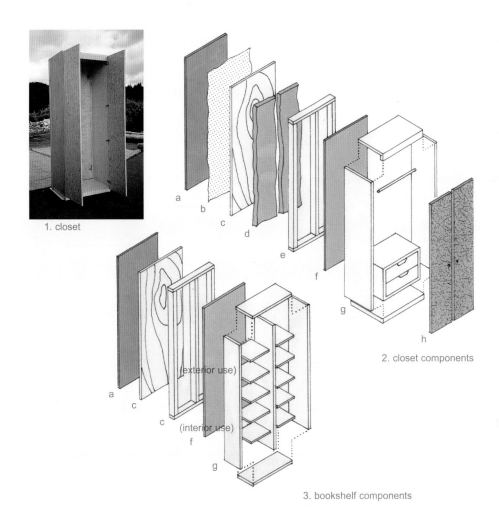

1. closet

2. closet components

3. bookshelf components

Furniture House, Lake Yamanaka, Yamanashi,
Japan, 1995
OPPOSITE: Constructing furniture units; view of
completed closet unit
BOTTOM ROW (left to right): Installing plywood
floor; bringing furniture units on site; installing
furniture units; completing the furniture unit
installation; installing the roof

Ban built his first Furniture House on a hill near Lake Yamanaka (later overlooking his Paper House) with Mt. Fuji visible in the distance. Two events helped inspire Ban's Furniture Houses. The first was designing the Library of a Poet, where he realized that bookshelves were as capable as paper tubes in supporting the roof. The second was working on the reconstruction of Kobe following the 1995 earthquake. There, Ban saw the severity of injuries and damage caused by falling furniture and realized its strength as a primary structural component. Both buildings use prefabricated furniture as both structural and space-defining elements.

This 116-square-meter house is comprised of thirty-three full-height, prefabricated "pieces" of furniture. Before the furniture units were installed, coated plywood panels were fitted on top of a cast concrete floor. Then the furniture units—each 2.4 meters by 90 cm by 45 to 75 cm, depending upon its use, and weighing 90 kilograms—were arranged on top of the panels according to the room plans and in consideration of vertical and lateral forces. Wooden studs were attached to the back of the units to contribute to the overall load-bearing support. Adjacent units were joined by screws, while precut beams spanned the pieces to form the roof framework. Because the furniture units were confined primarily to the interior, most of the exterior walls, especially the east facade, could be glazed and offered sweeping vistas.

There were multiple benefits to this construction. It shortened the on-site construction period and reduced the quantity of leftover materials that needed to be transported away from the site upon completion. The prefabricated system also reduced labor requirements, since each unit was not only self-supporting but relatively small and could easily be handled by one worker. All of this significantly lowered overall construction costs.

To date Ban has completed five furniture houses, each different in terms of its size, materials, and the further simplification and refinement of the construction process.

Furniture House, Lake Yamanaka, Yamanashi,
Japan, 1995
OPPOSITE LEFT: Living/dining area with
bookshelves
CENTER: Kitchen area
LEFT: Plan and section, 1:200
BELOW: Axonometric view

1 Entrance
2 Living/dining/kitchen
3 Terrace
4 Japanese room
5 Bedroom

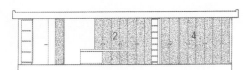

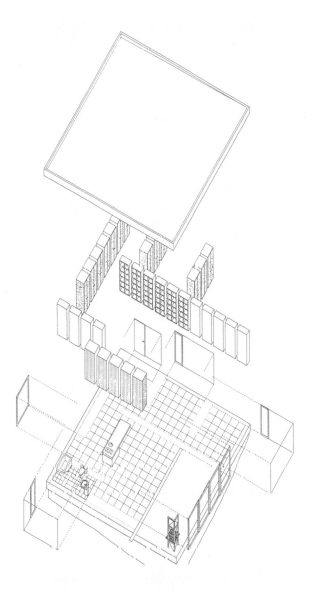

NINE-SQUARE GRID HOUSE

COMPLETION DATE: November 1997
LOCATION: Hadano, Kanagawa, Japan
STRUCTURAL ENGINEERS:
Hoshino Architect & Engineer —
Shuichi Hoshino

Nine-Square Grid House, Hadano, Kanagawa,
Japan, 1997
BELOW: Site plan, 1:800
RIGHT: Universal floor, living/dining/kitchen
areas

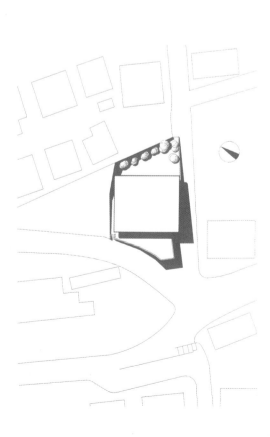

This house, located in a bedroom community outside of Tokyo, was built as a permanent residence for a couple without children. It is a version and further refinement of Ban's Furniture Houses, starting with the idea of balloon-frame construction. Ban substituted steel studs for wood in the furniture units, allowing the interior to be free of load-bearing walls. This creates a house with essentially just two walls: the east and west facades contain the furniture units, while the north and south sides completely open up to views of a private garden and distant hills, respectively.

Each furniture unit contains three components, and there are a total of six units, three on each side. Each unit measures 3.25 x 2.75 x 0.9 meters and serves a variety of storage functions, from holding air-conditioning equipment and a washer/dryer to refrigerator storage and clothes closets. They are constructed of steel studs and plywood panels, and insulated with glass wool.

The interior has a large, square floor area measuring 10.4 meters on each side. This universal floor space can be partitioned into as many as nine square areas by sliding full-height hollow wood doors along tracks inset in the floor and ceiling. When they are not being used, the doors can be stored in any of the ten "pockets" that project along the north, west, and east sides.

Nine-Square Grid House, Hadano, Kanagawa,
Japan, 1997
OPPOSITE LEFT: Open interior and west
wall unit
CENTER: Living/kitchen area with partitions
LEFT: Axonometric view
BELOW: Installing the steel stud
furniture units
BOTTOM: Kitchen/dining area with
partitions, view to the north

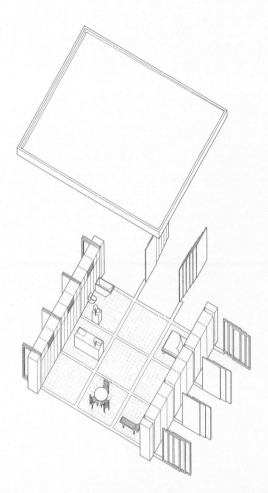

Nine-Square Grid House, Hadano, Kanagawa,
Japan, 1997
BELOW (top to bottom): Plan and section,
1:200; dining area with partitions
RIGHT: South facade, showing open interior

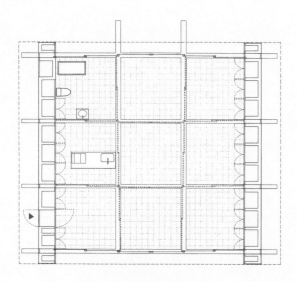

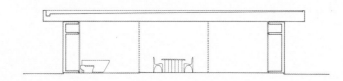

INSTITUTE, CENTRE D'INTERPRÉTATION DU CANAL DE BOURGOGNE

PROJECTED COMPLETION: 2003
LOCATION: Pouilly-en-Auxois, France
ASSOCIATE ARCHITECT:
Jean de Gastines Architecte
DPLG — Jean de Gastines,
Damien Gaudin
STRUCTURAL ENGINEERS:
Terrell Rooke and Associates —
Eric Dixon

BELOW LEFT: Site plan, 1:2000
BELOW RIGHT: Detail of shelf angle, 1:40 and 1:8
OPPOSITE TOP LEFT: North facade, view of exhibition space
OPPOSITE TOP RIGHT: Detail of exhibition space and shelf angle exhibit displays
OPPOSITE BOTTOM: Plan and section, 1:300; axonometric view, 1:400

This institute, dedicated to the history of the Canal de Bourgogne, is a 269-square-meter glass box, open to the surrounding landscape, containing gallery space and offices. The steel frame structure is based on the Furniture House system, with storage units as the main supports. Each unit is made of readily available perforated-steel shelf angles, which are used throughout the building for a wide range of functions, including display units within the exhibition space, storage cabinets, and wall partitions. These shelf angles are placed on a grid, but within the grid there is the possibility for multiple arrangements, an important feature for an exhibition space. The gallery area, located along the south side, comprises two-thirds of the building and is set up as permanent exhibition space. The motivation for Ban to design the exhibition space was based on integrating the structural system with the overall representation of the building. Essentially, he wanted the structure of the building to "disappear" and reveal only the display units and exhibition material.

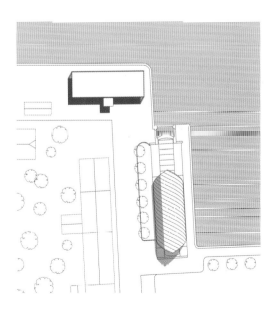

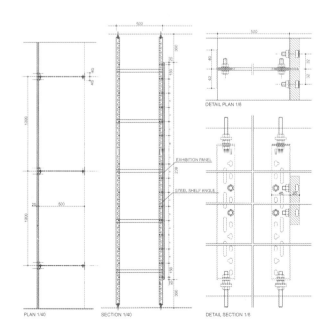

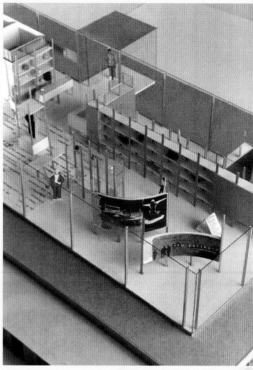

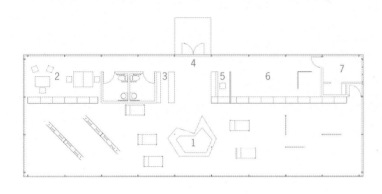

1 Exhibition space
2 Office
3 Shop
4 Entrance
5 Reception
6 Learning center
7 Mechanical

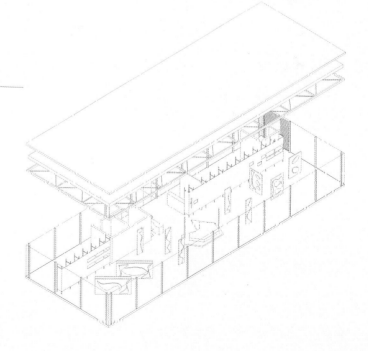

SAGAPONAC HOUSE

PROJECTED COMPLETION: 2004
LOCATION: Sagaponack, Long Island,
New York, United States
ASSOICATE ARCHITECT:
Dean Maltz Architect — Dean Maltz,
Justin Shaulis, Andrew Lefkowitz
STRUCTURAL ENGINEERS:
Robert Silman Associate, PC —
Nat Oppenheimer, Helena Meryman

BELOW LEFT: Site plan, 1:2000 (1"=160')
BELOW RIGHT: First floor plan, 1:600
(1"=50')
BOTTOM LEFT: Two views of the model
in plan
BOTTOM RIGHT: Bird's eye view of model
OPPOSITE: Study diagram of Mies van der
Rohe's Brick Country House (1924)
OPPOSITE BOTTOM LEFT: Model of
furniture unit
OPPOSITE BOTTOM RIGHT: Detail of furniture
unit 1:60 and 1:10

1 Entrance
2 Living/dining
3 Breakfast room
4 Kitchen
5 Bedroom
6 Master bedroom
7 Porch
8 Pool
9 Parking

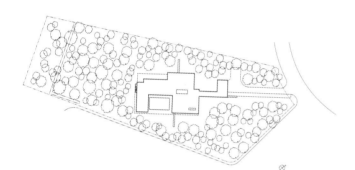

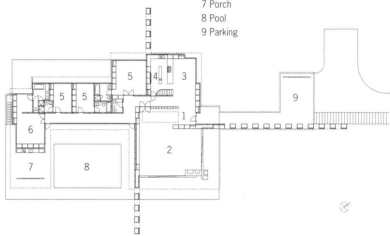

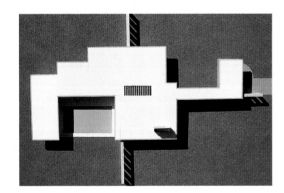

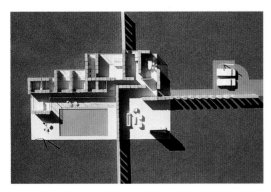

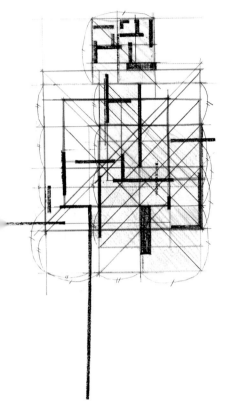

In 2001, Ban and thirty-three other prominent architects were selected to design houses for a new 100-acre enclave in Long Island called The Houses at Sagaponac. This residential community, developed by The Brown Companies in association with Richard Meier, is characterized by "simplicity and elegant modesty;" its houses vary in size from 1,800 to 4,000 square feet, with prices ranging from $800,000 to $2 million.

Sagaponac House, also called Furniture House 5, has some 4,000 square feet of floor area, including four bedrooms, four bathrooms, and an open living and dining space. Its plan is based on Ludwig Mies van der Rohe's unbuilt Brick Country House (1924); Ban reinterpreted the plan to suit the program, structural system, and site.

The design process deviated from Ban's normal practice, as there was no particular client associated with the project, so the program and space requirements had to be universal. In addition, the developer assumed all responsibilities associated with site administration at the construction stage, which meant that the architect had to relinquish control over the quality of construction. For these reasons, he decided to use the prefabricated Furniture House system he had been developing since 1993.

With this house Ban employed a new and improved structural method that does not rely on the 2 x 4 wood studs that his other Furniture Houses use. Instead, the corners are reinforced on the boxes and panels—the two basic structural units for the house—with wood triangular pieces. This gives the units strength in the lateral direction and prevents buckling.

Of the eighty furniture units in the house, all made out of plywood with a maple veneer, there are ten different types, ranging from wardrobe cabinets to bookcases to garden storage cabinets. Each has a standard measurement depending upon whether it is a box or a panel and whether it is an exterior or interior unit. In general, the exterior units are five inches deeper to accommodate insulation, waterproofing, and an exterior, white maple-veneered plywood panel.

The construction and assembly process is similar to the other houses in this series; the units are factory manufactured and finished, then transported to the site and attached to the floor slab according to the function of the individual unit. The installation of the roof—a truss I-joist system—follows.

Since this is Ban's first Furniture House in the United States, compromises were inevitable in fabricating the units, but he attempted to reduce the number of such concessions. For example, after a lengthy search, Ban and his team found a factory that would make the units as well as apply the exterior panels, reducing on-site work and the overall cost of building.

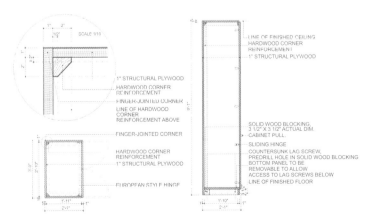

■ SAGAPONAC HOUSE

Experiment date _____ October 2001

Location _____ Tokyo National University of Fine Arts
and Music, Department of Architecture,
Faculty of Fine Arts, Tokyo, Japan

Performed by _____ Dr. Minoru Tezuka
Prof. Yoshiaki Tsuboi

Test Report Profile

In previous Furniture Houses, sideboards supporting cabinet shelves were never used for structural purposes. In this project, vertical framing is eliminated and the sideboards are combined with backboards to create a wooden structure in the shape of a steel C-channel. Due to its shape, the structure can bear the lateral forces parallel to the backboard, and although its efficiency decreases, it is also able to bear lateral forces in the perpendicular orthogonal direction. Boards attached as stiffeners in the ceiling and floor act as bracing reinforcements for the C-shaped structure. Wooden horizontal members are secured to the ceiling and floor stiffeners by lag screws, and these horizontal members are also glued to the sideboard and backboard to transmit the forces to the foundations. In order to connect the sideboard to the backboard, a wooden piece with a right-triangle cross-section was glued in the corner where the edges of the sideboard and backboard form a right angle. Since the unified strength of the connection needed to be confirmed, shearing tests were carried out on the glued connection between the sideboards and backboard.

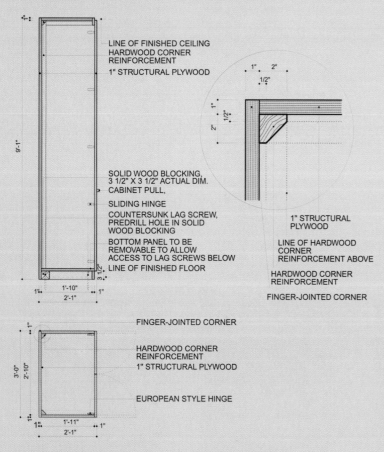

LINE OF FINISHED CEILING
HARDWOOD CORNER REINFORCEMENT
1" STRUCTURAL PLYWOOD

SOLID WOOD BLOCKING, 3 1/2" X 3 1/2" ACTUAL DIM.
CABINET PULL,
SLIDING HINGE
COUNTERSUNK LAG SCREW, PREDRILL HOLE IN SOLID WOOD BLOCKING
BOTTOM PANEL TO BE REMOVABLE TO ALLOW ACCESS TO LAG SCREWS BELOW
LINE OF FINISHED FLOOR

1" STRUCTURAL PLYWOOD
LINE OF HARDWOOD CORNER REINFORCEMENT ABOVE
HARDWOOD CORNER REINFORCEMENT
FINGER-JOINTED CORNER

FINGER-JOINTED CORNER
HARDWOOD CORNER REINFORCEMENT
1" STRUCTURAL PLYWOOD
EUROPEAN STYLE HINGE

SUPPLEMENTARY FIGURE Detail plan/section of furniture unit.

Vertical framing is eliminated and the sideboards combine with the backboards to create a wood structure in the shape of a C-channel.

Shearing Test
1-1 _____ Test Specimens
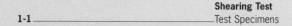

The sideboards and backboard are made from 24mm thick white birch plywood and the connecting joint is made from glue-laminated wood with a triangular cross-section. Ten sets of these connections were fabricated (J1–J10 shown in Figure 1). A water-based polymer isocyanate wood adhesive with a short pressing time was used to glue the joint and the sideboard and backboard together. Furthermore, the sideboard and backboard were connected using halving joints.

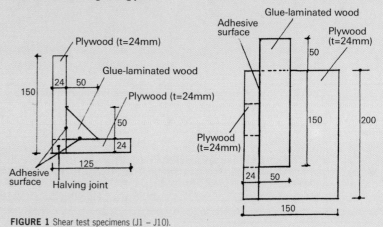

FIGURE 1 Shear test specimens (J1 – J10).

Shearing Test
1-2 _____ Test Procedures

As shown in Figure 2 and Figure 3, vertical load was applied to the glue-laminated triangular cross-section joint. The displacement between the jig attached to the underside of the joint and the testing bed was measured. The loading speed was 250kgf/min. Further, steel plates were placed on the testing bed and offset from the surface of the plywood so as not to obstruct a segregation fracture in the plywood.

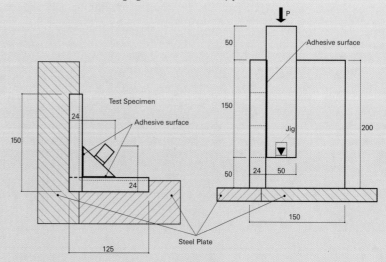

FIGURE 2 Shearing test procedures.

FIGURE 3 Shearing test procedures.

TABLE 1 Shear test result.

Specimen number	Maximum load (kgf)	Adhesive strength (kgf/cm²)	Failure Conditions
J1	4060	26.8	Segregation fracture in layers of plywood Shearing fracture of joint member Insufficient bonding
J2	2100	14.1	Shearing fracture of joint member Insufficient bonding
J3	2845	18.6	Segregation fracture in layers of plywood Shearing fracture of joint member Insufficient bonding
J4	4165	28.6	Segregation fracture in layers of plywood Shearing fracture of joint member Insufficient bonding
J5	3560	23.7*	Compressive fracture of joint member
J6	4020	27.7*	Compressive fracture of joint member
J7	3250	22.0	Segregation fracture in layers of plywood Shearing fracture of joint member Insufficient bonding
J8	3585	24.1*	Compressive fracture of joint member
J9	3275	21.8*	Compressive fracture of joint member
J10	3590	24.1*	Compressive fracture of joint member

*Determined by laminated bamboo's compressive strength not the adhesive strength.

Shearing Test
1-3_____Test Results

Figure 4 shows the load-relative displacement relationship. Among the test results, specimen J4 had the highest strength and specimen J2 had the lowest strength. The proportional limit load of specimen J2 was about 1tf and J4 was 3tf. These test results are evidence that there was insufficient bonding strength in specimen J2, as it had begun sliding at a lower applied load in comparison to specimen J4. Table 1 lists the state of destruction of each specimen along with its maximum load and adhesive strength value calculated from dividing the maximum load by the adhered surface area. Shear fracture of the joint member, segregation fracture in the layers of the plywood, and insufficient bonding were observed in four specimens. Maximum loads of five specimens were determined by the compressive strength of the stiffener (reinforcing material). Shear fracture of the joint member and insufficient bonding caused the lowest adhesive strength (=14.1kgf/cm²).

Shear fracture of the joint member and insufficient bonding caused the lowest adhesive strength (=14.1kgf/cm²).

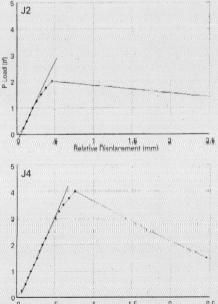

FIGURE 4 Shear test: load-relative displacement relationship.

SKIN

SKIN

A defining characteristic of skin is its ability to adapt. The skins of humans and animals grow hair, shed dead layers, change color when exposed to the sun, wrinkle with age, and regenerate when injured. Plants respond similarly as seasons change. The skin of a building, too, can adapt, changing from opaque during the day to a glowing translucent box at night; its surface can vacillate between an unbroken plane and a wall punctured with openings. A building's skin can transform its color, texture, and even its structure as it fluctuates between one state and the next.

Ban's architecture uses an enormous variety of building envelopes. He has referred to them as a cardigan sweater, an outer layer that is changeable, that can be opened or buttoned up as conditions demand. Some of his buildings have soft, organic, and pliable layers that play well against the harder surfaces and urban context in which they are placed. Other surfaces and facades actually move—allowing for either complete privacy or complete openness.

Ban's skins serve multiple functions—providing privacy and enclosure, views, egress, insulation—and often utilize preexisting materials in a new context. At the House for a Dentist, Ban introduced granulated Styrofoam, inserting it between hollow polycarbonate panels for insulation and privacy. On the south side of the house, a three-story-high ivy screen insures privacy while allowing ventilation and filtered natural light through the courtyard facade.

Ban has used an ivy screen in a number of projects, although its implementation in later buildings has served structural purposes as well as the need for privacy. In Ivy Structure 2, the screen creates privacy in a dense residential neighborhood while also providing the primary structural support for the inner glazed cube of the apartment building. Ban's play with "what's holding up what" is especially pronounced here; the ivy blankets the structural screen, implying that the vine provides support.

His most clever combination of material and building skin may be the Curtain Wall House, which includes a two-story-high curtain that surrounds the two sides facing the street. The curtain acts as a second skin—the first being the glazed sliding doors—and both can be opened completely for full exposure to the street or closed as tightly as a cocoon.

With the Naked House, Ban created a similar double skin with white, corrugated fiberglass-reinforced plastic on the exterior and a white nylon membrane stretched over wood studs for the interior walls. During the day sunlight filters through the opaque panels and the nylon makes the interior glow; at night the interior emits light, becoming a beacon in the landscape. The most interesting aspect of the house is its interior—a two-story loft containing rolling boxes that act as bedrooms for the family members.

This ability to transform a surface and space radically is commonplace in traditional Japanese architecture. *Shitomido*, early moveable panels that date back to the eleventh century, were hinged at the top so they could swing up and hook to metal rods suspended from the ceiling or from the exterior eaves. *Shoji*, panels made of light wood strips to which sheets of translucent rice paper are pasted, were used on the exterior of Japanese houses and protected by *amado*, an outer sliding door made of wood. For the interior, *fusuma* were used—panels similar to *shoji* but with a heavier opaque paper surface. Moving any of these panels could change the function as well as the size of a space to suit the activities of the moment.

Ban has investigated the idea of transformative skins in numerous projects, including the Paper House, a series of case study houses, the Picture Window House, and, most recently, a series of stacking shutter projects—the Glass Shutter House, Shutter House for a Photographer, Paper Art Museum (PAM), and the Temporary Guggenheim Tokyo (TGT). These projects demonstrate how space can be converted and surface metamorphose; the latter group of stacking shutter projects reveals the ability to eliminate the facade completely.

In the Glass Shutter House, a large outdoor space intended for a restaurant is created when the shutters are opened, and in his unbuilt design for TGT, Ban included stacking shutters to allow views of the Tokyo skyline when they are opened. PAM's two buildings offer two different solutions—one a stacking shutter and the other more akin to *shitomido*, but each variation creates a fluid relationship with the lush gardens that surround the buildings. In the Shutter House for a Photographer, which seems impermeable on the exterior, the series of inner courtyards between living spaces opens, one onto one another, creating a free-flowing, universal floor.

Ban's buildings have thick skins. The thickness, however, has less to do with density and more with gauge or measure. The surfaces respond effectively to circumstances around them: they offer protection and light but can disappear when desired. It is the integration of skin and structure that provides the real substance to these projects. While the visual effects are delicate, the physicality of the whole is prominent and robust.

LEFT: Ivy Structure 2, Azabu, Tokyo, Japan, 2000, partial view of glass facade.
RIGHT: Naked House, Kawagoe, Saitama, Japan, 2000, detail of translucent wall.

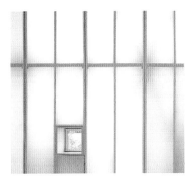

HOUSE FOR A DENTIST

COMPLETION DATE: February 1994
LOCATION: Setagaya, Tokyo, Japan
STRUCTURAL ENGINEERS:
Hoshino Architect & Engineer —
Shuichi Hoshino, Akira Teraoka

BELOW: Site plan, 1:800
RIGHT: Living/dining area and terrace,
view to the south

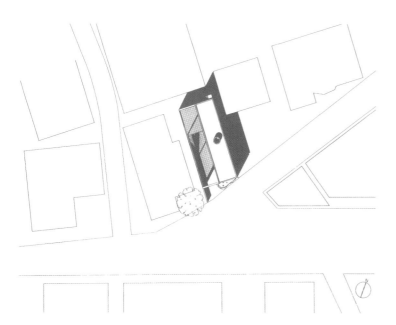

For this house and workplace, which is oriented lengthwise on a narrow rectangular lot in a residential neighborhood in Tokyo, the client wanted a three-story concrete building. A dentist's office occupies the ground floor, with living quarters on the two floors above. Due to poor soil conditions and a short construction period, Ban ruled out pile construction and chose instead a relatively light structural system that uses just three reinforced-concrete walls—for the parallel front and rear facades and for a central cylinder that runs the full height of the house. Lateral bracing for the main wall or front facade is provided by the perpendicular walls, giving stability in all directions. The floors are made of laminated wood.

The building's great sense of openness was achieved through two main factors. The first is the open-air courtyard that comprises half of the house's official floor area of 144 square meters. The court's southern boundary is a three-story-high, ivy-covered screen that ensures privacy and allows for ventilation and filtered natural light. Stairs and an upper deck lead to the living spaces above. Inside, both the office and residence have views of the courtyard and of a cherry tree that stands at the southern corner of the site. Ban minimized the number of solid walls, allowing for a greater use of glass; the entire courtyard facade, for instance, is glazed. The street facade is concrete, affording privacy for the client. The north facade is also glazed, but here Ban inserted hollow polycarbonate sliding panels filled with granulated Styrofoam for insulation and privacy. These panels can be opened to create a "see-through" building.

House for a Dentist, Setagaya,
Tokyo, Japan, 1994
OPPOSITE LEFT: Ivy screen (left)
and courtyard
OPPOSITE CENTER: Living area
OPPOSITE RIGHT: Dental clinic at
basement level
BELOW (left to right): Basement plan,
first floor plan, second floor plan, 1:400
BOTTOM: Section, 1:400

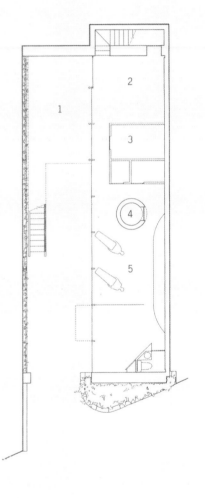
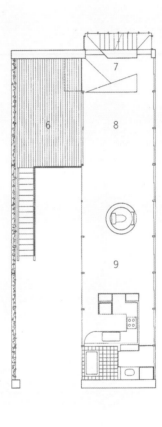
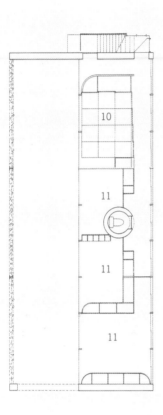

1 Parking
2 Office
3 Storage
4 X-ray room
5 Clinic
6 Terrace
7 Entrance
8 Living room
9 Dining room
10 Japanese room
11 Bedroom

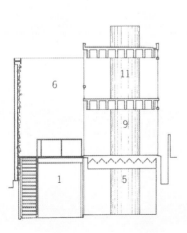

House for a Dentist, Setagaya,
Tokyo, Japan, 1994
BELOW: Axonometric view
CENTER: East facade at night
OPPOSITE: South facade

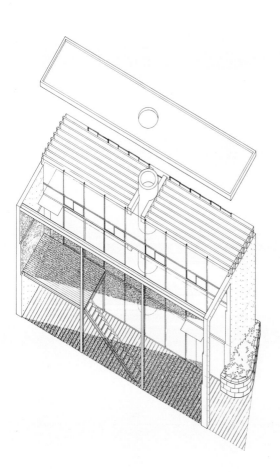

CURTAIN WALL HOUSE

COMPLETION DATE: July 1995
LOCATION: Itabashi, Tokyo, Japan
STRUCTURAL ENGINEERS:
Shuichi Hoshino Architect &
Engineer — Shuichi Hoshino

BELOW: Site plan, 1:600
OPPOSITE: East facade

The client for this steel-frame building owned a traditional Japanese-style house in a dense Tokyo neighborhood. Ban's design, built on the same site after the old house was razed, is a contemporary reinterpretation of traditional homes that incorporates contemporary materials.

An understated entrance on the first floor connects to a studio and to stairs leading up to the main living space on the second floor and then to bedrooms on the top floor. Although the total floor area is 179 square meters, the house feels even more expansive. The monumental, two-story-high curtain that spans the second and third floors can be pulled back and the sliding glass doors along the east and south facades opened to reveal a wide deck that wraps around two sides of the house. The open facades and deck extend the interior so that it can be completely exposed to the street, an unusual gesture in an urban dwelling. Standing on the deck, watching the activities of streetlife below, can seem like being on the prow of a ship. This double "curtain" wall can also be closed to control temperature, light, and privacy, and create a cocoonlike environment.

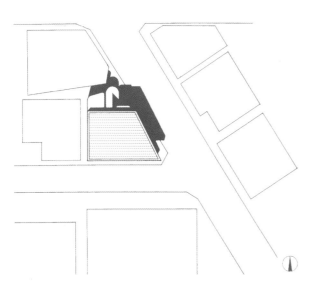

Curtain Wall House, Itabashi, Tokyo,
Japan, 1995
BELOW (left to right): South facade;
dining area and terrace;
east facade with curtains drawn
OPPOSITE (left to right): First floor plan,
second floor plan, third floor plan,
section, 1:200

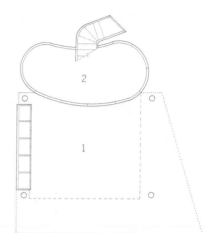 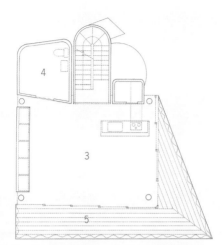 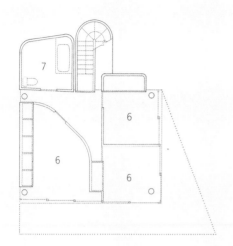

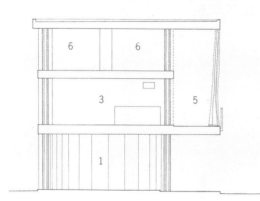

1 Studio
2 Parking
3 Living/dining/kitchen
4 Utility
5 Terrace
6 Bedroom
7 Bathroom

Curtain Wall House, Itabashi, Tokyo,
Japan, 1995
LEFT: Southeast facade
BELOW: Axonometric view

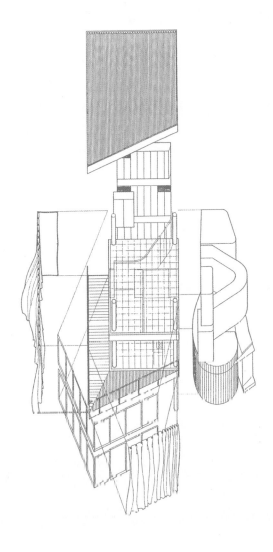

IVY STRUCTURE 2

COMPLETION DATE: January 2000
LOCATION: Azabu, Tokyo, Japan
STRUCTURAL ENGINEERS:
Hoshino Architect & Engineer —
Shuichi Hoshino, Noriko Komiyama

BELOW: Site plan, 1:1200
OPPOSITE: Entrance facade

Ivy Structure 2, an apartment and a gallery building located on an unusually shaped site in a predominantly residential neighborhood, is a three-story-high structure. The longest of the site's four sides is parallel to the street, while a condominium block, a large restaurant, and an embassy are adjacent or nearby. Privacy and flexible floor space were important criteria for the client.

Ban's three-story glass cube is surrounded on three sides by a semidetached, full-height ivy screen. This functions as an outer wall—allowing the tenants and owner maximum privacy without sacrificing openness—and as the primary structural support for the 711-square-meter cube, which contains three apartments, an art gallery, and an office space. Just as the ivy is dependent upon the screen for support, the main building relies on the exterior screen to counteract lateral forces. When the screen disappears behind a blanket of ivy, it appears as if the plant is anchoring the entire building.

Additional structural support is derived from terraces and "flying buttresses" at the corners of the cube, which redistribute lateral forces to the ivy screen. Metal-framed circular columns, placed on a grid of nine smaller, equilateral squares, minimize the vertical forces within the building. Support from the flying buttresses and terraces allows the diameter of the columns to be reduced on the upper floors and bracing and bearing walls to be eliminated. The building thus has a very flexible floor plan.

Ivy Structure 2, Azabu, Tokyo, Japan, 2000
BELOW (left to right): Detail of flying
buttress; living area in second-floor
apartment; aerial view from southwest,
with insulating pool on roof
OPPOSITE TOP LEFT: Axonometric view
OPPOSITE RIGHT (top to bottom): Section,
third floor plan, second floor plan, first floor
plan, basement plan, 1:600

Ivy Structure 2 has multiple layers of skin. The glass curtain wall, for example, can be shaded on the south and west facades with a skin of exterior blinds that unfurl mechanically. A pool of water on the roof creates a layer of added insulation during the summer, while the multifunctional ivy screen acts as the outermost skin.

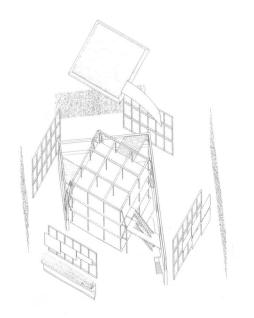

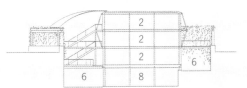

1 Entrance
2 Living/dining
3 Kitchen
4 Bedroom
5 Terrace
6 Garden
7 Gallery
8 Shop

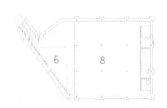

NAKED HOUSE

COMPLETION DATE: November 2000
LOCATION: Kawagoe, Saitama, Japan
STRUCTURAL ENGINEERS:
Hoshino Architect & Engineer —
Shuichi Hoshino, Takashige Suzuki

BELOW: Site plan, 1:2000
OPPOSITE: Interior living/dining area with
mobile rooms

The client's vision for this house, which is set in an agricultural region a short distance from Tokyo, was the guiding force for the architect. His requirements were very specific: three generations would occupy the house—his wife and their two children, a nine-year-old boy and a seven-year-old girl, and his 75-year-old mother. The budget was also strictly set at about $200,000. In a statement faxed to Ban, he expressed a desire for a warehouse-like structure that "provides the least privacy so that the family members are not secluded from one another, a house that gives everyone the freedom to have individual activities in a shared atmosphere, in the middle of a unified family."

The house sits by the Shingashi River and is surrounded by rice paddies and fields dotted with greenhouses. In fact, Ban's design takes on the character of a greenhouse; the house's external walls are translucent, made of two layers of corrugated fiberglass-reinforced plastic. This material is mounted on wood-stud frames with the fiber running in both horizontal and vertical directions to help structural reinforcement and insulation. The studs support the curved roof's thirty-four arched trusses. A drop ceiling conceals these trusses, although diagonal steel braces attached to the studs from the inside are exposed. A 15-inch gap separates the exterior plastic panels from the interior wall, which is made up of nylon membrane panels attached to the wood studs with Velcro. These panels can be removed for cleaning. The air pocket between the walls acts as an insulator and contains bracing for the wood joists. Added insulation in the form of five-hundred bags stuffed with polyethylene "noodles" normally used for packaging material is inserted in this gap and between the studs. Seen from the outside of the house, or through the translucent panels inside, these "noodle" cushions have a wonderful visual effect.

The two-story loftlike space of the interior suited the communal aspect of the client's requirements. Measuring 25 meters by 6.7 meters (excluding car park), its north and south facades are punctured only by an entrance vestibule and small terrace, respectively, as well as small square ventilation windows. The east and west facades, on the other hand, can open completely. Doors and louvered windows in the bathroom open onto a covered porch, while to the west, glass panels slide into pockets so the interior living space can expand onto another covered porch with views of the river and adjoining fields.

Naked House, Kawagoe, Saitama, Japan, 2000
BELOW LEFT (top to bottom): Plan, 1:200;
diagram of variable room layouts, 1:400
BELOW RIGHT (top to bottom): Section, 1:200;
detail of mobile room, 1:100
OPPOSITE LEFT: Living area with mobile rooms
OPPOSITE RIGHT: Dining area, with kitchen area
behind curtains

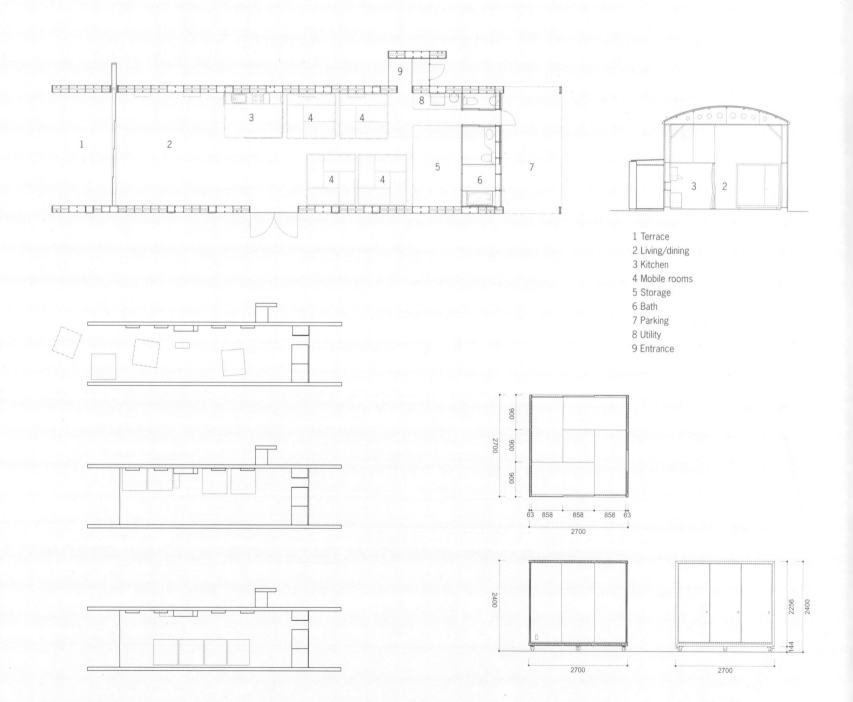

1 Terrace
2 Living/dining
3 Kitchen
4 Mobile rooms
5 Storage
6 Bath
7 Parking
8 Utility
9 Entrance

Particularly distinctive elements inside are the four boxes mounted on casters—mobile private retreats for each family member. The two larger boxes for the adults, each 3.6 by 2.7 meters, and the two smaller boxes for the children, each 2.7 by 2.7 meters, have tatami mat floors. To minimize the boxes' weight, private belongings are kept to a minimum and each wood-frame box is made of lightweight paper honeycomb panels clad with wood. The boxes can be pushed together; when their sliding panels are open they form one large interior space. They can also be moved to the perimeter of the house, where there are hookups for heating and cooling units.

The only fixed elements in the interior are one-and-a-half bathrooms and kitchen and storage areas. These latter two spaces are wrapped by large white curtains that can be pulled open or shut. Ban's careful layering of different skins—from the exterior's reinforced translucent panels to the nylon panels inside—ultimately creates a glowing box with the delicacy and beauty of a shoji screen.

Naked House, Kawagoe, Saitama, Japan, 2000
OPPOSITE: Entrance facade at night
BELOW LEFT (top to bottom): Detail plan
of wall, 1:20; interior wall of removable
nylon membrane panels
BELOW RIGHT: Axonometric view

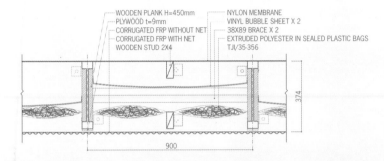

WOODEN PLANK H=450mm
PLYWOOD t=9mm
CORRUGATED FRP WITHOUT NET
CORRUGATED FRP WITH NET
WOODEN STUD 2X4

NYLON MEMBRANE
VINYL BUBBLE SHEET X 2
38X89 BRACE X 2
EXTRUDED POLYESTER IN SEALED PLASTIC BAGS
TJI/35-356

374

900

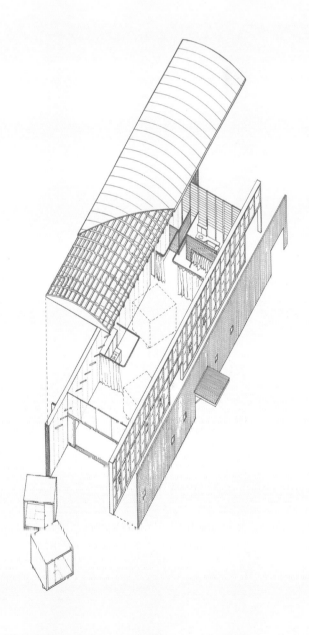

PICTURE WINDOW HOUSE

COMPLETION DATE: February 2002
LOCATION: Izu, Shizuoka, Japan
STRUCTURAL ENGINEERS:
Hoshino Architect & Engineer —
Shuichi Hoshino, Takashige Suzuki

BELOW: Living/dining/kitchen area,
view to the east

Picture Window House, Izu, Shizuoka,
Japan, 2002
BELOW: East facade
OPPOSITE: Living/dining area and terrace

This year-round residence within commuting distance from Tokyo is located on a hill with an unobstructed view of the Pacific Ocean. Ban's immediate response to the site was to frame the panorama with architecture that would create a continuity between the wooded site and the ocean. In effect, he conceived of the whole house as a picture window.

The two-story, 273-square-meter house is a steel-frame structure with a second-floor truss spanning 20 meters. The first floor is thus completely open and columnless, allowing the 20-meter-long, 2.5-meter-high south wall to become a single window. Four bedrooms on the second floor face south toward the ocean; their views are only minimally obstructed by diagonal bracing. A completely glazed corridor runs along the north side of the house. A bathroom incorporated into this hall is separated by a glazed door and white curtain. The idea of a picture window is maintained on all sides of the house regardless of issues of privacy or the particular functions of the space.

The first-floor living area has only minimal insertions—stairs, kitchen counter, and cabinets. All other requirements, including a bathroom, entrance vestibule, and back stairs, have been consolidated on the east and west sides of the house. When the sliding glass doors at the north and south are opened, a true architecture of transparency is revealed.

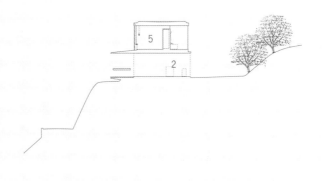

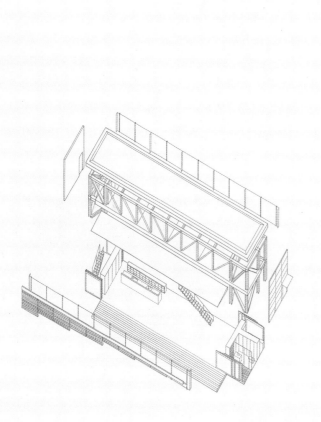

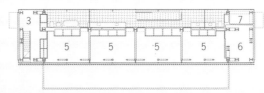

1 Living/dining
2 Kitchen
3 Study
4 Entrance
5 Bedroom
6 Storage
7 Open to below

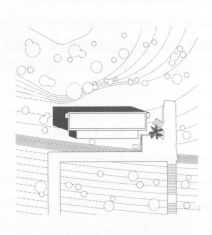

PICTURE WINDOW HOUSE _____ 213

Picture Window House, Izu, Shizuoka, Japan, 2002
OPPOSITE FAR LEFT (top to bottom):
Axonometric view, site plan, 1:1500
OPPOSITE TOP RIGHT (top to bottom): Section,
second floor plan, first floor plan, 1:400
OPPOSITE BOTTOM (left to right): Second floor
bathroom and hallway, bedroom on second floor
BELOW: West facacde

GLASS SHUTTER HOUSE

COMPLETION DATE: April 2003
LOCATION: Meguro, Tokyo, Japan
STRUCTURAL ENGINEERS:
Shuichi Hoshino Architect & Engineer —
Shuichi Hoshino

BELOW LEFT: Site plan, 1:800
BELOW RIGHT: Facade of street
OPPOSITE: North facade with all shutters open

The site for Ban's Glass Shutter House is in a neighborhood that borders a busy commercial district, a transitional zone between shopping and living. It is an appropriate location for this multifunctional building, whose client is a culinary scholar. His requirements included a restaurant on the ground floor, a studio kitchen for photography sessions, and a living area for a family of three.

An 8-meter-high glazed wall, based on a rolling shutter system used in storefronts, stands on the north and west sides of the building. Ban's version, however, translates the aluminum grille into 1-meter by 35 cm glass panels that can be mechanically opened to allow outdoor dining and living.

The building site is long, narrow, and slightly trapezoidal. The northern boundary—facing the street—is 8.7 meters wide, and the south side is 6.3 meters wide. Half of the site is left open as exterior space; the actual building has a footprint 4 meters wide and 16 meters deep. In addition, the northern half of the site is officially zoned as a street, since at one point the city was considering widening the

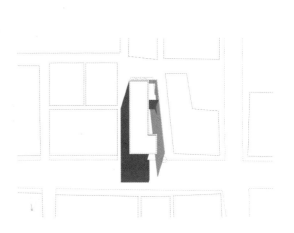

right-of-way. Although this idea was abandoned, regulations still stipulated that the building could not exceed two stories. As a result, the north side has only two levels—the restaurant and second-floor studio—while the southern half has all three levels.

Using the glass shutter system, Ban combined storefront imagery with a building that has a multifunctional program and complicated site. This new type of urban dwelling is characterized by a movable skin that can quickly transform it from a public space into a private residence.

Glass Shutter House, Meguro, Tokyo, Japan, 2002
OPPOSITE LEFT: Two views of the courtyard
with shutters opened and closed
OPPOSITE RIGHT: View of restaurant and terrace
in the evening
LEFT: View of interior
BELOW LEFT: Axonometric view
BELOW RIGHT (top to bottom): Third floor plan,
second floor plan, first floor plan, section, 1:250

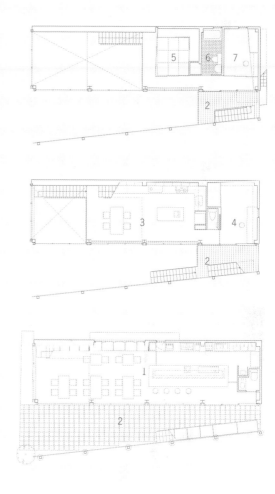

1 Restaurant
2 Terrace
3 Kitchen studio
4 Study
5 Japanese room
6 Bathroom
7 Bedroom

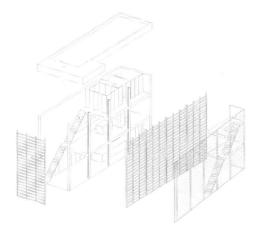

PAPER ART MUSEUM

COMPLETION DATE: September 2002
LOCATION: Mishima, Shizuoka, Japan
STRUCTURAL ENGINEERS:
Hoshino Architect & Engineer —
Shuichi Hoshino, Takashige Suzuki

BELOW (left to right): East facade with stacking shutters closed; site plan, 1:1600
OPPOSITE: East facade with stacking shutters open

This museum (A) and contemporary gallery (B), located outside Tokyo, are devoted to the art and manufacture of paper. The client is an established paper manufacturer who wanted to build one of the few paper art museums to present not only his own collection of paper but also displays of Japanese graphic design and contemporary art.

With a total floor area of 1,479 square meters, the museum is a square volume that Ban divided into tripartite three-story-blocks: offices on the south or garden side, exhibition space on the north, and a multifunctional middle space or atrium. Bridges connect the north and south sides on each level, and a glass room is added as a fourth story on the garden side. The museum is connected to the gallery by an entrance vestibule, with the museum located at the west end of the site and the

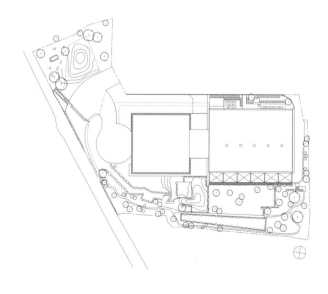

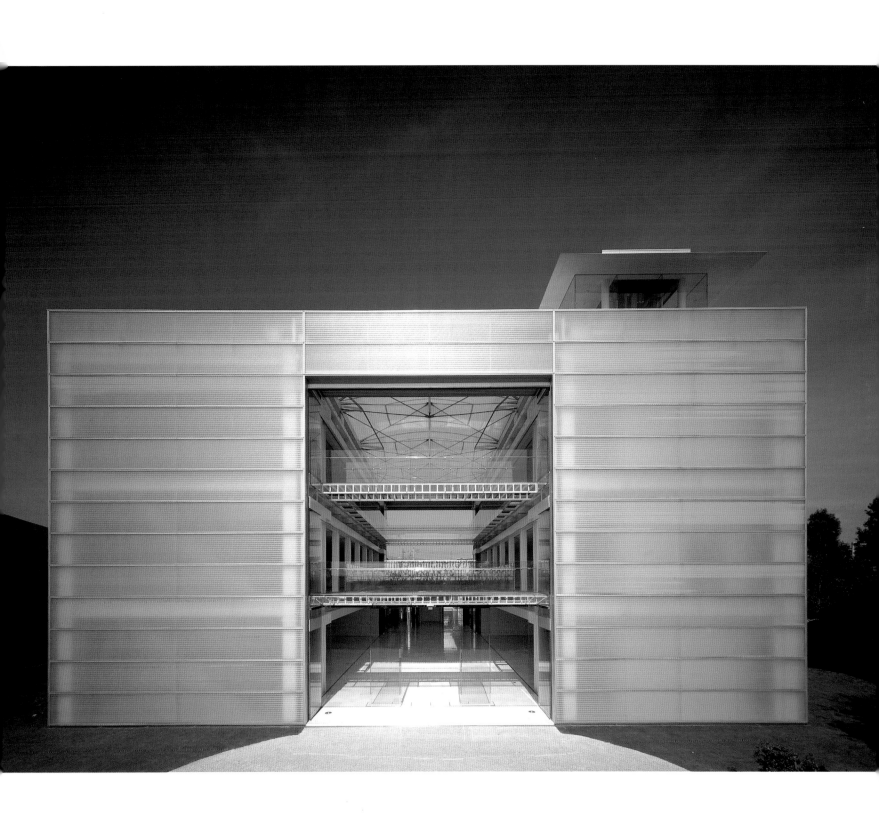

Paper Art Museum A, Mishima, Shizuoka, Japan, 2002
OPPOSITE: Interior atrium
ABOVE LEFT: Offices below, samples room center, and lecture room above
ABOVE RIGHT: View through atrium to the garden
BELOW (left to right): section through PAM A and B, cross-section through PAM A, 1:600
BOTTOM (left to right): first floor plan, second floor plan, third floor plan, fourth floor plan, 1:600

1 Entrance
2 Foyer
3 Atrium
4 Exhibition space
5 Office
6 Samples room
7 Lecture room
8 Reception
9 Roof
10 Gallery

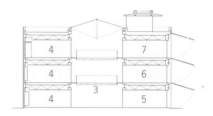

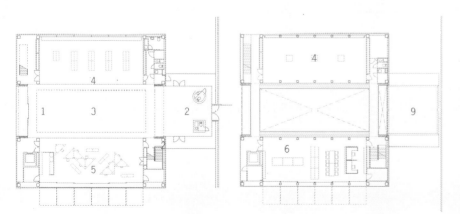

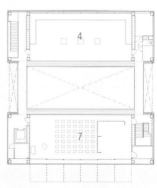

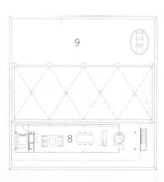

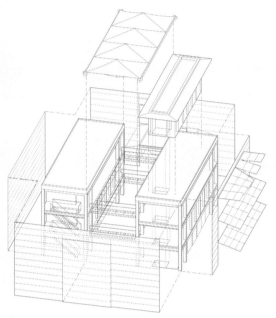

Paper Art Museum A, Mishima, Shizuoka,
Japan, 2002
OPPOSITE LEFT: West facade with
translucent FRP panels
OPPOSITE RIGHT: Axonometric view
BELOW: South facade with vertical
shutters closed (left) and open (right)

one-story contemporary gallery to the east. Each building is of steel-frame construction, but their skins are different. For the museum, Ban used a double layer of glass and fiberglass-reinforced plastic panels (FRP) on the exterior that can be moved in a variety of ways. On the south side facing the garden, panels on all three floors can be lifted vertically to create an awning or *shitomido*, a type of vertical shutter used in Japanese domestic architecture for centuries. On the east and west facades, FRP panels are used in the stacking shutters, which can open to a height of 10 meters, completely exposing the three-story interior atrium to the outdoors. This transformation of the three facades provides spatial continuity between interior and exterior. The only stationary elevation is the north side, which is composed of silica calcium boards that both provide thermal insulation and, on the inside, function as an exhibition surface.

The 924-square-meter contemporary gallery is an existing structure that Ban was asked to renovate. A similar transformation occurs on its south facade. This entire side is composed of six sets of translucent fiberglass-reinforced plastic (FRP) shutters that look like *shoji* screens when closed. On the exterior, Ban installed the track for the shutters so that the panels slide outward, creating a 5-meter-deep awning. The interior gallery extends outside and reconnects with the surrounding landscape.

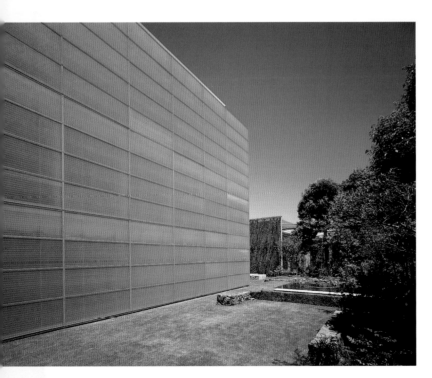

Paper Art Museum B, Mishima, Shizuoka,
Japan, 2002
ABOVE: South facade with shutters closed and
open
RIGHT: Before and after drawings of the renovated
factory building
BELOW (left to right): Plan and section, 1:400
OPPOSITE: Interior gallery and garden

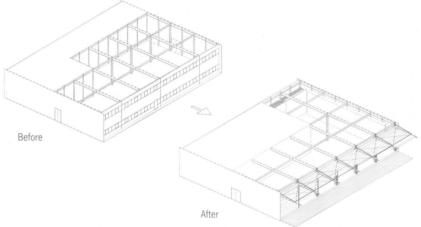

Before

After

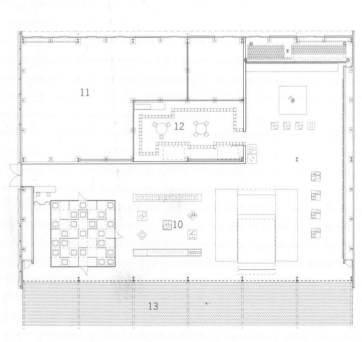

10 Gallery
11 Storage
12 Preparation room
13 Terrace

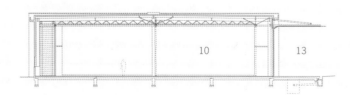

COMPLETION DATE: August 2003
LOCATION: Minato, Tokyo, Japan
STRUCTURAL ENGINEERS:
Hoshino Architect & Engineer —
Shuichi Hoshino, Takashige Suzuki

BELOW LEFT: Site plan, 1:1000
BELOW RIGHT: Sequential views of
shutters closing (construction images)
OPPOSITE LEFT (top to bottom):
Axonometric view, 1:500; second floor plan,
first floor plan, basement plan, section,
1:400
OPPOSITE RIGHT (top to bottom): Bird's eye
view of model, showing second floor interior
stacking shutters and perimeter walls;
view of model showing first floor interior
stacking shutters without perimeter walls;
view of photography studio in basement

This house and studio for a professional photographer and his family is located in the middle of
a dense residential neighborhood in Tokyo. The site is long and narrow—9.6 by 23.4 meters—and is
surrounded by private residences, an apartment building, and an embassy compound. Within this
density, Ban created a perimeter wall of greenery to shield a very introspective building.

A series of inner courtyards inside the house is accessible through a combination of doorways and
seven sets of stacking shutters. By using industrial stacking shutters instead of a conventional glass
curtain wall, Ban allows for a physical and visual continuity between all of the rooms.

The building is organized on a grid, with a loose checkerboard arrangement of rooms that alternate
between interior and exterior spaces. The rooms vary in size according to the program as well as to
the specific number of grid modules. The smallest module is a steel column that not only acts as part
of the structural core but also becomes a vertical node connecting all of the interior floors.

The ceiling height in the different spaces is also variable. Single-story spaces are reserved for the dining
room, kitchen, and bedrooms located on the first floor. The photography studio, first-floor living
room, and outdoor courtyards are all double-height. Adding variation to the outdoor experience is the
height of the rolling shutters themselves—three sets are double-height (5.4 meters) and four sets
are single-story (2.6 meters). The complex, three-dimensional network of spaces is knitted together
by the transforming nature of the stacking shutters.

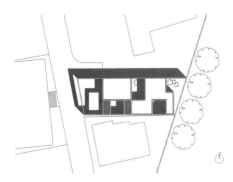

Studio
Darkroom
Entrance
Parking
Living room
Dining room
Kitchen
Courtyard
Master bedroom
0 Bedroom

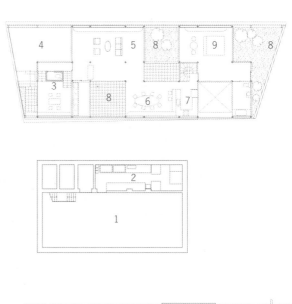

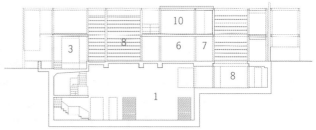

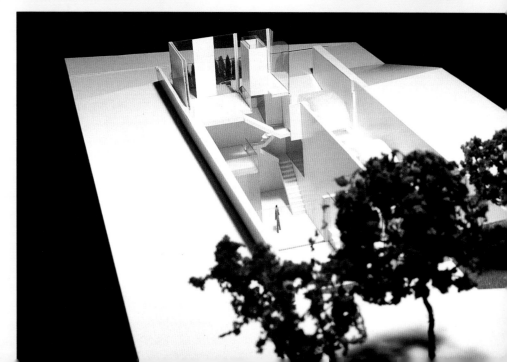

TEMPORARY GUGGENHEIM TOKYO

DESIGN DATE: April 2001–August 2001
LOCATION: Odaiba, Tokyo, Japan
STRUCTURAL ENGINEERS:
VAN Structural Design Studio —
Shigeru Ban, Satoshi Higuchi

Temporary Guggenheim Tokyo, Odaiba, Tokyo,
Japan, 2001; Phase 1
BELOW LEFT: Aerial view of model
BELOW RIGHT: Model, view of main exhibition
gallery made of paper tubes
OPPOSITE TOP: Model, view of monumental
colonnade along east facade
OPPOSITE BOTTOM: Section and first floor
plan, 1:1200

PHASE 1

In 2001, Ban competed with two other architects—Zaha Hadid and Jean Nouvel—to design a
temporary satellite in Tokyo for New York's Solomon R. Guggenheim Museum. Ban created three
different designs that responded to changes in requirements at different phases of the project.

The basic requirement for the first phase was to design a 7,000-square-meter building that would
have a lifespan of two years. The time frame for design and construction was one year. Ban's design,
a two-story, post-and-beam paper-tube structure that included a monumental colonnade along the
entrance facade, was reminiscent of his earlier Japan Pavilion in Hannover.

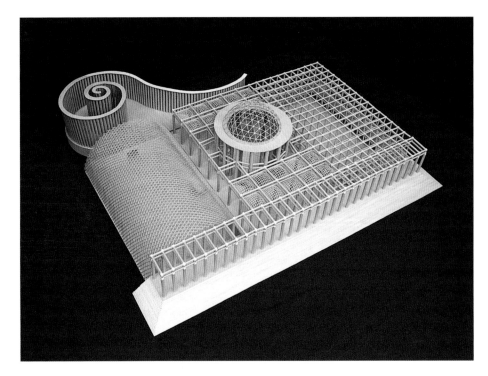

1 Lobby
2 Museum shop
3 Gallery
4 Rotunda
5 Storage

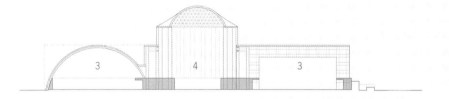

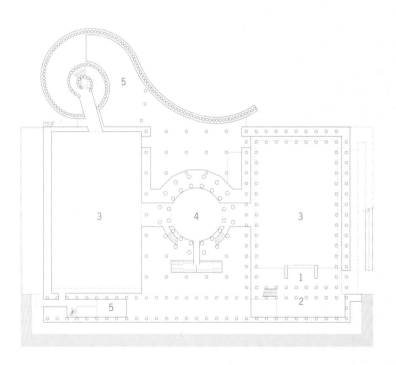

Temporary Guggenheim Tokyo, Odaiba,
Tokyo, Japan, 2001; Phase 2
BELOW: Computer model of main facade
with shutters partially open
OPPOSITE TOP: Model of Phase 2, entrance
facade showing stacked shipping containers

OPPOSITE MIDDLE (left to right): Computer
model image of east facade with shutters
partially open; partial view of exhibition
gallery with paper-tube exhibition space
OPPOSITE BOTTOM (left to right):
Longitudinal section and cross-section,
1:1200

PHASE 2

In the second phase, exhibition space was consolidated into one story with a maximum height of
30 meters. The life span of the building was extended to ten years, while the design and construction
phase was reduced to ten months. In response, Ban changed materials and chose a more efficient
building system. Although regulations accepted a paper-tube structure as viable, he was also required
to use either concrete or steel for further fire protection. His proposal was to make two parallel
stacks of shipping containers that reached a height of approximately 30 meters. A series of nine stacking
shutters were to be installed along the ocean side; the structure would act like an airplane hanger.
Inside was a secondary paper-tube structure measuring 23 by 30 by 84 meters that would define the
exhibition space. A transparent membrane roof covered this paper-tube insertion as well as the
exterior—creating a "double-skin" for easier climate control. This combination of materials made the
building easy to disassemble, transport, and rebuild in another location.

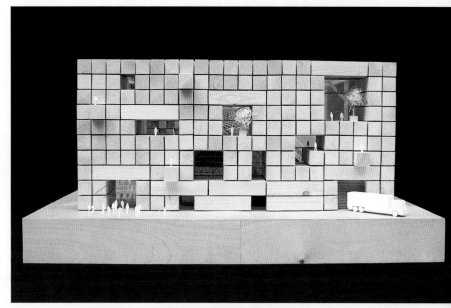

1 Exhibition space
2 Media wall
3 Office
4 Museum shop
5 Café

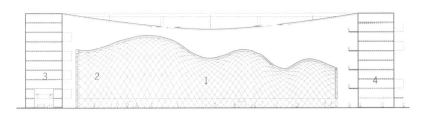

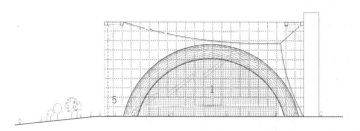

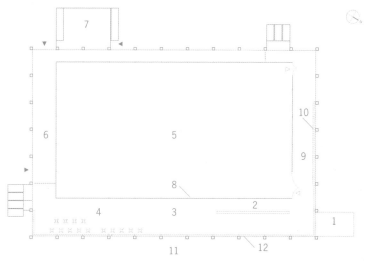

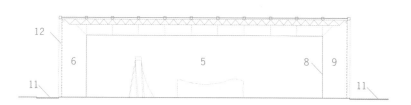

1 Entrance
2 Admissions
3 Lobby
4 Café
5 Exhibition space
6 Preparation space
7 Storage
8 Fly curtain
9 Museum shop
10 Media wall
11 Pond
12 Stacking shutters

Temporary Guggenheim Tokyo, Odaiba,
Tokyo, Japan, 2001; Phase 3
OPPOSITE TOP: Computer rendering
of east facade with stacking shutters open
on all four sides
OPPOSITE MIDDLE (left to right): Plan and
section, 1:1400
OPPOSITE BOTTOM: Diagram sequence
showing transportable museum

(left to right): museum, disassembling the
building, loading components into shipping
containers, easy transport by ship
BELOW (left to right): Computer renderings
of varying positions of the rolling shutters
and interior white "fly curtain"
BOTTOM: Computer simulations of various
Fiberglass Reinforced Panels (FRP) used for
the shutters

PHASE 3

In the final version, Ban simplified his scheme, developing the stacking shutter idea within an overall
steel-frame structure. All four sides of the museum were made of transparent fiberglass stacking
shutters, and the exhibition space was defined by a series of "fly curtains" made of a translucent white
membrane. When the fiberglass stacking shutters were closed, the museum appeared to be a glowing,
translucent cube. When retracted, the white membrane became a second skin that could in turn
be peeled back to reveal the event or exhibition inside.

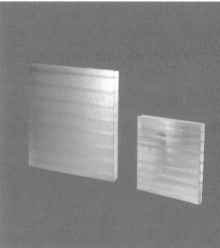

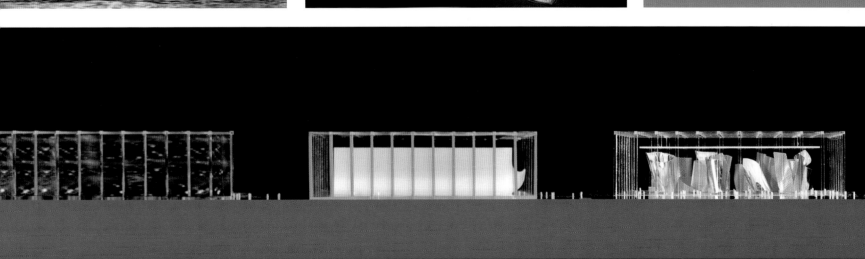

1. Emilio Ambasz Exhibition
Location: Axis Gallery, Tokyo, Japan
Exhibition Date: 1985

2. Alvar Aalto Exhibition
Location: Axis Gallery, Tokyo, Japan
Exhibition Date: 1986

3. Judith Turner Exhibition
Location: Axis Gallery, Tokyo, Japan
Exhibition Date: 1986

4. Villa TCG
Location: Chino, Nagano, Japan
Project Team: Shigeru Ban
Structural Engineers: Keishosha — Junichi Igarashi
Mechanical Engineers: Urban Mechanical Engineering
General Contractors: Shelter Home
Principal use: Villa
Site area: 1,139.53m^2
Building area: 109.57 m^2
Total floor area: 150 m^2
Structure: Wood; 1 basement and 2 stories
Design Date: January 1986 – April 1986
Construction Date: August 1986 – December 1986

5. Villa K
Location: Chino, Nagano, Japan
Project Team: Shigeru Ban
Structural Engineers: Keishosha — Junichi Igarashi
Mechanical Engineers: Urban Mechanical Design
General Contractors: Hirabayashi Komuten
Principal use: Villa
Site area: 1,219.8 m^2 Building area: 88.4 m^2
Total floor area: 115 m^2
Structure: Wood; 3 stories
Design Date: October 1986 – February 1987
Construction Date: April 1987 – August 1987

6. Three Walls — Studio for an Architect
Location: Setagaya, Tokyo, Japan
Project Team: Shigeru Ban, Junko Saito
Structural Engineers: Keishosha — Junichi Igarashi
Mechanical Engineers: Kawaguchi Mechanical Engineering
General Contractors: Matsumoto Corporation
Principal use: Atelier and Residence
Site area: 71 m^2 Building area: 54 m^2
Total floor area: 194 m^2
Structure: Reinforced concrete; 4 stories
Design Date: January 1985 – June 1987
Construction Date: September 1987 – July 1988

7. M Residence
Location: Setagaya, Tokyo, Japan
Project Team: Shigeru Ban, Jun Matsumori
Structural Engineers: Akira Watanabe Architect & Engineers
Mechanical Engineers: Urban Mechanical Engineering
General Contractors: Heisei Construction
Principal use: Residence
Site area: 139 m^2
Building area: 61 m^2
Total floor area: 148 m^2
Structure: Reinforced concrete, part-steel frame; 3 stories
Design Date: July 1987 – April 1988
Construction Date: June 1988 – January 1989

8. Paper Arbor — Paper Tube Structure 01
Location: Design Expo '89, Nagoya, Aichi, Japan
Project Team: Shigeru Ban, Toshihiro Kiyoshige
Associate Architects: ArchiNetwork
Structural Engineers: Yoshiaki Tsuboi, Toshifumi Matsumoto
General Contractors: Nomura Display
Principal use: Arbor Site area: 8730 m^2
Building area: 22 m^2 Total floor area: 22 m^2
Structure: PTS (Paper Tube Structure); 1 story
Design Date: July 1988 – May 1989
Construction Date: July 1989

9. Emilio Ambasz Exhibition
Location: La Jolla Museum of Contemporary Art, La Jolla, California, U.S.A.
Exhibition Date: 1989

10. Nova Oshima — Zanotta Furniture Exhibition
Location: TEPIA, Tokyo, Japan
Exhibition Date: 1989

11. Odawara Festival Main Hall — Paper Tube Structure 02
Location: Odawara, Kanagawa, Japan
Project Team: Shigeru Ban, Takeshi Sato
Structural Engineers: Gengo Matsui, Yoshiaki Tsuboi, Toshifumi Matsumoto, Minoru Tezuka
Mechanical Engineers: Chiku Engineering Consultants
General Contractors: Odawara Construction Union
Principal use: Festival hall
Site area: 8,265 m^2 Building area: 1,226 m^2
Total floor area: 1,243 m^2
Structure: PTS (Paper Tube Structure); 2 stories
Design Date: July 1989 - December 1989
Construction Date: January 1990 – April 1990

12. East Gate of Odawara Festival — Paper Tube Structure 03
Location: Odawara, Kanagawa, Japan
Project Team: Shigeru Ban, Takeshi Sato
Structural Engineers: Gengo Matsui, Minoru Tezuka
General Contractors: Shoko Bijutsu
Principal use: Festival Gate Building area: 100 m^2
Structure: PTS (Paper Tube Structure); 1 story
Design Date: July 1989 – December 1989
Construction Date: January 1990 – April 1990

13. Villa Torii
Location: Suwa, Nagano, Japan
Project Team: Shigeru Ban, Toshihiro Kiyoshige
General Contractors: Rinyu Home
Structural Engineers: Minoru Tezuka
Mechanical Engineers: Urban Mechanical Engineering
Principal use: Villa
Site area: 1,209 m^2 Building area: 103 m^2
Total floor area: 167 m^2
Structure: Wood, 3 stories
Design Date: November 1988 – July 1989
Construction Date: August 1989 – December 1990

14. Library of a Poet — Paper Tube Structure 04
Pages 16 – 21
Location: Zushi, Kanagawa, Japan
Project Team: Shigeru Ban, Hiromi Okusa
Structural Engineers: Gengo Matsui, Minoru Tezuka, Kazuo Ito
General Contractors: Kadomatsu Komuten
Principal use: Library Site area: 270 m^2
Building area: 35 m^2 Total floor area: 42 m^2
Structure: PTS (paper tube truss structure); 2 stories
Design Date: January 1990 – June 1990
Construction Date: September 1990 – February 1991

15. Studio for Vocalists
Location: Setagaya, Tokyo, Japan
Project Team: Shigeru Ban, Toshihiro Kiyoshige
Structural Engineers: Toshifumi Matsumoto
Mechanical Engineers: Sou Engineering
General Contractors: Takagi Komuten
Principal use: Residence
Site area: 146 m^2 Building area: 84 m^2
Total floor area: 137 m^2
Structure: Reinforced concrete; 1 basement and 2 stories
Design Date: March 1989 – January 1990
Construction Date: February 1990 – March 1991

16. I House — Case Study House 01
Location: Koganei, Tokyo, Japan
Project Team: Shigeru Ban, Masao Yamazaki
Structural Engineers: Hoshino Architect & Engineer — Shuichi Hoshino
General Contractors: Sanken Kougei
Principal use: Residence
Site area: 120 m^2 Building area: 48 m^2
Total floor area: 89 m^2
Structure: Wood, 2 stories
Design Date: April 1990 – October 1990
Construction Date: November 1990 – May 1991

17. Villa Kuru
Location: Chiisagata, Nagano, Japan
Project Team: Shigeru Ban, Hiromi Okusa
Structural Engineers: Hoshino Architect & Engineer — Shuichi Hoshino
Mechanical Engineers: Urban Mechanical Engineering
General Contractors: Toshin Doken
Principal use: Villa
Site area: 1,279 m^2 Building area: 91 m^2
Total floor area: 165 m^2
Structure: Reinforced concrete, wood (roof); 1 basement and 1 story
Design Date: November 1989 – June 1990
Construction Date: July 1990 – July 1991

18. PC Pile House — Case Study House 02
Pages 154 – 157
Location: Susono, Shizuoka, Japan
Project Team: Shigeru Ban, Tadanori Maekawa
Structural Engineers: Gengo Matsui, Hoshino Architect & Engineer — Shuichi Hoshino
General Contractors: Ishiwata Corporation
Principal use: Villa and Atelier
Site area: 516 m^2 Building area: 118 m^2
Total floor area: 112 m^2
Structure: Pre-cast concrete piles and wood; 1 story
Design Date: October 1990 – July 1991
Construction Date: August 1991 – May 1992

19. Housing at Shakujii Park
Location: Nerima, Tokyo, Japan
Project Team: Shigeru Ban, Masao Yamazaki
Structural Engineers: Matsumoto Structural Design — Toshifumi Matsumoto
Mechanical Engineers: Chiku Engineering Consultants
General Contractors: Heisei Construction
Principal use: Multi-unit Housing
Site area: 1,289 m^2 Building area: 448 m^2
Total floor area: 1,837 m^2
Structure: Reinforced concrete bearing wall; 1 basement and 4 stories
Design Date: July 1989 – June 1990
Construction Date: July 1990 – June 1992

20. Complex by Rail Road
Location: Shibuya, Tokyo, Japan
Project Team: Shigeru Ban, Toshihiro Kiyoshige, Masao Yamazaki
Structural Engineers: Matsumoto Structural Design — Toshifumi Matsumoto
Mechanical Engineers: Chiku Engineering Consultants
General Contractors: Tomoe Corporation
Principal use: Shop, Office, and Residence
Site area: 264 m^2 Building area: 191 m^2
Total floor area: 1,029 m^2
Structure: Reinforced concrete; 1 basement and 6 stories
Design Date: August 1989 – May 1991
Construction Date: May 1991 – December 1992

21. A Factory at Hamura-Dengyosha
Location: Hamura, Tokyo, Japan
Project Team: Shigeru Ban, Tadanori Maekawa, Tetsuo Yamakoshi
Structural Engineers: Hoshino Architect & Engineer — Shuichi Hoshino, Akira Teraoka
Mechanical Engineers: Chiku Engineering Consultants
General Contractors: JV of Mitsui Construction, Matsumoto Corporation
Principal use: Office and Factory
Site area: 968 m^2 Building area: 448 m^2
Total floor area: 1490 m^2
Structure: Steel frame and pre-cast concrete; 4 stories
Design Date: July 1991 – April 1992
Construction Date: May 1992 – February 1993

22. Emilio Ambasz Exhibtion
Location: Tokyo Station Gallery, Tokyo, Japan
Exhibition Date: 1993

23. House of Double-Roof — Case Study House 03
Location: Lake Yamanaka, Yamanashi, Japan
Project Team: Shigeru Ban, Tetsuo Yamakoshi
Structural Engineers: Hoshino Architects & Engineer — Shuichi Hoshino, Akira Teraoka
General Contractors: Marukaku Kenchiku
Principal use: Villa Site area: 368 m^2
Building area: 73 m^2 Total floor area: 73 m^2
Structure: Wood and steel frame; 1 story
Design Date: May 1991 – August 1992
Construction Date: August 1992 – August 1993

24. House for a Dentist *Pages 186 – 191*
Location: Setagaya, Tokyo, Japan
Project Team: Shigeru Ban, Makiko Tsukada
Structural Engineers: Hoshino Architect & Engineer — Shuichi Hoshino, Akira Teraoka
Mechanical Engineers: ES Associates
General Contractors: Heisei Construction
Principal use: Dental clinic and residence
Site area: 183 m^2 Building area: 75 m^2
Total floor area: 223 m^2

1

3

5

7

9

11

13

15

17

19

2

4

6

8

10

12

14

16

18

20

Structure: Reinforced concrete and wood;
1 basement and 2 stories
Design Date: June 1992 – April 1993
Construction Date: May1993 – February 1994

25. Miyake Design Studio Gallery
— Paper Tube Structure 06
Location: Shibuya, Tokyo, Japan
Project Team: Shigeru Ban, Yoko Nakagawa
Structural Engineers: Gengo Matsui, Minoru Tezuka, Shuichi Hoshino
General Contractors: Nomura Display
Principal use: Gallery Site area: 128 m^2
Building area: 86 m^2 Total floor area: 86 m^2
Structure: PTS (Paper Tube Structure); 1 story
Design Date: January 1993 – September 1993
Construction Date: December 1993 – February 1994

26. Furniture House 1 — Case Study House 04
Pages 164 – 169
Location: Lake Yamanaka, Yamanashi, Japan
Project Team: Shigeru Ban, Yoko Nakagawa
Structural Engineers: Gengo Matsui, Minoru Tezuka, Shuichi Hoshino
General Contractors: Marukaku Kenchiku
Principal use: Villa Site area: 562 m^2
Building area: 111 m^2 Total floor area: 103 m^2
Structure: Furniture structure; 1 story
Design Date: June 1992 – September 1993
Construction Date: December 1993 – April 1995

27. Paper House — Paper Tube Structure 05
Pages 22 – 27
Location: Lake Yamanaka, Yamanashi, Japan
Project Team: Shigeru Ban, Shigeru Hiraki
Structural Engineers: Gengo Matsui, Minoru Tezuka, Kazuo Ito, Nobunori Yamada
General Contractors: Marukaku Kenchiku
Principal use: Villa Site area: 499 m^2
Building area: 100 m^2 Total floor area: 100 m^2
Structure: PTS (Paper Tube Structure); 1 story
Design Date: October 1990 – July 1994
Construction Date: October 1994 – July 1995

28. Curtain Wall House — Case Study House 07
Pages 192 – 197
Location: Itabashi, Tokyo, Japan
Project Team: Shigeru Ban, Yoko Nakagawa, Shigeru Hiraki
Structural Engineers: Hoshino Architect & Engineer — Shuichi Hoshino
General Contractors: Heisei Construction
Principal use: Studio and Residence
Site area: 110 m^2 Building area: 75 m^2
Total floor area: 179 m^2
Structure: Steel frame; 3 stories
Design Date: September 1993 – September 1994
Construction Date: November 1994 – July 1995

29. 2/5 House — Case Study House 06
Location: Nishinomiya, Hyogo, Japan
Project Team: Shigeru Ban, Takashi Nakagawa
Structural Engineers: Hoshino Architect & Engineer — Shuichi Hoshino
Mechanical Engineers: ES Associates
General Contractors: Matsumoto Corporation
Principal use: Residence
Site area: 511 m^2 Building area: 182 m^2
Total floor area: 507 m^2
Structure: Reinforced concrete and steel frame; 1 basement and 2 stories
Design Date: February 1991 – March 1994
Construction Date: May 1994 – August 1995

30. Paper Log House-Kobe
— Paper Tube Structure 07 *Pages 34 – 37*
Location: Nagata, Kobe, Japan
Project Team: Shigeru Ban, Mamiko Ishida
Structural Engineers: Minoru Tezuka, TSP Taiyo — Eiichiro Kaneko
General Contractors: Volunteers
Principal use: Temporary housing
Building area: 16 m^2 Total floor area: 16 m^2
Structure: PTS (Paper Tube Structure); 1 story
Design Date: May 1995 – June 1995
Construction Date: July 1995 – September 1995

31. Paper Church — Paper Tube Structure 08
Pages 42 – 47
Location: Nagata, Kobe, Japan
Project Team: Shigeru Ban, Shigeru Hiraki
Structural Engineers: Gengo Matsui, Shuichi Hoshino, TSP Taiyo-Mihoko Uchida
General Contractors: Volunteers
Principal use: Church, community hall
Building area: 168 m^2 Total floor area: 168 m^2
Structure: PTS (Paper Tube Structure); 1 story
Design Date: March 1995 – July 1995
Construction Date: July 1995 – September 1995

32. Furniture House 2
Location: Fujisawa, Kanagawa, Japan
Project Team: Shigeru Ban, Shigeru Hiraki
Structural engineers: Minoru Tezuka
General contractors: Tsuchiya Kensetsu
Principal use: Residence
Site area: 151 m^2 Building area: 76 m^2
Total floor area: 116 m^2
Structure: Furniture structure; 1 story
Design Date: February 1995 – September 1995
Construction Date: October 1995 – March 1996

33. Nova Oshima Showroom
— Container Structure
Location: Meguro, Tokyo, Japan
Project Team: Shigeru Ban, Yoko Nakagawa
General Contractors: TSP Taiyo
Principal use: Temporary Showroom
Site area: 500 m^2 Building area: 289 m^2
Total floor area: 289 m^2
Structure: Aluminum container (rental) and steel frame (roof); 1 story
Design Date: August 1993 – December 1993
Construction Date: March 1994 – October 1996

34. Tazawako Station *Pages 158 – 163*
Location: Tazawako, Akita, Japan
Project Team: Shigeru Ban, Takashi Nakagawa
Structural Engineers: Gengo Matsui, Sadakazu Yoda
Mechanical Engineers: ES Associates
General Contractors: Daiichi Kensentsu Corporation
Principal use: Train Station and Information Center
Site area: 4,423 m^2 Building area: 761 m^2
Total floor area: 991 m^2
Structure: Pre-cast concrete piles and steel frame, partly wood; 2 stories
Design Date: November 1994 – June 1996
Construction Date: August 1996 – March 1997

35. Wall-Less House — Case Study House 08
Location: Karuizawa, Nagano, Japan
Project Team: Shigeru Ban, Shigeru Hiraki
Structural Engineers: Hoshino Architect & Engineer — Shuichi Hoshino
General Contractors: Maruyama Komuten
Principal use: Villa
Site area 330 m^2 Building area: 85 m^2
Total floor area: 60 m^2
Structure: Steel house; 1 story
Design Date: August 1995 – September 1996
Construction Date: October 1996 – August 1997

36. Paper Stage Design for Mannojo Nomura
Location: Ginza, Tokyo, Japan
Project Team: Shigeru Ban, Tatsuya Matsuyama
General Contractors: Kabukiza Theater Stage and Okamura
Principal use: Stage set
Structure: PTS (Paper Tube Structure)
Completion date: October 1997

37. Hanegi Forest
Location: Setagaya, Tokyo, Japan
Project Team: Shigeru Ban, Mamiko Ishida
Structural Engineers: Hoshino Architect & Engineer — Shuichi Hoshino, Kiyoko Yamashita
Mechanical Engineers: Satohide
General Contractors: Satohide
Principal use: Multi-unit Housing
Site area 1,034 m^2 Building area: 554 m^2
Total floor area: 984 m^2
Structure: Steel frame; 3 stories
Design Date: May 1995 – September 1996
Construction Date: September 1996 – November 1997

38. Nine-Square Grid House
— Case Study House 09 *Pages 170 – 175*
Location: Hadano, Kanagawa, Japan
Project Team: Shigeru Ban, Tatsuya Matsuyama
Structural Engineers: Hoshino Architect & Engineer — Shuichi Hoshino
General Contractors: Ishiwata Kensetsu
Principal use: Residence
Site area 335 m^2 Building area: 125 m^2
Total floor area: 124 m^2
Structure: Steel furniture structure; 1 story
Design Date: March 1996 – January 1997
Construction Date: February 1997 – November 1997

39. Paper Dome — Paper Tube Structure 09
Pages 48 – 53
Location: Masuda, Gifu, Japan
Project Team: Shigeru Ban, Yoko Nakagawa, Tatsuya Matsuyama
Structural Engineers: Minoru Tezuka, VAN Structural Design — Shigeru Ban, Satoshi Higuchi
General Contractors: Ikehata Komuten
Principal use: Workshop
Site area: 3,300 m^2 Building area: 445 m^2
Total floor area: 445 m^2
Structure: PTS (Paper Tube Structure); 1 story
Design Date: March 1996 – March 1997
Construction Date: December 1997 – January 1998

40. Ivy Structure 1
Location: Suginami, Tokyo, Japan
Project Team: Shigeru Ban, Shigeru Hiraki, Tatsuya Matsuyama
Structural Engineers: Hoshino Architect & Engineer — Shuichi Hoshino, Noriko Komiyama
General contractors: Heisei Kensetsu
Principal use: Residence
Site area: 216.48 m^2 Building area: 108.23 m^2
Total floor area: 108.23 m^2
Structure: Steel frame; 2 stories
Design Date: May 1996 – August 1997
Construction Date: September 1997– June 1998

41. Furniture House 3
Location: Tsurumi, Kanagawa, Japan
Project Team: Shigeru Ban, Shigeru Hiraki
Structural Engineers: Minoru Tezuka, Hoshino Architect & Engineer — Shuichi Hoshino
General Contractors: Marukaku Kenchiku
Principal use: Residence
Site area: 240.79 m^2 Building area: 118.75 m^2
Total floor area: 170 m^2
Structure: Furniture structure and steel; 2 stories
Design Date: July 1997 – January 1998
Construction Date: February 1998 – July 1998

42. Paper Emergency Shelters for UNHCR
— Paper Tube Structure 10 *Pages 28 – 33*
Location: Byumba Refugee Camp, Rwanda
Principal use: Emergency Shelter for Refugees
Size: W 3.5m x L 4.0m x H 1.7m
Total number of shelters built: 50
Structure: Paper Tube Structure
Construction date: February 1999
Monitoring and observation: February 1999 – September 1999

43. Nemunoki Children's Art Museum
Pages 54 – 59
Location: Kakegawa, Shizuoka, Japan
Project Team: Shigeru Ban, Mamiko Ishida
Structural Engineers: Minoru Tezuka; VAN Structural Design – Shigeru Ban, Naoyuki Sasaki
General contractors: TSP Taiyo
Principal use: Museum
Site area: 1,464.00 m^2 Building area: 320.2 m^2
Total floor area: 299.71 m^2
Structure: Paper honeycomb triangular lattice structure and steel
Design Date: June 1998 – February 1999
Construction Date: February 1999 – May 1999

44. Ivy Structure 2 *Pages 198 – 201*
Location: Azabu, Tokyo, Japan
Project Team: Shigeru Ban, Shigeru Hiraki
Structural Engineers: Hoshino Architect & Engineer — Shuichi Hoshino, Noriko Komiyama
General Contractors: Iwamoto Gumi
Principal use: Residences and Gallery
Site area: 429.1 m^2 Building area: 253.7 m^2
Total floor area: 711.06 m^2
Structure: Steel frame; 1 basement and 3 stories
Design Date: January, 1998 – April, 1999
Construction Date: April 1999 – January 2000

21

23

25

27

29

31

33

35

37

39

22

24

26

28

30

32

34

36

38

40

45. Paper Log House-Turkey
— Paper Tube Structure 11 *Pages 38 – 39*
Location: Kainasli, Turkey
Project Team: Shigeru Ban, Keina Ishioka
Associate Architects: Mine Hashas,
Hayim Beraha, Okan Bayikk
General Contractors: Volunteers
Principal use: Temporary housing
Floor area: 19 m² (3100m x 6100m)
Structure: Paper Tube Structure
Design Date: September 1999 – December 1999
Construction Date: December 1999 – January 2000

46. Paper Arch — Paper Tube Structure 12
Pages 68 – 71
Location: The Museum of Modern Art, New York, USA
Project team: Shigeru Ban, Yoko Watanabe
Associate Architects: Dean Maltz, Architect
— Dean Maltz, Kamonsin Chathurattaphol
Structural Design: Preliminarily Design: Takenaka
Corporation — Yoshio Tanno, Keiichi Hasegawa
Construction Design: Buro Happold Consulting
Engineers PC, New York – Craig Schwitter, Cristobal
Correa, Laura Fuentes
Construction Management: Sciame Construction Co., Inc.
General Contractors: Atlantic Heydt Corporation
Principal use: Installation
Building Area: 586 m²
Structure: Paper Tube Structure
Design Date: August 1999 – April 2000
Construction Date: April 2000

47. Japan Pavilion, Expo 2000, Hannover
— Paper Tube Structure 13 *Pages 60 – 67*
Location: Hannover, Germany
Project Team: Shigeru Ban, Nobutaka Hiraga,
Shigeru Hiraki, Jun Yashiki
Consultant: Frei Otto
Structural Engineers: Buro Happold
— Michael Dickson, Paul Westbury, Paul Rogers,
Greg Hardie, Klaus Leiblein
General Contractors: Takenaka Europe GmBH
Principal use: Exhibition pavilion
Site area: 5,450.0 m²
Building area: 3,090.0 m²
Total floor area: 3,015.8 m²
Structure: Paper Tube Structure and timber
Design Date: July 1997 – August 1999
Construction Date: September 1999 – May 2000

48. GC Osaka Building
— Wooden Fire Protection 01 *Pages 92 – 97*
Location: Chuo, Osaka, Japan
Project Team: Shigeru Ban, Nobutaka Hiraga,
Souichro Hiyoshi
Associate Architects: Marunouchi Architects and
Engineers — Mitsuaki Matsuo
Structural Engineers: VAN Structural Design Studio
— Shigeru Ban
Mechanical Engineers: Marunouchi Architects
and Engineers
Fire Engineers: Kajima Corporation — Tomio Oouchi
General Contractors: Kajima Corporation
Principal use: Office, showroom
Site area: 602.08 m²   Building area: 348.76 m²
Total floor area: 2,108.19 m²
Structure: Steel frame, steel-reinforced
concrete basement

Design Date: September 1998 – June 1999
Construction Date: July 1999 – June 2000

49. Uno Chiyo Memorial Museum
Location: Iwakuni, Yamaguchi, Japan
Project Team: Shigeru Ban, Nobutaka Hiraga,
Mamiko Ishida
Consultant: Frei Otto
Structural Engineers: Arup-Tokyo — Shigeru Hikone,
Arata Oguri; Arup-Dusseldorf — Rudiger Lutz
Principal use: Museum
Site area: 4,000 m²   Building area: 1,089.4 m²
Total floor area: 1,300 m²
Structure: LVL (wickerwork) roof and steel columns;
1 basement and 2 stories
Design Date: January 1999 – September 2000

50. Naked House — Case Study House 10
Pages 202 – 207
Location: Kawagoe, Saitama, Japan
Project Team: Shigeru Ban, Mamiko Ishida,
Anne Scheou
Structural Engineers: Hoshino Architect & Engineer
— Shuichi Hoshino, Takashige Suzuki
General Contractors: Misawaya Kensetsu
Principal use: Residence
Site area: 516 m²   Building area: 183 m²
Total floor area: 138.5 m²
Structure: Wood structure (TJI); 1 story
Design Date: May 1999 – April 2000
Construction Date: May 2000 – November 2000

51. Veneer Grid Roof House
— Case Study House 11
Location: Chiba, Japan
Project Team: Shigeru Ban, Mamiko Ishida, Jun Yashiki
Structural Engineers: VAN Structural Design
— Shigeru Ban, Naoyuki Sasaki
Principal use: Residence
Site area: 494.52 m²   Building area: 101.88 m²
Total floor area: 163 m²
Structure: Veneer lattice frame structure; 1 story
Design Date: October 1998 – July 2000
Construction Date: August 2000 – May 2001

52. Imai Hospital Daycare Center
— Plywood Structure 03 *Pages 98 – 103*
Location: Odate, Akita, Japan
Project Team: Shigeru Ban, Nobutaka Hiraga,
Soichiro Hiyoshi, Keita Sugai
Structural Engineers: TIS & Partners
— Norihide Imagawa, Koh Sakata
Mechanical Engineers: ES Associates
General Contractors: Obayashi Corporation
Principal use: Daycare center
Site area: 235.20 m²   Building area: 131.20 m²
Total floor area: 73.84 m²
Structure: Timber structure
Design Date: February 2000 – December 2000
Construction Date: December 2000 – May 2001

53. Temporary Guggenheim Tokyo 1, 2, 3
Pages 228 – 233
Location: Odaiba, Tokyo, Japan
Project Team: Shigeru Ban, Nobutaka Hiraga,
Mamiko Ishida
Structural Engineers: VAN Structural Design Studio
— Shigeru Ban, Satoshi Higuchi

Principal use: Museum
Site area: 17,980 m²
Building area: 1) 8,569 m², 2) 7,920 m², 3) 8,360 m²
Total floor area: 1) 7,783 m², 2) 8,500 m², 3) 9,350 m²
Structure:
1) Paper Tube Structure; 2 stories
2) Paper Tube Structure and Steel Structure;
1 story; Office/Storage: Shipping containers
3) Steel Structure; 1 story
Design Date: April 2001 – August 2001

54. Paper Log House-India
— Paper Tube Structure 14
Pages 40 – 41
Location: Bhuj, India
Project Team: Shigeru Ban, Keina Ishioka
Associate Architect: Kartikeya Shodhan Associates
— Kartikeya Shodhan
General Contractors: Volunteers
Principal use: Housing
Structure: Paper Tube Structure
Design Date: February 2001 – March 2001
Construction Date: March 2001 – September 2001

55. Picture Window House
Pages 208 – 213
Location: Izu, Shizuoka, Japan
Project Team: Shigeru Ban, Nobutaka Hiraga,
Jun Yashiki
Structural Engineer: Hoshino Architect & Engineer
— Shuichi Hoshino, Takashige Suzuki
General Contractors: Daido Kogyo
Principal use: Residence
Site area: 880.50 m²
Building area: 158.63 m²
Total floor area: 273.81 m²
Structure: Steel frame; 2 stories
Design Date: December 1999 – February 2001
Construction Date: March 2001 – February 2002

56. Rietberg Museum Competition — Zürich
Location: Zürich, Switzerland
Project Team: Shigeru Ban, Nobutaka Hiraga,
Mamiko Ishida, Kentaro Ishida, Yukie Ikeda,
Tamaki Terai, Hajime Masubuchi, Grant Suzuki
Associate Architect: Arndt Geiger Hermann
— Thomas Geiger, Michael Rüegg;
Stücheli Architekten — Stefan Beck
Structural Engineers: Arup, London
— Chris Luebkeman; SKS Ingenieure AG
— Theo Weber, Christoph Schenk
Mechanical Engineers: Arup, London — Chris Trott
Geotechnical Engineers: Arup, London
— Timothy JP Chapman
Landscape: Vetsch Nipkow Partner — Beat Nipkow
Graphic Design: Hara Design Institute, Nippon Design
Center Inc. — Kenya Hara, Yuji Koiso
Site area: 12,000 m²
Total floor area: 3,200 m²
Design Date: November 2001 – February 2002

57. Church in Roppongi
Location: Roppongi, Tokyo, Japan
Project Team: Shigeru Ban, Nobutaka Hiraga,
Mamiko Ishida, Jun Yashiki
Principal use: Church
Site area: 855.7 m²   Building area: 324.89 m²
Total floor area: 607.31m²

Structure: Reinforced concrete, steel
Design Date: April 2002 – May 2002

58. Eda Multi-Unit Housing Competition
Location: Eda, Tokyo, Japan
Project Team: Shigeru Ban, Nobutaka Hiraga,
Mamiko Ishida, Hajime Masubuchi, Kentaro Ishida,
Keita Sugai, Grant Suzuki, Tamaki Terai, Keina Ishioka
Structural Engineers: Hoshino Architect & Engineer
— Shuichi Hoshino, Takashige Suzuki
Site area: 3,137 m²   Building area: 2,234 m²
Total floor area: 8,069 m²
Design Date: March 2002 – May 2002

59. Bamboo Furniture House
— Furniture House 04 *Pages 132 – 137*
Location: Great Wall at Shui Guan, China
Project Team: Shigeru Ban, Wakako Tokunaga
Structural Engineers: Minoru Tezuka
General contractors: SOHO China
Mechanical Engineering: SOHO China
Principal use: Villa .   Building area: 400 m²
Total floor area: 276 m²
Structure: Laminated bamboo; 1 story
Design Date: October 2000 – April 2001
Construction Date: June 2001 – June 2002

60. Atsushi Imai Memorial Gymnasium
— Plywood Structure 04 *Pages 104 – 111*
Location: Odate, Akita, Japan
Project Team: Shigeru Ban, Nobutaka Hiraga,
Soichiro Hiyoshi, Keita Sugai
Structural Engineers: TIS & Partners — Norihide
Imagawa, Yuuki Ozawa
Mechanical Engineering: ES Associates
General Contractors: Obayashi Gumi
Principal use: Gymnasium, swimming pool
Site area: 2041.9 m²   Building area: 940.6 m²
Total floor area: 980.9 m²
Structure: Timber structure, reinforced concrete;
1 story
Design Date: February 2000 – August 2001
Construction Date: August 2001 – August 2002

61. Wickerwork House *Pages 112 – 113*
Location: Chino, Nagano, Japan
Project Team: Shigeru Ban, Mamiko Ishida,
Kentaro Ishida
Structural Engineers: Arup Japan — Arata Oguri,
Tatsuo Kiuchi
Principal use: Villa
Site area: 1171 m²   Building area: 203.56 m²
Total floor area: 158.76 m²
Structure: Sandwich board (FRP, formed urethane,
weaved plywood), steel edge beam
Design Date: June 2001 – September 2002

62. Paper Art Museum *Pages 218 – 225*
Location: Mishima, Shizuoka, Japan
Project Team: Shigeru Ban, Nobutaka Hiraga,
Tadahiro Kawano, Keina Ishioka
Structural Engineers: Hoshino Architect & Engineer
— Shuichi Hoshino, Takashige Suzuki
Mechanical Engineers: Chiku Engineering Consultants
General Contractor: Obayashi Corporation
Principal use: Museum
Site area: 6,277.69 m²
Built area: 1,672.40 m² (PAM B 924.76 m²,

 41
 43
 45
 47
  49
 51
 53
 55
 57
 59

 42
44
 46
48
50
 52
54
 56
   58
60

PAM A 719.77 m^2)
Total floor area: 2,437.11 m^2 (PAM B 924.76 m^2, PAM A 1479.31 m^2)
Structure: Steel frame; 4 stories
Design: February 2000 – April 2001
Construction Dates: May 2001 – September 2002

63. Bamboo Roof — Bamboo Gridshell 01
Pages 142 – 143
Location: Rice University Art Gallery, Houston, Texas, USA
Project Team: Shigeru Ban, Mamiko Ishida, Grant Suzuki
Structural Engineers: Arup, London — Cecil Balmond, Charles Walker, Benedikt Schleicher
Principal use: Installation
Site area: 163.88 m^2 Building area: 120.4 m^2
Structure: Laminated bamboo, steel poles
Design Date: August 2002 – October 2002
Construction Date: November 2002

64. Plastic Bottle Structure 01
Location: Shanghai Art Museum, Shanghai, China
Project Team: Shigeru Ban, Tamaki Terai
Structural Engineer: Minoru Tezuka
Principal use: Installation Building Area: 30 m^2
Structure: Plastic bottles, acrylic
Design Dates: September 2002 – November 2002
Construction Date: November 2002

65. World Trade Center Competition
Location: New York, New York, U.S.A.
Designers: Team THINK
Shigeru Ban Architects — Shigeru Ban, Nobutaka Hiraga, Kentaro Ishida; Dean Maltz, Architect — Dean Maltz, Hirosugi Mizutani, Andrew Lefkowitz; Rafael Vinoly Architects; Frederic Schwartz Architects; Ken Smith Landscape Architects
Engineers: Arup, Buro Happold, Schlaich Bergermann und Partner
Contributors: William Morrish, David Rockwell, Janet Marie Smith
Site area: 64,750 m^2 (16 acres)
Total Floor area: 604,000 m^2
Design Date: September 2002 – February 2003

66. Paper Studio — Paper Tube Structure 15
Location: Keio University, Fujisawa, Kanagawa, Japan
Project Team: Shigeru Ban, Mamiko Ishida, Grant Suzuki
Structural Engineers: Minoru Tezuka
Construction: Students
Construction Assistance: Taiyo Kensetsu — Toshihiro Tokushige, TSP Taiyo
Principal Use: Design studio
Building area: 147.5 m^2 Total floor area: 122.7 m^2
Structure: PTS (Paper Tube Structure); 2 stories
Design Date: May 2002 – July 2002
Construction Date: August 2002 – March 2003

67. Glass Shutter House — Case Study House 12
Pages 214 – 217
Location: Setagaya, Tokyo, Japan
Project Team: Shigeru Ban, Nobutaka Hiraga, Keita Sugai
Structural Engineers: Hoshino Architect & Engineer — Shuichi Hoshino
Mechanical Engineers: Chiku Engineering Consultants
General Contractors: Heisei Construction
Principal use: Residence, restaurant
Site area: 132.89m^2 Building area: 73.67m^2
Total floor area: 151.79m^2
Structure: Steel frame; 3 stories
Design Date: June 2001 – November 2001
Construction Date: November 2001 – April 2003

68. "Territoire Partages, L'Archipel Metropolitain" Exhibition
Location: Pavillon de L'Arsenal 21, Paris, France
Project Team: Shigeru Ban, Mamiko Ishida
Associate Architect: Jean de Gastines Architecte DPLG — Jean de Gastines, Ivan Fouquet
Principal use: Exhibition
Total floor area: 750 m^2
Exhibition Date: October 2002 – March 2003

69. Planning and Design of Haihe Square and Heiping Road Area Competition — Tianjin
Location: Tianjin, China
Project Team: Shigeru Ban, Nobutaka Hiraga, Mamiko Ishida, Kentaro Ishida, Keita Sugai, Keina Ishioka, Grant Suzuki, Tamaki Terai, Tomoo Nitta
Structural Engineers: Kawaguchi & Engineers — Mamoru Kawaguchi, Yuji Aso, Xiaodun Wang
Urban Strategy: Masami Kobayashi, Hiroyuki Niino, Hiroshi Koike
Financial Strategy: Yasuharu Murahashi
Landscape: Tokyo Landscape Architects
Environmental & Fire Prevention: Takenaka Corp.
Transportation Systems: Toyota Motor Corporation, ITS Planning Division
Acoustics: Nagata Acoustics
Site area: 720,000 m^2 (72 hectares)
Total floor area: 1,460,000 m^2
Design Date: January 2003 – March 2003

70. New School of Business, American University of Beirut — Competition
Location: Beirut, Lebanon
Project Team: Shigeru Ban, Nobutaka Hiraga, Mamiko Ishida, Kentaro Ishida, Tamaki Terai, Keita Sugai, Keina Ishioka, Grant Suzuki
Associate Architect: Bernard Khoury Architects — Bernard Khoury, Joseph Chartouni
Structural Engineers: Arup — Richard Terry, Pat Dallard, Arata Oguri
Mechanical & Environmental Engineers: Arup — Chris Trott, Stephen Hill
Economic Engineers: LACECO Architects & Engineers — Marwan Saleh, Ziad Namani
Landscape: Toru Mizutani
Site area: 4,900 m^2
Building Area: 4,300 m^2
Total floor area: 13,000 m^2
Design Date: March 2003 – May 2003

71. 76 rue Saint Antoine à Paris — Competition
Location: Paris, France
Project Team: Shigeru Ban, Grant Suzuki, Kentaro Ishida, Tamaki Terai, Keina Ishioka, Keita Sugai
Jean de Gastines Architecte DPLG — Jean de Gastines, Veronique Assens, Monica Perez del Rio
Structural Engineers: RFR — Matt King, Mitsu Edwards
Economist: Camebat — Gilles Pasquier
Site area: 236.5 m^2
Total floor area: 1,037.5 m^2
Design Date: April 2003 – May 2003

72. Amsterdam Paper Dome — Paper Tube Structure 16
Location: Ijburg, Amsterdam, Holland
Project Team: Shigeru Ban, Mamiko Ishida, Kentaro Ishida
Associate Architects: STUT Architecten — Wouter Klinkenbijl
Structural Engineers: Minoru Tezuka; abt Consulting Engineers — Walter Spangenberg; Octatube — Mick Eekhout, Erik van Baars
Principal use: Theater
Total floor area: 485 m^2
Structure: PTS (Paper Tube Structure); 1 story
Design Date: June 2002 – April 2003
Construction Date: April 2003 – June 2003

73. Boathouse, Centre d'Interpretation du Canal de Bourgogne *Pages 72 – 73*
Location: Pouilly-en-Auxois, France
Project Team: Shigeru Ban, Anne Scheou
Associate Architect: Jean de Gastines Architecte DPLG — Jean de Gastines, Damien Gaudin
Structural Engineers: Buro Happold — Paul Westbury, Geoffrey Werran; Terrell Rooke and Associates — Eric Dixon
Principal use: Boathouse
Building area: 295 m^2 Total floor area: 295 m^2
Structure: Paper Tube Structure, 1 story
Design Date: September 1998 – August 2002

74. Shutter House for a Photographer
Pages 226 – 227
Location: Minato, Tokyo, Japan
Project Team: Shigeru Ban, Nobutaka Hiraga, Anne Scheou, Tomoo Nitta
Structural Engineers: Hoshino Architect & Engineer — Shuichi Hoshino
General Contractors: Iwamoto Gumi
Principal use: Residence
Site area: 291 m^2 Building area: 142 m^2
Total floor area: 465 m^2
Structure: Concrete, steel-reinforced concrete, steel
Design Date: February 2000 - August 2002
Construction Date: September 2002 –

75. Institute, Centre d'Interpretation du Canal de Bourgogne *Pages 176 – 177*
Location: Pouilly-en-Auxois, France
Project Team: Shigeru Ban, Anne Scheou
Associate Architect: Jean de Gastines Architecte DPLG — Jean de Gastines, Damien Gaudin
Structural Engineers: Terrell Rooke and Associates — Eric Dixon
Mechanical Engineers: Noble Ingenierie
Contractors: Deblangey (concrete work), ACML (steel structure)
Principal use: Museum
Building area: 280 m^2 Total floor area: 265 m^2
Structure: Steel frame; 1 story
Design Date: November 2000 – May 2001
Construction Date: January 2002 –

76. Schwartz Residence *Pages 138 – 139*
Location: Sharon, Connecticut, USA
Project Team: Shigeru Ban, Mamiko Ishida, Wakako Tokunaga
Associate Architect: Dean Maltz, Architect — Dean Maltz, Justin Shaulis, Andrew Lefkowitz, Mara Dorkin, Hirosugi Mizutani
Structural Engineers: Buro Happold — Craig Schwitter, J. Cohen, Cristobal Correa
Principal use: Residence
Site area: 437,000 m^2 (108 acres)
Building area: 1,050 m^2 Total floor area: 1,644 m^2
Structure: Bamboo box beam, steel column, concrete block
Design Date: February 2001 – September 2002

77. Forest Park Pavilion — Bamboo Gridshell 02 *Pages 140 – 141*
Location: St. Louis, Missouri, USA
Project Team: Shigeru Ban, Mamiko Ishida, Grant Suzuki
Associate Architects: Dean Maltz, Architect — Dean Maltz, Justin Shaulis, Andrew Lefkowitz
Structural Engineers: Arup, London - Cecil Balmond, Charles Walker, Martin Self, Benedikt Schleicher
Principal use: Pavilion Building area: 1009 m^2
Structure: Laminated bamboo
Design Date: July 2001–

78. Sagaponac House — Furniture House 05
Pages 178 – 179
Location: Long Island, New York, USA
Project Team: Shigeru Ban, Mamiko Ishida, Wakako Tokunaga, Tamaki Terai
Associate Architect: Dean Maltz, Architect — Dean Maltz, Justin Shaulis, Andrew Lefkowitz
Structural Engineers: Robert Silman Associate, P.C. — Nat Oppenheimer, Helena Meryman
Mechanical Engineers: Stanislav Slutsky PE, Consulting Engineers
Principal use: Residence
Site area: 6,578 m^2 Building area: 573.5 m^2
Total floor area: 465.5 m^2
Structure: Wood, part steel
Design Date: September 2001 – May 2003
Construction: June 2003 –

79. Mul(ti)houses
Location: Mulhouse, France
Project Team: Shigeru Ban, Anne Scheou, Grant Suzuki
Associate Architect: Jean de Gastines Architecte DPLG — Jean de Gastines
Structural Engineers: Atelier des Constructions-Jean-Marc Weill
Mechanical Engineers: Delphi, CTH
Economist: Camebat
Principal use: Social housing
Site area: 1742 m^2 Building area: 258.5 m^2
Total floor area: 1200 m^2 Structure: Steel
Design Date: September 2001 – April 2002

80. Hanegi Forest Annex
Location: Setagaya, Tokyo, Japan
Project Team: Shigeru Ban, Mamiko Ishida, Keina Ishioka
Structural Engineers: Hoshino Architect & Engineer — Shuichi Hoshino, Takashige Suzuki, Ryuji Kotani
Mechanical Engineers: ES Associates
Principal use: Atelier
Site area: 221.65 m^2 Building area: 106 m^2
Total floor area: 112 m^2
Structure: Steel and wood
Design Date: September 2001 –

61

63

65

67

69

71

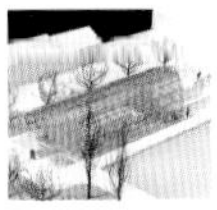
73

75

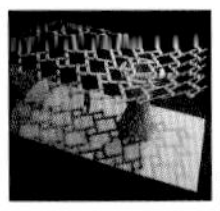
77

79

62

64

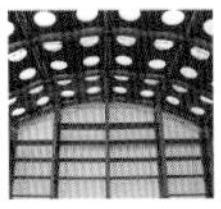
66

68

70

72

74

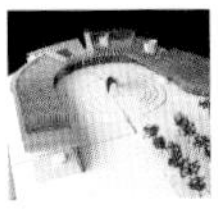
76

78

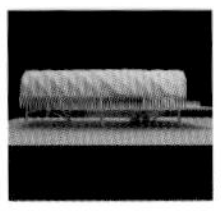
80

Awards

2002_____Best House in the World, World Architecture Awards 2002, Naked House
2001_____Finishing Technology Prize, Japan Society, GC Osaka Building
Gengo Matsui Award, Japan Pavilion, Hanover Expo 2000
Best Building in Europe, World Architecture Awards 2001, Japan Pavilion,
Hannover Expo 2000
New Office Award, Nikkei, GC Osaka Building
2000_____Berlin Art Award, Akademie der Kunste, Germany, Japan Pavilion,
Hannover Expo 2000
1999_____ar+d Award, Architectural Review, United Kingdom, Paper Church
Architecture for Humanity, United States, Paper Loghouse
1998_____Tohoku Prize, Architectural Institute of Japan, Tazawako Station
1997_____Best Young Architect of the Year, The Japan Institute of Architects
1996_____Innovative Award, Tokyo Journal
Yoshioka Prize, Japan
Kansai Architects Award, The Japan Institute of Architects
1995_____Mainichi Design Prize
1993_____House Award, Tokyo Society of Architects
1989_____Grand Prize, Arflex Design Competition
1988_____Display of the Year, Japan, "Alvar Aalto" Exhibition
1st Prize, Osaka Industrial Design Contest, L-Unit System
1986_____2nd Prize, Design Competition for the redevelopment of Shinsaibashi, Osaka
Display of the Year, Japan, "Emilio Ambasz" Exhibition

Industrial Design

1998_____Carta Collection, Cappellini
1993_____L-Unit System — final version, Nishiwaki Kohso
1988_____Multi Purpose Exhibition Panel, Itoki
1986_____Interior Light — J. T. Series, Daiko

Graphic Design

1987_____Book Design, *The Garden for Rabbits*, Mutsuro Takahashi
1987_____Calendar Design, Judith Turner, Naka Kogyo
1986_____Book Design, *Judith Turner, Photographer*

Publications

2001_____*Shigeru Ban*, Princeton Architectural Press, New York
2000_____*Shigeru Ban*, Galerie Renate Kammer, Junius Verlag GmbH, Germany
1999_____*Shigeru Ban, Projects in Process to Japanese Pavilion, Expo 2000
Hannover*, TOTO Shuppan, Japan
1998_____*Shigeru Ban, 17 realisations/works*, Institut Francais d'Architecture, France
1998_____*Paper Tube Architecture from Rwanda to Kobe*, Chikuma Shobo Publishing
Co., Ltd., Japan
1998_____*Shigeru Ban*, JA30, The Japan Architect Co. Ltd., Japan
1997_____*Shigeru Ban*, GG portfolio, Editorial Gustavo Gili, S.A., Spain

Exhibitions

2003_____GA Japan 2002 — Rietberg Museum Competition, GA Gallery, Tokyo
Paper, Wood & Bamboo — Structural Innovation in the Work of Shigeru Ban,
Harvard Design School, Cambridge, Massachusetts
GA Houses 2003 — Shutter House for a Photographer, GA Gallery, Tokyo
2002_____Recent Projects, La Galerie d'Architecture, Paris
Recent Projects, Arc en reve, Bordeaux, France
GA Houses 2002 — Schwartz Residence, GA Gallery, Tokyo
Bamboo Roof, Rice University Art Gallery, Houston, Texas
2001_____GA Houses 2001 — Paper Green Houses, GA Gallery, Tokyo
GA Japan 2001 — Hanegi Forest Annex, GA Gallery, Tokyo
Recent Projects, AEDES East Forum, Berlin
Recent Projects, Zumtobel Light Forum, Vienna, Austria
2000_____Paper Show by Takeo & Nippon Design Center, Spiral Hall, Tokyo
GA Houses 2000 — Naked House, GA Gallery, Tokyo
Venice Biennale, Venice, Italy
Japan Pavilion, Renate Kammer Architektur und Kunst, Hamburg, Germany
1999_____GA Houses 1999 — Veneer Grid Roof House, GA Gallery
SHIGERU BAN, Projects in Process, Gallery MA
Future Show, Bologna, Italy
ARCHI LAB, Orleans, France
Shigeru Ban, Ifa, France
Cities on the Move, Hayward Gallery, London
Un-Private House, MoMA, New York
Paper Tea House, Space TRY, Tokyo
1998_____'97 JIA Prize for the best young Architect of the year, Osaka and Tokyo
GA Japan League '98, GA Gallery
1997_____Resurrection of Topos 3, Hillside Terrace Gallery, Tokyo
GA Japan League '97, GA Gallery, Tokyo
Stool Exhibition 3, Living Design Center OZONE, Tokyo
1996_____Paper Church and Volunteers at Kobe, Kenchikuka Club, Tokyo
1995_____Paper Church, Matsuya Gallery, Ginza, Tokyo
Paper Church and Volunteers, INAX Gallery, Osaka, Japan
1994_____GA Japan League '94, GA Gallery, Tokyo
Architecture of the Year '94, Metropolitan Plaza, Tokyo
GA Japan League '95, GA Gallery, Tokyo
1993_____Chairs by Architects, Hanegi Museum, Tokyo
GA Japan League '93, GA Gallery, Tokyo
Hardwares by Architects, Hanegi Museum, Tokyo
1990_____Virgin Collections, Guardian Garden, Tokyo
Last Decade 1990, Matsuya Gallery, Ginza, Tokyo
1989_____Neo-Forma, Axis Gallery, Tokyo
1988_____Models from Architect's Ateliers, Matsuya Gallery, Ginza, Tokyo
S. D. Review '88, Hillside Terrace Gallery, Tokyo
1987_____40 Architects under 40: Tokyo Tower Project, Axis Gallery, Tokyo
1985_____Adam in the Future, Seibu Shibuya, Tokyo
S. D. Review '85, Hillside Terrace Gallery, Tokyo
1984_____Japanese Designer in New York, Gallery 91, New York

Shigeru Ban

2001–present	Professor, Keio University
2000	Visiting Fellow, Donald Keen Center, Columbia University
2000	Visiting Professor, Columbia University
1996–2000	Adjunct Professor of Architecture, Nihon University
1995–99	Adjunct Professor of Architecture, Yokohama National University
1995	Established NGO: VAN (Voluntary Architects Network)
1995–99	Consultant of United Nations High Commissioner for Refugees (UNHCR)
1993–95	Adjunct Professor of Architecture, Tama Art University
1985	Established private practice in Tokyo, Japan
1984	Bachelor of Architecture, Cooper Union School of Architecture
1982–83	Worked for Arata Isozaki, Tokyo, Japan
1980–82	Cooper Union School of Architecture
1977–80	Southern California Institute of Architecture
1957	Born in Tokyo

Nobutaka Hiraga—Partner

1998–present	Joined Shigeru Ban Architects as Partner
1987	Established Archi Network, Principal
1980–87	Y. Ashihara Architect & Associates
1971–80	Sasagawa Architects & Partners
1971	Bachelor of Architecture, Tokyo University of Fine Arts
1949	Born in Tokyo

Mamiko Ishida—Associate

2002–present	Shigeru Ban Architects, Associate
1995–02	Shigeru Ban Architects
1988–94	Antonin Raymond Architectural Design Office Inc.
1988	Bachelor of Architecture, Musashino Art University
1966	Born in Tokyo

Staff

Keina Ishioka
Anne Scheou
Keita Sugai
Tomoo Nitta
Tamaki Terai
Grant Suzuki

International Partners

Dean Maltz Architect, New York
Dean Maltz — Partner
Justin Shaulis
Andrew Lefkowitz

Jean de Gastines Architecte DPLG, Paris
Jean de Gastines — Partner

Former Staff

Junko Saitoh
Kiyoshi Matsumori
Masako Wada
Toshihiro Kiyoshige
Takeshi Sato
Hiromi Okusa
Masao Yamazaki
Yoko Nakagawa
Tadanori Maekawa
Tetsuo Yamakoshi
Takashi Nakagawa
Tatsuya Matsuyama
Makiko Tsukada
Shigeru Hiraki
Yoko Watanabe
Soichiro Hiyoshi
Tadahiro Kawano
Jun Yashiki
Wakako Tokunaga
Kentaro Ishida

Acknowledgments

I am especially grateful to Karen Stein, editorial director at Phaidon Press in New York, for the opportunity to undertake this project, and to Megan McFarland, senior editor, whose patience and professionalism were paramount to the book's completion. Also, my thanks to Terence Riley, The Philip Johnson Chief Curator in the Department of Architecture and Design at The Museum of Modern Art, who initially encouraged me to pursue this project, and, later, Paul Warwick Thompson, Director, Cooper-Hewitt, National Design Museum, who allowed me the time to continue the project until its completion. Other individuals and firms who have been extremely supportive in shaping the book are Frei Otto, konyk architecture, Dean Maltz of Dean Maltz Architects, Judith Turner, and Cristobal Correa, senior engineer at Buro Happold Consulting Engineers. Kenya Hara and Kayoko Takeo of Hara Design Institute have designed an elegant publication, and Rise Endo has so tirelessly and perfectly coordinated all of the material for the book that working with her has been one of the most enjoyable parts of this project.

The book would not have been possible without the full participation of Shigeru Ban and his office. Especially helpful have been Grant Suzuki and Yukie Ikeda, who never tired of tracking down answers to my many questions. And most gracious, understanding, and articulate has been Shigeru, who has been a constant source of amazement and pride for me as I've watched him maneuver through his very busy world.

Last, but definitely not least, is my home team: Craig, Ana, and Alex. They have given me a gift to pursue this journey, and I hope it has allowed them their own personal adventures.

Matilda McQuaid

McQuaid is Exhibitions Curator and Head of the Textiles Department at the Cooper-Hewitt, National Design Museum in New York. Her essays on architecture, textiles, and fiber art have appeared in numerous journals and museum publications.

Shigeru Ban Project Team

Project Manager
Grant Suzuki

Graphic Design
Kenya Hara
Kayoko Takeo
Hara Design Institute,
Nippon Design Center

Material Tests Authors
Minoru Tezuka
Grant Suzuki

Contributors
Birte Böttger
Yukie Ikeda
Kentaro Ishida
Yasushi Ishikawa
Julia Jamrozik
Chigusa Kasori
Masahito Kinjo
Maria Kouloumbri
Yoshie Narimatsu
Sergio Pirrone
Emi Saitoh
Tina Tajitsu
Tamaki Terai
Nahoko Wada

Illustration Credits

Abbreviations: l=left, r=right, t=top, c=center, and b=bottom.
All photographs by Hiroyuki Hirai except those noted below.
Satoshi Asakawa: 131 (l), 132 – 137, 236 (#59)
Shigeru Ban Architects: 28 – 33, 36, 38, 39, 44, 50, 56, 63 (bl), 68, 69, 70, 72 (l), 73 (t), 91, 100 (c), 109, 112, 113, 130 (l), 139, 140, 141 (l), 142 (bl), 153 (r), 157 (t), 166, 167, 173 (t), 177 (t), 226, 227, 228, 229, 231, 233, 235 (#42), 236 (#45, #46, #49, #53, #56, #57, #58), 237 (#61, #64, #68, #69, #70, #71, #72)
Jean de Gastines Architecte DPLG: 177
Dean Maltz, Architect: 178 – 179
Hiroshi Osaka: 234 (#3)
Takanobu Sakuma: 35, 153 (l), 235 (#30)
Takashi Sekiguchi: 13, 89, 129, 151, 183
Yukio Shimizu: 15 (l), 234 (#2)
Toshihiro Sobajima: 72 (c, r), 73 (b)
Grant Suzuki: 91 (l), 142 (t, br), 143, 237 (#63, #66)
Kartikeya Shodhan Associates: 40 – 41, 236 (#54)
Takenaka Corporation: 62, 63 (tl, tc, tr, cl)
Kayoko Takeo: 130 (r), 131 (r)
Team THINK: 237 (#65)
Judith Turner: 71

All photographs in the Material Tests are credited to the respective test performers, except Appendix 1 and 2 of p. 76 credited to Shigeru Ban Architects.

All drawings © Shigeru Ban Architects, with the exception of those noted below:
Kartikeya Shodhan Associates, Ahmedabad: 40
Buro Happold Consulting Engineers PC, New York: 71 (r)
Arup: 140 (hand sketch details), 141 (r),142 (l)

Phaidon Press Limited
Regent's Wharf
All Saints Street
London N1 9PA

Phaidon Press Inc.
180 Varick Street
New York, NY 10014

www.phaidon.com

First published 2003
Reprinted 2004, 2005
© 2003 Phaidon Press Limited

ISBN 0 7148 4194 3

Designed by Kenya Hara and Kayoko Takeo, Hara Design Institute, Nippon Design Center

Printed in China